4   non-random mutations Sebastopol 2004
    in the meta language

p. 30,31 More than one way to say something
         synonymous codons allow for mutation without affecting the protein

33   certain areas only one way for
     the codons to express an amino
     acid

33   error checking from communication
     theory

34   strict spelling required for the
     cut & paste of a patch

60   staircase analogy

77   synonyms

106 The meta drug - attacks
     strategies

111 slips not repaired correctly

111 not on or off, but modulation

112,113 area of the genome where
         creativity occurs - the "slip"
         repetitive letters - "hot spot"

112 well written code

119 opportunity for evolution at
     the cellular level

121 "Extra copy" of block of code
127 not a single human only gene family
128 variation is most likely to be
     successful in our anti-body genes.
     Pathogen binding site is most
     likely to vary

130,131 focussed mutation - high rate of change
         among synonymous codons

131 commented out = "stop" codons

138 4...then of computer code

Darwin in the Genome

Molecular Strategies in Biological Evolution

Lynn Helena Caporale

McGraw-Hill

New York   Chicago   San Francisco
Lisbon   London   Madrid   Mexico City   Milan
New Delhi   San Juan   Seoul   Singapore
Sydney   Toronto

The *McGraw·Hill* Companies

Library of Congress Cataloging-in-Publication Data

Caporale, Lynn Helena.
    Darwin in the genome : molecular strategies in biological evolution /
Lynn Helena Caporale.
        p.   cm.
    ISBN 0-07-137822-7 (hardcover)
    1. Evolution (Biology).   2. Molecular evolution.   3. Genomes.
I. Title.

QH366.2 .C367 2002
576—dc21
                                                    2002009570

1 2 3 4 5 6 7 8 9 0 DOC / DOC 0 8 7 6 5 4 3 2

ISBN 0-07-137822-7

This book is printed on recycled, acid-free paper containing a
minimum of 50% recycled de-inked fiber.

With love,
to Mom and Dad

and to our next generation—
Brooks, Michael, Parker, and Rockella

Contents

Preface

I was in a new world, and . . . could not help speculating on what my wanderings there . . . might bring to light.

—Alfred Russel Wallace[1]

Long ago, consciousness began to emerge within life on Earth. Now, at the very moment when we are alive, consciousness is starting to comprehend the extraordinary information that each of us carries inside on the thin ribbons of our genome. What will we find, now that we can peer so deep within ourselves?

Just four hundred years ago, lenses were ground, placed together in a tube, and turned toward the night sky. Galileo's revelations did not require the see-to-the-edge-of-time spacecraft-mounted telescopes of our day. He looked through lenses with the strength of the 12× binoculars that today we carry so casually to examine the markings on a bird overhead. By turning such simple lenses to the sky, he showed us something that directly contradicted the overwhelming evidence of our senses. Contrary to what seemed so obvious every day from the sunrise, to the movement of the sun across the sky, to its setting on the opposite horizon, and its predictable rise the next day, we learned that the sun does not revolve around the Earth. We were certain that the sun circled around us, but in fact it does not.

When we learned that we are not at the very center of all that there is, our view of who we are and our place in the universe was dramatically changed (although there was, and in many ways still is, resistance to this change in perspective). Yet this revolution in our comprehension of the world and our place in it was, I believe, small, very small, compared to the change in our comprehension of the world and our place in it that is about to occur as we look inside at our own genome, and at the genomes of other creatures.

The initial impulse for this book came when I organized and cochaired a conference that may well represent a landmark in discussions of evolution. This gathering was filled with enthusiastic discussions among people whose work varies from sitting at computers to studying the life that lives within beautiful shells along the beach. I was convinced that the research we discussed, and, since then, the new discoveries that continue to capture our imagination, could be shared with a broad range of readers. For nonscientists, I worked hard to break through the barrier of technical language to share the heart of these ideas and discoveries with you, but if you find that I have failed to do this in some spots, I also worked hard to make it possible to skip some sections and pick up the train of thought. There is a glossary in the back to help out, too. For readers who are professional scientists, I ask of course for patience as I explain some things that you may already have learned. (For everyone, I have inserted a few brief word games, which a friend of mine dislikes intensely and has characterized as "typos on steroids"; if you agree with him, jump over them.) I ask all readers to share with me in reflecting on what the implications of these new discoveries might be.

On the shelves of a bookstore, imaginative writings are thought to be confined to the fiction section, but in fact imagination drives scientists as much as it does novelists. Indeed, much as a novel is enhanced when its locations are described in factual detail and its characters made to seem real, so nonfiction can be more inspiring when the reader is taken into the imagination of the scientist. In such writing, as in the mind of a good scientist, the boundaries between data and imagination must be made very clear. In this book, I have worked to weave a wide range of research into a coherent vision, while describing much that remains the subject of active current investigation and even controversy. Some sections, which it is my job to indicate clearly, step into the realm of scientists' imagination, suggesting where new discoveries may lead.

As one of the founders of the field of molecular biology, Max Delbrück, pointed out, "Any living cell carries within it the results of billions of years of experimentation by its ancestors." The steps of this long journey are inscribed in our DNA, and in the DNA of all the living creatures that share our time on Earth. There are messages in our genome for each of us; they come from our diverse ancestors, and they outline our path across past ages, in other forms, to here. If we strain to listen, will our genome help us to comprehend how mutation and selection ever could have led to us—to

me, sitting here and writing, and to you, sitting there and reading? I have
written this book to explore these very questions.

Our genome encodes many types of information. Perhaps the best
studied is the information that encodes our proteins. Other information
controls which proteins are made in a cell in our heart, or in our brain, or
in our thumbs. But it is clear that there is room in our genome for other
types of information that we are only now beginning to perceive. This information can be found in the spaces between genes, and even doubled up
along the stretches of DNA that encode our proteins. Early examples of
such multiple messages involved information encoding proteins that ran
together along a piece of DNA in different reading frames, something like
you find tthhee itrw ol emtetsesrasg easl tmeirxneadt iunpg here. In fact, it
was this ability to transmit more than one message through the same
stretch of DNA that first led to my writing about evolution, as described in
Chapter 13.[2] As will be explained in this book, I have proposed that this
extra coding potential has been harnessed[3] by natural selection to improve
the probability of survival. Some scientists may disagree with my interpretation of the data before us, leading to interesting discussions about data;
in studies of the genome, data are coming very quickly now. Some people
do seek data that show that their ideas are right, and discard data that are
not consistent with their preconceived ideas, but that is not science.

Because this book mentions evolution, it may attract religious debate,
but faith is, of course, something entirely different. This book addresses scientific research, not faith. But knowledge does have implications. Rather
than view evolution as a no-holds-barred fight to the death, I find that the
discoveries described in this book harmonize with the teachings of many
great religions: that people are brothers and sisters; that we should respect,
welcome, and share with others; and that reverence should extend to other
forms of life. Indeed the intellectual, practical, political, and philosophical
implications of being able to read the information within genomes reach
into everyone's lives and emphasize the importance of diversity for survival. This includes biodiversity and, especially, should lead us to treasure
the diversity of our own species.

On a practical level, the knowledge that we gain from looking into our
genome will facilitate medical research and also may teach us ways to
design novel coding systems for our computers. By bringing our consciousness into the analysis of microbe and tumor genomes, our new skills should
strengthen our hand in the age-old battle against these adversaries, as discussed in this book. Some private messages in each person's genome may

warn of susceptibility to certain diseases, but other information will reassure people that there are other diseases that they are less likely to suffer. Many observations lead to caution in the face of proposals to fix "errors" in the human genome.

When I was a little girl sitting at my desk in school, I was asked to draw a circle around a picture of a ball and to connect it, with a line, to the word *ball*. I assume you too had workbooks in which you connected pictures and words, one at a time. In retrospect, it was a lot like that when we first began to look at our DNA, connecting one gene to one protein. But now that we finally can see the genome as a whole, we are learning new ways to read DNA that go beyond letters and words, to understand decision-making networks and hierarchies.[4] Physically, a genome may be a string of letters along a strand of the DNA double helix, but functionally it is an interconnected, highly cross-referenced system. In the more than 3 billion letters of our genome, there are concepts to pull out, ideas in one place that are connected to and built up from ideas in other places. All of biology, including our journey to this place, is waiting within us to be pieced together into an integrated living, whole. I feel fortunate to have become a biochemist at this extraordinary moment in history, and I invite you to join me on this journey of discovery into our genome, to explore what our "wanderings there might bring to light."

Prologue
Chance Favors
the Prepared Genome

*Delicate, elusive . . . is that mysterious principle known
as "Organization," which leaves all other mysteries con-
cerned with life stale and insignificant by comparison.*

—Loren Eiseley, *The Immense Journey*

There was a moment in time when the dust itself edged, in slow motion,
over a boundary into life. It entered onto a path strewn with dangers,
uncertainty, and creativity. It spread its growing skill across the Earth until
it learned how to fly at will and how to sit still here, and to discuss its own
evolution. Those who do not believe that we have evolved from life forms
that are invisible to the naked eye—and even those who do—find it hard
to *conceive* of how this journey, relying only on random mutation and survival of the "fittest," could have succeeded. It seems almost inconceivable
that there has been enough time for mere molecules to organize themselves
into a being that could compose music, travel to the moon and back, and
indeed analyze its own genome. How did we get this far, even once, in only
billions of years? How could we have happened so randomly?

In the greatest achievement in human intellectual history, the information in our genome, the product of billions of years of evolution, is now
opening before us. What answers does our genome hold to the Big Questions
that whisper to us all? What does it say of the immense journey it has taken
as it has passed through uncounted life forms to be carried within us as we
sit here, discussing our origins and our fate?

It has been well over a century since Charles Darwin and Alfred Russel Wallace first proposed that from among the natural variations in a population, the "most fit" individuals would tend to survive in greater numbers, passing their selected variations on to their progeny. But when Darwin and Wallace proposed that evolution happens through variation and then selection, they did not know the mechanism by which the varied traits were inherited. Science at that time was still was about a century away from uncovering the chemistry of heredity. And, although Darwin and Wallace had each traveled from England to the Pacific Ocean, they had not traveled to Gregor Mendel's garden at Brno and so had never talked to their contemporary about how traits might be transmitted between generations. (What a conversation that would have been!)

For his part, Mendel went beyond the general understanding that we resemble our parents and showed that traits, such as whether the peas borne by the plants in his garden were wrinkled or smooth in form or yellow or green in color, were inherited independently of each other in a way that was *predictable*.[1] Mendel used careful statistics to work out the "laws" of heredity. He could anticipate the mix of smooth and wrinkled, yellow and green peas borne by tall and dwarf plants from generation to generation, but he could not explain how this worked. We now know that the predictability of the peas comes from the fact that the inherited variations of the peas are encoded in separately assorting stretches of the DNA of pea chromosomes.

Of course, the naturalists and the statistician/monk did not have a chance to travel forward in time to kick ideas around with researchers who studied the mechanisms of mutation, but some decades after Darwin, Mendel, and Wallace were gone, their ideas were incorporated into the then more recent work to form our current understanding of evolution: Variations among organisms are due to variations in genes; variation is due to different "versions" of genes (giving, for example, green peas or yellow peas, green eyes or blue eyes) and mutation of the DNA that makes up our genes. From this variation, selection picks the most "fitted."

When we say "fit" in our daily lives, this usually leads into a conversation about workouts, but for the moment I would like to talk about personality quirks. Imagine that a developer built new homes in an isolated canyon. The homes were very desirable, but the developer had a prohibitive personality quirk: He would allow only certain cars through the gate on the road that led to the canyon. No one understood why their car was allowed through the gate or turned away, but I can tell you: The imaginary developer let families get through the gate only if at least one child in the car was wearing a blue T-shirt. The natural consequence was that among the people who settled in the valley, there was a higher proportion of children who tended to wear blue T-shirts than there were in the general population. After a couple of generations, the isolated canyon became crowded, and the developer's grandchildren built homes in the next canyon over. The developer's grandchildren inherited the developer's quirky attention to T-shirts, but they were so used to blue, from its enrichment in the first canyon, where they too lived, that they did not favor blue at the new barrier. They would admit only families that had a child wearing a yellow T-shirt.

After generations of families getting through gates controlled by generations of quirky developers, the tenth canyon was inhabited by families that, without thinking about it, each day dressed their several children in different-colored T-shirts. These colorful families were the ones that had the best chance of having one of their children wearing the "right" color T-shirt and thus being able to get across barrier after barrier, from the canyon enriched in blue to the canyon enriched in yellow and beyond.

As genomes travel from generation to generation across evolutionary time, we face something far more serious than quirky developers. Pathogens are among the life-and-death challenges that allow only some children to pass into the next generation. Just as the imaginary developers let families who varied the colors of their children's T-shirts get through, pathogens let genomes get through that varied their progeny enough to avoid the pathogens' biochemical tricks.

You can be too careful. True, a genome must be conserved as it is passed from generation to generation. To reproduce a genome, it is necessary to be careful in copying DNA and to repair errors. But having all progeny be exactly the same may not be the safest strategy. In fact, Darwin and Wallace and their contemporaries were impressed with the tremendous variation they observed within each species, from birds to beetles. Now, the genome, which had been hidden from their view, is becoming a landscape for a new kind of naturalist to explore. This naturalist views the variations within each species using a different kind of binoculars. Far from being carried on a strap, these "binoculars" involve laboratory infrastructure and computers to read and analyze each species' DNA. The variation that these naturalists study is not limited to that between feathers and limbs; rather, what captures our imagination is the variation among worm or flower or human, or bacterial genomes.

What has made evolution so hard for many to accept is the assumption that it depends upon random mutation for the generation of new variations. Momentarily sloppy, the gene-copying mechanism drops something, messes up, and passes on a mistake to a probably unfortunate member of the next generation. Through sheer luck, the change in the DNA, the accident, may turn out OK, so that the child who inherits it survives and passes it on. Rarely, through even greater luck, the change may turn out to be for the better; with those rare lucky accidents, the random mistake makes a fitter child (or fawn or tadpole or sprout or bacterium), one that is favored by natural selection. Slowly, over unfathomable lengths of time, from one rare, lucky mutation after another, these rare fitter children in turn give birth rarely and accidentally to even fitter children; and so, at its stumbling pace, evolution proceeds, selecting any advantage in a wing or a protein, one by one.

That variation comes from random mutation of DNA was not, of course, Darwin's proposal. But just as Darwin and Wallace could not incorporate into their theories what they did not know about genes, when our current understanding was developed, there was a lot that we did not know about genomes. In this book I will propose that it is time to incorporate our new discoveries into our understanding of evolution. As Baldomero Olivera, whose work will be discussed in Chapter 3, pointed out when describing his observations, "Unconventional hypotheses for these unusual data merit serious consideration."

The work described in this book has led me to the conclusion that natural selection must work not just on each individual mutation, but also on the very *mechanisms* that generate genetic variation—as it does on all biological functions. The research discussed in this book leads to the conclusion that mutations are not all accidents and that mutations are not always random. Our genomes, and those of other life forms, have evolved mechanisms that *create* different kinds of mutations in their DNA, and they reuse and adapt useful pieces of DNA, even to the point that there are genomic "interchangeable parts." Biochemical mechanisms can arise that tend to focus genetic variation, resulting in "hot spots" of genetic change at certain places in the genome. The probability of genetic change at any given point in the genome is dependent upon the surrounding sequence of the DNA, the environment, and the proteins that are present in the cell that interact with the DNA; for example, specific types of mutation can be increased in our immune system.

Evolution may not have been reaching for the goal of two eyes and a brain and two arms and two legs, but it didn't just stumble onto us through clumsy wandering. Randomness fades in a world that rewards each step of getting better at finding food, avoiding predators, or adapting to recurring challenges. As the dust organized, it faced selection. Over time, there emerged something that, viewing the effects now, we might call *strategies*—

such as the ability to actively generate diversity—that enabled life to emerge from the darkness of random wandering. Because the mechanisms that change the genome fall under selective pressure, I propose, based on the new observations discussed in this book, that information can flow back from survival to the places in the genome that affect the generation of the diversity that we see around us, and that this will make genomes become more efficient at adapting and evolving. If one of the predictable characteristics of the world is that it changes over the course of generations, natural selection will lead to organisms that are more efficient at adapting to an environment that may change.

These discoveries do not refute the theory of natural selection developed by Darwin and Wallace, but instead provide a deeper understanding of how natural selection leads to organisms that are better adapted to their world. Natural selection acts on all biological properties. That means that natural selection acts not only on fins and wings, but also on the mechanisms that change a genome. With time, it turns out, the "fittest" genomes, the "successful" genomes—the ones that survive—are the genomes that evolve what here I will call mutation strategies. Some readers may disagree with this use of the word *strategies*, as I am, after all, discussing groups of molecules. But I use this word to emphasize that the molecular mechanisms I will describe in this book have the effect of anticipating and responding to challenges and opportunities that continue to emerge in the environment.

The first strategy for survival clearly is to generate diversity. The long-term survival, or fitness, of a genome often depends upon the diversity of its descendants. Genomes have evolved biochemical mechanisms that actively diversify themselves. The more diverse the progeny, the better the chance that at least some progeny will be different in a way that allows them to survive or even thrive, whether they are in an isolated canyon, a salt cave, a hot spring in Yellowstone National Park, or an irradiated can of meat—for life can survive in all of these places.

Miroslav Radman, whose work is discussed in Chapter 8, described it this way: "The generation of a large repertoire of biological diversity [is] the evolutionary equivalent of buying a large number of lottery tickets."[2] The lottery winners are those who survive natural selection. You don't want everyone in your family to buy a ticket that has the same number.

We must have sunlight to construct vitamin D in our skin, but too much sun will burn us. With dark skin to protect against sunburn, a child can survive at the Equator. With lighter skin to let in more sunlight, a child can be wrapped in warmer and warmer coverings and begin a journey away from the Equator. The world inhabited by these children can be very different from the world that best suited their parents. If the world may become different, it is an advantage for some children to be different too.

If the ability to generate diversity is a useful skill, the fact that genomes can generate genetic diversity in more than one way provides an even greater advantage.[3] To prepare for various levels of selection, the genome too can change just a little, a little more, or still more between generations. Maybe one quirky developer admits applicants to the new canyon not on the basis of the color of their shirts, but on the style of their top shirt buttons. Another issue in getting into some canyons may be the size of the car (too big?) or the strength of its engine (too weak?). A genome's ability to grow and to explore new organizational structures would be severely constrained if its options were limited to changes in the molecular equivalent of the top shirt button. A single letter along a strand of the DNA double helix can change to another letter, but also a patch of letters may expand, be replaced, or be removed, or some pieces of the genome might be rearranged. By now a diverse set of biochemical mechanisms of change has emerged, each mechanism generating a different type, rate, and extent of diversity.

A second strategy that has emerged in genomes, and that will be discussed starting with Chapter 7 in this book, is the reuse of useful pieces of genetic information. This is exemplified by the spread among bacteria of information that encodes resistance to antibiotics. Other useful genetic information, such as how to digest a new food source, also can come into a bacterial genome from outside—in other words, from a genome that was not its parent. As in a port city in a nation of immigrants, within bacteria new genetic ideas arrive, are put together, survive, prosper, and can thrive. Useful genetic information that is already within a genome also can be adapted for a new job, molded by making an extra copy of a piece of DNA, moving the copy around, and tinkering. Shuffling DNA around within our genome can have risks and do damage, leading, in people, to "birth defects." But, as the roof falls, albeit ever so slowly, in, sitting still also has its risks. In the high-stakes game of evolution and survival, genomes don't take time to reinvent the wheel. They network, copy, vary, and explore the potential of the information they already hold inside them.

As is described in several chapters, genetic change is not something that strikes all parts of a genome evenly. It also has become clear that, as illustrated in Chapter 8 by Evelyn Witkin's work with sunburned bacteria, the likelihood and type of genetic change, or mutation, can vary depending upon which molecules a cell contains. In other words, rather than being purely passive, the genetic change that a cell experiences can become somewhat conditional on, for example, which proteins the cell itself makes.

Under some conditions, one bacterium may become more open to new ideas, more likely to swallow DNA; a neighbor might feed it a gene that encodes a recipe for destroying an antibiotic.

While a genome evolves a balance between faithful copying of itself and exploration through mutation, this is a difficult balance to get right. Perhaps it can never really be "right" because the right balance between fidelity and exploration may change as threats and opportunities in the environment change. As Nobel laureate Barbara McClintock, whose work will be described in Chapter 15, said, "In the future attention . . . will be centered on the genome . . . sensing the unusual and unexpected events, and responding to them."

It is becoming clearer and clearer that some classes of nonrandom mutations are very appropriate to the needs of the organism. In this book, I will discuss recent information that supports this new understanding of evolution, which I first proposed in the technical literature in the early 1980s.[4] These ideas attract controversy, but the evidence coming from sources as diverse as the bacteria that cause Lyme disease and our own immune system is growing strong. The work of Richard Moxon and others demonstrates that mutations can become more likely at the very spots in pathogen genomes that speed their race to get a grip on us and to survive. We too are the survivors of many battles with pathogen across the ages, and so those parts of our genome that encode our immune response are creative sites of focused mutation.

To reject purely random mutation as the current substrate of genome evolution is not to reject Darwin and Wallace. Indeed, while Darwin's name may be connected to the phrase "survival of the fittest," this book emphasizes these words of his: "I have called this principle, by which each slight variation, if useful, is preserved, by the term Natural Selection."[5] Among the variations that I propose are preserved, when useful, are intrinsic variations in the probability of mutation along the genome, as described, for example, in Chapter 4.

The flow of information from the biological effects of genetic change to the intrinsic variations in the type, location, and probability of mutation and the mechanisms that generate mutations is not a simple loop, for we are not adjusting an aileron to restore level flight but must survive the unexpected. Still, intrinsic differences in genetic variation would *tend* to focus in classes of places along a genome where these mutations are more likely to be creative, and tend to move away from areas where changes have done more harm than good. This is a tendency, an adjustment, and not an absolute; for still, now, many mutations do damage. This adjustment would emerge because those genomes that accidentally keep losing important information will have fewer descendants across the generations and thus will be less likely to survive. In contrast, genomes will tend to endure when their most likely mutations create effective responses to their most likely challenges, as is detailed in this book. As the fittest molecular strategies emerge through natural selection, by the survival of the descendants of the genomes that encode them, those who remain in the world tend to be those whose ancestors were lucky enough to keep making more creative mistakes. Any genome that we find today, including our own, has been successful, because it has survived through the molecular equivalent of countless canyon gates—though, of course, it has survived only this far, so far.

A genome can't predict what will happen to the next generation, nor can you or I. But genomes have faced some challenges over and over again, such as in host/pathogen battles, and this has left its mark on the genome. A genome evolves a "worldview" of which types of changes, under what types of circumstances, may yield a new function and are less likely to destroy something essential. While a genome can't predict the future, a genome that has been so prepared by experience is likely to be favored by chance. For me, evolution becomes more conceivable when it is viewed through such a "strategic" biochemical window. The ability to evolve and adapt is an acquired skill, responsive to the environment and acquired through the experience of genomes across generations. Through selection, genome structure emerges from randomness.

We live at an extraordinary moment in human intellectual history. Until now, the information that gives rise to all that we try to study in biology and medicine remained hidden from view, as if our eyes were covered by blindfolds. These blindfolds are becoming transparent, and soon they will fall off. The sequences of entire genomes are opening before us.

Varied genomes, based on similar chemistry, have spread across the Earth, taking advantage of opportunities, establishing themselves in new environments. After the asteroid hit, what emerged was not another *Tyrannosaurus Rex* but instead us. Each of us is, in a way, an experiment, and an example of the life-preserving, creative diversity expressed at our moment in time by the human genome. Indeed, we share with one another, no less than with the majesty of the redwoods and the doves, the fact that each of us is a unique creation of the barely tapped potential immanent in the first genomes on Earth.

1

Diversity or Death

"We are caught in an inescapable network of mutuality, tied in a single garment of destiny. Whatever affects one directly affects all indirectly."

—Rev. Martin Luther King, Jr.,
"Letter from the Birmingham City Jail," 1963

It was a mystery. There were very few of these lucky people, but there were a few. They surely had been exposed to HIV, but they simply did not get sick, not even after ten years. Each day each one faced the terror of knowing that the deadly virus had touched his body. And yet each one awoke, morning after morning, to the tentative joy that there was no sign that the virus had gained a foothold inside him. For each one of these lucky few, doctor after doctor—nurses, nutritionists, researchers, reporters, friends—hoped, hypothesized, and investigated. What was he eating, taking, doing differently? Or was it something in his genes? Yet as each was questioned, poked, and wondered over, it remained a mystery.

This mystery remained unsolved for a full decade after the HIV virus was discovered in people with AIDS. While this mystery remained unsolved, Ed Berger, at the National Institutes of Health near Washington, D.C., was studying a different HIV mystery. Berger was trying to figure out how HIV gets into cells. HIV does serious damage when it invades the T cells of our immune systems, but it can't get into just any cell. To get inside a T cell, HIV needs to find a gate it can crash, a *receptor* on the T-cell surface. The receptor is a protein called CD4. But if we force a cell that does not normally let HIV in to put the receptor protein CD4 on its surface, HIV still cannot get into that cell. So CD4 is not the whole answer. Berger thought that there must be another molecule, a *coreceptor*, needed along with CD4 to let HIV in. He was right. Berger discovered the coreceptor, called CXCR4.[1]

CXCR4 allows HIV to spread from T cell to T cell. Finding CXCR4 led investigators to another coreceptor, a protein called CCR5 that looks a lot like CXCR4. CCR5 also can let HIV into cells, but it lets HIV into different cells. Unlike CXCR4, CCR5 is not found at the entry to most T cells. HIV needs to get into T cells in order to destroy the immune system, but first it needs to get into our bodies. CCR5 opens the front door to HIV. For most people, CCR5 is what helps the virus get into the very first cells it infects, where it first touches a person. These cells usually are not T cells.

Most HIV particles that attach to CCR5 and infect us cannot get into T cells and thus cannot directly harm our immune system. But, once CCR5 has let HIV inside some of our cells, the deadly invader has penetrated the barrier between being outside of us and being inside us. It has gained a foothold in our bodies; it is living with us, within us.

Once inside, HIV experiments. It floats around, poking and prodding, and exploring. It mutates, and these mutations inevitably produce a small change on its surface that it can use to attach to the coreceptor door. Once HIV's coreceptor binding site mutates to a form that binds to CXCR4, it has evolved the key to let itself into T cells. It continues to mutate and can become an even more unwelcome guest, discovering the keys to additional doors.[2]

If the HIV in other cells didn't mutate into a form that could get into the T cells, we might all be infected with HIV without even knowing that HIV exists. This is not a reassuring thought. In fact, I find this haunting: How many other viruses already have found their way inside me, changing, exploring, trying out new keys, perhaps doing no harm—for now?

Berger had set out to solve the coreceptor mystery, but his work also explained the mystery of the people who remained healthy after they were exposed to HIV. The discovery of the coreceptors CXCR4 and CCR5 not only explained how HIV gets into cells, but also, unexpectedly, revealed why those few lucky people were so resistant to HIV.

The answer to the mystery was that the lucky survivors' CCR5 coreceptor was different. It was damaged—it was missing a piece, and so couldn't let HIV in. HIV could not get a foothold in their bodies; it could not get in the door. Out of all the countless molecules in a human body, this one mutation—one small change in one protein—was enough to keep HIV out of the cells of a few lucky people and so saved their lives.

Like all breakthroughs, the discovery of mutant CCR5 answered one question but also led to so many others. How did these lucky people get the unusual CCR5 protein? Obviously it was in their genes, which came from their parents, but what generated the mutant protein in their parents' genes, or their parents' ancestors' genes? Which ancestors were they? Other primates, indeed other mammals, have CCR5 receptors too. Had the ancestors of the HIV-resistant people already encountered HIV, or perhaps another pathogen that uses the same coreceptor to get in? Perhaps small-pox?[3] If so, how did *their* ancestors prepare for it and survive?

Or, had the genes of their ancestors, and our ancestors, somehow "learned," by surviving infection after infection for generation after generation, that something like HIV, another new pathogen, inevitably would come? To become a survivor, it may simply be enough for an individual to be a little different, in a way that provides no apparent advantage in fitness until a new, never before encountered pathogen appears. For an individual, such a difference is great luck; but at the level of the genome, it may reflect a strategy that has emerged in successful genomes, a way to be prepared for the unexpected.

The mechanism of evolution, natural selection, usually is described as "survival of the fittest." But as we look at genomes that have been handed down from generation to generation, what do we mean by survival? What do we mean by fittest? Survival demonstrates fitness: We gather that the *successful* ancestors, the ones whose genes made it to us, must have had the better genes. But what *is* "better"? "Better" is a moving target. Continents move; climates change; predators, competitors, food, and the atmosphere all evolve. We call mutations "errors," but from the perspective of evolution, the most serious error for a genome is to make no mutations.

Genomes can prepare for the unexpected by being diverse. If every one of us were the same, and a pathogen were to hit us suddenly and hard (especially before we had laboratories that could work more quickly than generations), we could be wiped out, all of us. The human genome would become extinct in the brief time it took for the pathogen to spread through the human community and do its work. Our libraries and our architecture would be left behind for the product of a future genome to decipher. The reptiles and now the mammals having had their day, perhaps the cephalopods would come next.

But, if every one of us were a little different, even in some small way, a few of us might be different in the very way that would protect against this new pathogen. Then a few of us would survive, and with the survivors the human genome also would survive. It would not become extinct, but would continue to come forward in time, as it came forward to live within us. It would survive in us, walking, through our descendants, into the future.

I think back before protease inhibitors, before antibiotics, before research labs, before we understood how a pathogen spreads (swamp air? drafts?), before we could fight back against pathogens. In that time before worldwide travel, a new pathogen like HIV could sweep through a local human community and kill nearly everyone in it. Indeed, it does not take a journey back in time to see this, just a journey to many places on the planet. HIV cuts huge holes in families, in communities, even in entire countries where there is no access to information about prevention or the right medicine for treatment. As I write this, I am reading a report from Allan Rosenfield, dean of Columbia University's School of Public Health,[4] pointing out that 28 million people in Africa are HIV-positive. There are 12 million HIV orphans; one-third of all adults in sub-Saharan Africa are infected. Parts of Asia are risking the same fate. The human genome will notice this.

In an unprotected community, a new pathogen with the right keys could kill everyone except those few who were just a little different, who had a mutant protein in the right place—like, for example, those with the mutant CCR5 coreceptor. After the pathogen had swept through the unprotected community, if the human genome remained there at all, it would have been touched by this tragedy. It would "remember"; it would have been adjusted. Among the survivors, and their children and their children's grandchildren, the mutant protein would no longer be rare; it would have become the common form of the protein, the one that everyone had. Examining the genome centuries later, we never would guess that it was ever otherwise. We might never be inspired to wonder what protection a now-lost form, or a minor, unnoticed new mutant form, might provide against a different pathogen another day. The pathogen, by removing those without the once-rare mutant protein, would have left behind a changed human genome to be shared by those who survived to live in the future.

This has happened before. There is clear evidence that a pathogen has marked our collective genome. This is a pathogen with which we are still doing battle, which kills the equivalent of one to three 747 loads of people every few hours. Most of the passengers on these imaginary 747s are little children, the majority of them under 5 years old. They've been bitten by mosquitoes and are suffering from the anemia of malaria, with two-thirds of their oxygen-carrying red blood cells destroyed. Every day, every week, last week, yesterday, today, it continues.

And for each person who dies, many more are ill; 300 to 500 million people suffer from malaria each year.[5] It is as if every single person in the United States, plus every single person in England, Germany, and Japan, were infected, each one shaking with the chills and sweating with the fever caused by this persistent pathogen. Of course, few of the real victims are lying in beds in the United States, England, Germany, and Japan. Most of malaria's direct victims lie in a belt across the middle of the Earth, a belt containing close to half of the people in the world. Their parents do not anchor our evening news, nor edit our daily newspapers, nor write the advertisements that shout to us on TV; but these children share with us this moment in time, in the continued evolution and sculpting of the human genome—and the human genome takes notice.

With hundreds of millions of victims across the centuries, including today, the human genome has felt the pressure of the malaria parasite. Of a group of children, friends and brothers and sisters, all bitten by infected mosquitoes, one child comes down with a sudden fever, with seizures, and slips into a coma. Left untreated, half of these ill children die; but even without treatment, half of them live. And some children, even though they are attacked by malaria, don't get very sick. In the genomes of these sur-vivors, some genes are different. Just as HIV kills those who lack the mutant CCR5, leaving as survivors those with the rare version, malaria too has sculpted the human genome.

This sculpting of our genome, this battle with malaria, is not without its victims. For these victims, too, the struggle is painful. Tears roll down the cheeks of an infant screaming in pain. She cannot explain it, but it feels as if countless nails are being driven through her body. Her red blood cells, the carriers of desperately needed oxygen, are bent out of shape and are jam-ming up her blood vessels. Her nerves, sensing the lack of oxygen, are ex-ploding in pain. There were over 300,000 of these children, born last year,[6] in a tropical band across Africa and in families whose ancestors lived in these places, suffering from what we have come to call sickle cell disease. What happened to leave so many children suffering in, of all places, the paradise of our imaginations, the tropics?

Biochemically, at first glance, it is a minor thing that is causing so much suffering for the little girl—a change in a single amino acid in one protein out of many tens of thousands of distinct proteins in her red blood cells. But this tiny change is in hemoglobin, a vital molecule that carries oxygen to all of our tissues. Surely such a mutation, one that messes up a vital molecule, damages the red blood cells, and causes so much pain, should have been removed from the human genome by natural selection long ago. But it has not been re-moved. In fact, this painful mutation seems to have thrived and spread.

This child's pain comes from the wounds of a battle the genome has fought against a tiny adversary, invisible to her unless someone were to give her a microscope. The tiny adversary is a protozoan, with its relatives called *Plasmodium*, that causes malaria. Both copies of her hemoglobin gene are altered, and the mutant protein encoded by these genes has sickled her red blood cells out of shape and jammed up her tiny blood vessels; but when only one of the copies of this hemoglobin gene is altered, as in the genome of each of the little girl's parents, it can be a good thing for people who live at sea level in the tropics, for it protects them against malaria. And so, as malaria continues to take down its jumbo-jet loads of people in the tropics every few hours, those who survive the attack are more likely to have a mutant hemoglobin within their red blood cells. In the tropics, the malaria parasite has left its mark on the human genome.

For malaria and mammals, the oxygen-carrying red blood cells have been a major theater of battle. The hemoglobin molecule, the molecule that catches oxygen in our lungs and delivers it through the body, has been a major battleground. Not only sickle cell hemoglobin, but also the thalas-semias, a swath of variants in hemoglobin structure and regulation, follow the anopheles mosquito that carries malaria. Surely, after all this time, the mammalian genome should have won; it should have evolved a way to keep the malaria parasite out of our cells. Indeed, we have changed. But so has our adversary. As the malaria parasite has sculpted our human genome, we surely have sculpted its genome, too.

We can change, but there is a limit to how drastically we can change our red blood cells. We can fool around only so much with our life-sustaining oxygen-carrying mechanism. And so the battle with our ancient adversary continues. Perhaps now that we finally are gaining the real-life equivalent of the magical secret decoder ring with the sequencing of the complete malaria genome, we will find a more effective vaccine or therapy and at last overcome malaria's bag of tricks. Perhaps our new level of consciousness will finally bring us complete victory over our ancient adversary. But not yet. For now, malaria continues to take down its 747 load of victims every few hours, last week, yesterday, and today, this afternoon. If you happen to glance at your watch again in a few hours, note that another planeload of children will be gone.

As we look into the forest at night, instinctively we fear snarling fangs and coiled vipers. But it is the once-invisible predators—protozoa such as malaria; bacteria such as the plague, typhus, and tuberculosis; and viruses such as smallpox—that take the largest toll on our species. Just as they still threaten us today, these tiny predators put selective pressure on our ancient ancestors. As our ancestors escaped from and banded together to capture the large predators, the predators we listen for when we wake up in the moonless forest at night, our genes have been doing battle with the tiny ones. And new ones keep emerging. Where does Ebola hide deep in the forest?

One evening in the mid-nineteenth century, Alfred Russel Wallace lay on his cot at the edge of the rain forest shivering with fever. He had traveled halfway around the world to study nature, and now, on an island in the Moluccas, he was getting a much closer view of it than he had planned. As he lay on his cot for hours each day, alternately shivering and sweating, he later wrote, "I had nothing to do but to think over any subjects then particularly interesting me." One day he began to think about Malthus's book *Principles of Population*, which he "had read about twelve years before." Wallace began to think about Malthus's "clear exposition of 'the positive checks to [population] increase'—disease, accidents, war, and famine." He connected the idea that disease, accidents, war, and food shortages, which would limit the ability of the human population to keep increasing, also could limit the increase of animal populations.[7] Animals breed so quickly, he reasoned, that there must be an enormous loss each year or "the world would long ago have been densely crowded with those that breed most quickly."

As he reflected on "the enormous and constant destruction which this implied," his mind focused on the question, "Why do some die and some live?" This was not a purely abstract question at that moment for Wallace, who was lying with a raging fever in a hut on an island far from home. For him, "the answer was clearly, that on the whole the best fitted live. From the effects of disease the most healthy escaped; from enemies, the strongest, the swiftest, or the most cunning; from famine, the best hunters or those with the best digestion; and so on. . . . That is, the fittest would survive."

Wallace's next thoughts were about dramatic changes in the environment and the great amount of individual variation there is within a species.

> Then at once I seemed to see the whole effect of this, that when changes of land and sea, or of climate, or of food-supply, or of enemies occurred—and we know that such changes have always been taking place—and considering the amount of individual variation that my experience as a collector had shown me to exist, then it followed that all the changes necessary for the adaptation of the species to the chang-

ing conditions would be brought about; and as great changes in the
environment are always slow, there would be ample time for the change
to be effected by the survival of the best fitted in every generation.[8]

With his own life threatened by disease, Wallace had discovered the idea
of natural selection, survival of the fittest, all on his own, before hearing the
idea from Darwin. While the phrase "survival of the fittest" seems to ring in
our ears, there is another, quieter phrase that needs some attention. Wallace
said that his realization of the role of natural selection was based on "considering the amount of individual variation that my experience as a collec-
tor had shown me to exist." Variation is an essential prerequisite to selection.

Variation comes from mutation: changes in a single genomic letter,
changes in a block of letters, and the rearranging of pieces of DNA. The
ultimate creative step in variation, for those who have survived to become
adults, is the cutting and pasting and mixing and sorting with the genome
of another adult that happens when we create a new life together—a child
created by mixing pieces of the genomes of all our ancestors.

Survival-of-the-fittest: The words are spoken as one word. But what
carries our own specific DNA forward in time? Our DNA survives in a
partnership with others, carried like candlelight passed through a branching
chain of individuals. As the torch is passed at the border of each new generation, our DNA gets cut up and mixed with DNA from other people. The
work of the other genes in the new mixture may increase or decrease each
gene's "fitness."

Ten generations from now, an eyeblink in evolution, if your DNA has
survived the journey, it will have been diluted to a mere thousandth of your
descendants' genomes. It will be mixed in with the genomes of thousands
of other people who are now alive, most of whom you do not know.
Perhaps a part of your DNA will find itself connected to the DNA of someone in the blue car, in the center lane that you passed yesterday morning,
or that person who stepped aside as you left the train in the subway, or the
child you saw in the arms of his mother, clinging to a tree, in a flood in a
distant land reported on the evening news. Together, at a time in a future
that we cannot clearly imagine and that we will not ourselves live to see, all
of you may share in the creation of a child.

With luck and fitness, these descendants will survive. Is this how, and
when, we tell that you were the fittest? The fittest what? The fittest when?
Now, or when future fragments of your genome encounter a new pathogen? What is "better"? What is fit when you are aiming at a moving target?
Fitness emerges as a strategy, not a goal; a process, not a place.

The pain and tears of the little girl with sickle cell anemia are her wounds in a struggle that is for us, for the survival of our shared genome. She is suffering because her parents carry important information in their genes, information to be shared, through her parents' children's children, with our children's children, information that protects against malaria. For even today, malaria is not tamed, and it is not caged: In 1999, at a camp about a 1½ hour drive from the Empire State Building, two 11-year old boys got malaria.

To survive, we must absorb this truth, that our genome's ability to change, to explore, to incorporate the discoveries of many individuals—and the diversity that results from this exploration—is a central part of our fitness. It is a lesson incorporated into our genome through billions of years of evolution. If we do not treasure human diversity, we risk an eternally broken chain, the end of our species, the loss of our future. If the human brain and the human heart do not learn fast enough what we have known in our bones, and in our eggs and sperm, for millennia, the genes that have brought us this far, through all of their diversity, will be wiped out. Our hopes, our future, indeed our very survival in a distributed, gene-mixing rebirth, depend upon our connections with one another. We are all, profoundly, siblings in the present, parents of the future.

2

The Magic Staircase

In this way an infinite variety of nucleotide [letter] sequences would be possible, to explain the biological specificity of DNA.

—Rosalind Franklin[1]

E ach time a skin cell divides to make two new cells or parents pass their DNA to a child, the information stored in the DNA must be copied very carefully. When I stop to think that the information in our DNA is stored in 3 billion pairs of pieces linked together in 46 strings, one string to a chromosome, I do not wonder that mistakes can be made in copying this information. In fact, I wonder why there aren't many *more* mutations. To copy so much, so carefully, takes precise machinery, as well as backup machinery that can fix essentially any error.

You might envision DNA as a carefully preserved reference library. The instructions needed to make a hand, an eye, an ear, a virus, a tulip, a bee, or a person are stored there, in code; so are the instructions for making molecular machines, including molecular machines that copy DNA and machines that can proofread their copy. Included in the DNA reference library, too, are the instructions for making a molecular machine that can decode the information encoded in a molecule of DNA and use it to build molecules of proteins.

When DNA is decoded, its information first is copied into another molecule, RNA, that travels like a messenger to a protein factory, where the information the RNA carries is translated into the strings of amino acids that we call proteins. Each amino acid in the protein is specified by a string of three letters in the DNA and RNA. For example, the letters CAG encode the instructions to put the amino acid Q into a protein.[2]

In an English-language library, information is stored using an alphabet of 26 letters, A through Z. In a DNA-language library, information is encoded using an alphabet of four letters, A, G, T, and C. Of course, these letters are not really letters, but chemicals called adenine, guanine, thymine, and cytidine. A and G are similar to each other, and are bigger than T and C. These four letters are strung together as if in words—GACGCTAGATGGATTAAC. . . .

For each protein in our bodies, there is a place in the DNA, which we refer to as a gene, where the order of these chemicals or letters specifies the order in which to connect amino acids in a string that will fold up to become that protein. A protein molecule may be part of a larger structure, like the fibers in our muscles, or it may be an enzyme, a catalyst that makes things happen much more rapidly than they would happen in a lifeless pond.

We may envision these genes being brought out by their cellular keepers, as if on velvet from a locked vault, for precise reading of their instructions—for faithful copying—and handed down with great care from parents to children. We may envision this precious DNA being carefully protected from dust, and certainly—to the greatest possible extent—from mutation.

But maybe the peaceful library is not such a good way to describe DNA, because DNA is not like the motionless double helix of textbook covers. Living DNA is active, dynamic, and busy. You can't assume that if you've seen one patch of double helix, you've seen them all. If it were a creation of performance art, a tourist attraction on a grand plaza, all guidebooks would recommend DNA as a "must visit." We would crowd around, look up, and be captivated. We would see two strong ribbons, twisted about each other to form a double helix, extending far up from our imaginary plaza. Running up the center of the double helix, as if the two helical ribbons were banisters, is a spiral staircase (see Figure 2-1). The steps of this staircase are all the same width and come in two color schemes: one part gold and part cobalt blue, the other part turquoise and part apricot.

At a scheduled time, starting from the top, the gold part of each step separates from its cobalt partner, and each turquoise patch separates from its apricot partner. Starting from the top, the two ribbons twirl and move apart. In the midst of the twirling, separating ribbons, two new helical ribbons begin to grow, one beside each of the original ribbons. To keep things from getting tangled, a ribbon is cut, its partner helix passes through it, and the ribbon ends are reconnected, precisely and quickly. Over and over, they

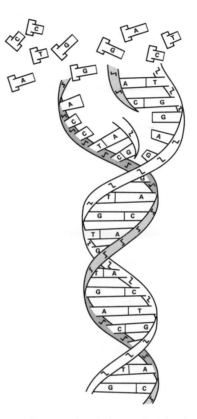

Figure 2-1 The magic staircase. Two strands spiral around each other, forming a double helix. Each strand is a string of the letters A, T, G, and C, connected by linkers. The information that DNA carries from generation to generation is encoded in the order of the letters in each strand. When DNA is duplicated, the strands separate; each strand specifies the order of letters in its new partner by the rule that where there is an A on one strand, there will be a T on the other; and where there is a G on one strand, there will be a C on the other.

are cut, twirl, and reattach, in an intricate choreography. Attentive spectators begin to notice a recurrent pattern.

It becomes obvious that you can predict the next color that will join a growing ribbon by looking at the strand of the original ribbon beside it. If there is a gold patch on the original ribbon, you can predict that it will attract a cobalt patch to form part of a new gold/cobalt step connecting the two ribbons; cobalt will attract gold, apricot patches will attract turquoise, and turquoise will attract apricot. Each of the two original strands is used as a template to direct the order of the colors in its new partner strand. When the swirling stops and two new double helices are before us, the color scheme in each is the same as that in the original double helix; the two new helical staircases are copies of the original, with the same two-color steps, gold/cobalt and apricot/turquoise.

We may watch, enthralled, as the beautiful sculpture spins in its complex choreography. But we know that there is more to the sculpture than its form and the patterns of its dance. The most captivating part is that messages are encoded in the sequence of cobalt, gold, apricot, and turquoise— C, G, A, and T. If we can break the codes, we can decipher extraordinary messages. These ribbons encode a life and create a foundation on which future generations can emerge.

In life, when a DNA double helix unravels to be copied, and the two new double helices grow alongside their partners, a rapidly acting copying machine, composed of proteins, has the job of making a careful match at every step. Some of the proteins in the machine are enzymes, the catalysts that attach the letters to each other. Some of the proteins hold the machinery together; others hold the machine to the DNA as it moves along.

The copying machine has to be careful, but it also has to be fast. To copy the 3 billion steps in each of our cells each time the cell divides takes about 8 hours, with each of about 1000 machines attaching about 80 new letters every second. One tiny missed match among the billions would be a mutation; the child would be different from the parent.

As the copying machine builds the chain, there are two steps to think about. First, the right letter must float into the machinery to become the new partner of a letter on the template strand (A floats in to pair with T, T to pair with A, G to pair with C, and C to pair with G). Once this new letter is in place, the enzyme creates a strong link to make the new letter part of the growing DNA chain.

Like beads in a necklace, the letters in DNA hang on linkers that attach them to the chain. DNA's linker is in part a sugar, deoxyribose, the D in DNA. To build the growing chain, the enzyme attaches the deoxyribose linker of the incoming T or A or G or C to the deoxyribose linker of the T or A or G or C that the enzyme has just attached to the growing chain one step before. How does the machinery get the correct letter into each step of the template strand? If a G floats into the empty space across from a T instead of T's correct partner, A, the shape of the step will be wrong. Because the G doesn't fit right, it tends to float away, leaving room for an A to float in. In contrast, if an A floats in, it fits quite comfortably, and thus it is more likely to stay long enough to be attached to the growing chain. In fact, when this was measured,[3] when copying a T, A was about 1000 times less likely to float away than G was. In DNA, the letter G (or guanine) is the closest in shape to A (adenine). When a C or another T floated in beside the T that was about to be copied, it was even more likely to slip away. Because the correct letter fits the best and stays in the machinery the longest, it is most likely to become part of the growing chain.

Not only does the wrong letter tend to slip away, but also, if the letter pair is the wrong shape, the copying enzyme seems to have a hard time reaching around the back to attach the new letter to the growing helix. In fact, it took four times as long to attach a G across from this T as it did to attach an A, and it took eight times as long to attach another T or a C.

Because it takes longer to attach the wrong letter, and during all that time the wrong letter has a high chance of slipping away, mistakes are infrequent. But whether it is copying a tiny genome or a human genome, occasionally the machine does make an error. In fact, in the example described above, a T-G pair was formed instead of a T-A pair once every 20,000 times the T was copied. T-C and T-T pairs were each formed only once every 500,000 times the T was copied.

If I made only one mistake every 500,000 times I made a decision, I would be pretty proud of myself. For DNA, however, this is good, but not good enough. In our two-stranded 3-billion-letter genome, one mistake every 20,000 to 500,000 times would be 12,000 to 300,000 mistakes every time one of our 50 trillion cells divides. At that rate, our genome would not come close to making it to an adult from a fertilized egg. In fact, our DNA copying machinery does much better than one mistake every 20,000 to 500,000 times, because it actually can proofread its work and, when it does insert the wrong letter, correct it on the fly. It can break the link it just made and get rid of the mistaken letter, the wrong partner, catching errors so fast that its accuracy is improved another 1000 times—it removes 999 of every 1000 errors.

Still, some mistakes remain after the copying machinery has moved on. One team looked at 414 mutations that were left after copying many examples of a 210-letter region of a gene in bacteria grown in their laboratory. There were different kinds of mistakes. In 7 of every 10 mistakes, the wrong letter was attached. Nearly half of these wrong-letter mistakes were of the same kind—a T, rather than a C, was paired with a G. Nearly 1 in 5 mistakes were deletions, where a whole patch of the DNA was left out. (More than half of these deletions occurred at one spot, over and over.) Nearly 1 in 10 mistakes involved the insertion of a patch of extra letters, and about 1 in 20 of the mistakes involved adding or removing a single letter.[4]

These copying errors are not left in the DNA, for there is yet another level of protection for the messages in DNA. A "mismatch repair" machine follows to correct the remaining mismatches between the template letters and their new partners. In the 210 letters of the bacteria's gene discussed in the last paragraph, mismatch repair corrected 996 of every 1000 errors, leaving only 4 of these errors behind. Just as some kinds of mutations happened more often than others, mismatch repair fixed some kinds of errors more reliably than it fixed others. It kept Cs from replacing Ts seven times better than it kept Ts from replacing Cs.[5] The mismatch repair machinery is especially careful to repair places where extra letters have been inserted or letters have been deleted.[6] Insertions and deletions generally are much more serious than a change in a single letter, because a deletion or insertion throws the whole message out of frame: mngitu ni ntelligibletot he rea der. But still, after all of this attention to detail, and the care taken before making the bond, and the proofreading and repair of mistakes, out of the 1000 errors that were left after careful copying and proofreading, 4 still remained.

Sometimes the DNA at a spot is badly damaged even before it is copied, perhaps by radiation or something else in the environment. It might be so badly damaged that the careful copying enzymes can't even recognize it. Was it once a T? When the machinery runs into a damaged letter, it simply stalls there, leaving a cell with a partly copied piece of DNA. What to do? Call in another DNA copying enzyme that can make a quick and dirty patch, so that the DNA copying machinery can move on.[7] This copier is not so demanding about the proper shape, so in an emergency it is able to attach something opposite the damaged piece and allow the copying to pass the block. This less finicky copier moves slowly and can be replaced by a more careful enzyme once it gets past the mistake. Later, other repair systems may be able to fix up the sloppy repair job. If not, where the DNA was damaged, for example by ultraviolet light, a mutation is left behind.

Just to copy the genome of the relatively simple bacterium *Escherichia coli* requires complex machinery. Its copying machine is made of 10 different kinds of proteins, some in more than one copy, so that there are 18 pieces to the machine that we know of so far. In addition to the protein enzymes that actually hook the new letters to the growing strand, there are the proofreaders, the proteins that hold the machinery together, and the proteins that hold the machinery on the DNA so that it doesn't float away. What a job. And this happens over and over again, each time the DNA is copied; this bacterial machinery copies 500 letters per second.

When the copy is faithful to the original, the message will be preserved; when an error is made and not caught in time, the message will change; there, the new cell will differ from the original. With the combined care of the copying, proofreading, and repair machinery, there is on the average only about one unrepaired error in every billion to 10 billion letters copied—about one mutation every time one of our cells divides. This mutation may have no effect, it may be bad, or it may even be a good thing. If it happens in our skin cells, we may never notice it, or it could lead to skin cancer. If it happens in what become sperm or egg cells, when we are passing DNA to our children, it is the substrate of evolution.

3

Predators Battle Prey in the Genome

And we too are impressions left by something that used to be here.

—Stephen Batchelor[1]

A shell caught the athlete's attention as he walked along a Pacific beach. It had an intricate, beautiful pattern, and it was large for a shell. He picked it up, and, looking closely at the treasure in his hand, scratched it with a pocketknife. Unfortunately, this shell was occupied, and the young man's scratching at the opening was interpreted as predation. The occupant reacted to defend itself. "Hey, I think this thing stung me," the man said. According to his mother, he felt no pain, just some numbness, but soon could not move his legs; he slipped into unconsciousness and, within 5 hours, he was dead.[2]

I learned about this deadly cone snail from Baldomero Olivera, a biochemist, who made good use of some free time he had when he returned to his native Philippines. He was waiting for equipment that he needed for his research on DNA to reach him from overseas. Olivera decided to use that waiting time to satisfy his curiosity about how cone snails, which come in many sizes and beautiful, collectable, patterns, kill their diverse prey.[3] By the time his equipment arrived, he was hooked on the snails.

Life on a reef is both rough and biochemically competitive. The beautiful killer cone shell contained a snail that lives by fishing. A cone snail can catch a fish. True, the snail would lose any race against a fish through the water. But after all, we do not catch most fish by swimming after them either. Some cone snails use a strategy that starts a bit like ours: The snail floats a "worm" in the water. This is not, of course, an actual worm; it is a part of the snail's body that looks like a worm. When the fish bites the "worm," the snail injects a cocktail of nerve and muscle toxins into the fish that, essentially, short-circuits it. The fish can't move, and the snail has its meal.

Olivera, working together with Lourdes Cruz, a professor in the Philippines, found more than one toxin in cone snails—many, many more. Each of the 500 cone snail species has at least 50 and sometimes even as many as 200 different toxins. Different species of cone snail kill different types of prey—fish, worms, even other kinds of snails. They have a cornucopia of toxins with a wide range of toxic effects, interfering with different types of nerve signals.

Cone-snail evolution was beginning to look like a toxin-generating machine. Olivera began to toy with the idea that cone snails might have evolved a genetic strategy for generating diverse toxins rapidly. If cone snails were able to evolve such a genetic strategy, it would give them an advantage in molecular evolutionary wars. A large and flexible repertoire of new toxins would enable the cone snails' progeny to adapt rapidly, across only a few generations, to changes in prey, predators, and competitors. In a fast-changing competitive environment, it is good to have a wide range of options.

Olivera's thinking about the evolution of cone-snail toxins began to focus on a mismatch between something everyone expected and something he observed. When two things that always match suddenly don't match, pay attention. There is something unusual afoot.

The standard explanation as to why cone snails have so many different toxins would be that the snails' DNA varied randomly and the snails that survived were the ones that got it right. This standard explanation began to unravel when Olivera noted that most of the variation between different toxin genes was focused in one corner of the gene. At first, it looked as if the standard "random mutation, then selection" theory could explain this focused genetic variation. Random mutation generates changes throughout the gene, this explanation says, but changes in most parts of the gene provide no selective advantage. If changes in a particular part of the gene provide no advantage, then a snail with those changes is no more fit than the starting snail, and so there is no reason to expect an increase in snails with changes in that part of the gene. Changes in some parts of the gene actually hurt the new snail, so those snails have a disadvantage; we won't see many of them or their children either. Changes in the side of the toxin gene that creates new toxins may actually help the snail survive, and so we get a lot of snails with changes in that corner of the toxin gene.

So, the standard theory explains, we see more changes in one part of the toxin genes because these changes generate new, improved toxins; changes that generate new, improved toxins would be the only changes favored by selection; changes anywhere else in the gene might not have been selected for—or might even have been selected against. Thus, random mutation and selection would explain why one region of the toxin gene has more changes. The standard explanation says that the toxin DNA only *appears* to change more quickly; change actually occurs randomly everywhere in the genome, but we do not see the other random changes because the snails that inherit them do not have any advantage.

The problem with the usual explanation was that only some of the frequent changes that Olivera found in one region of the toxin gene occurred in places that actually change the toxin protein itself. If many of the frequent changes in the toxin DNA were not changing the toxin protein, these specific changes couldn't be selected for by selecting for a better toxin. So why were these changes so much more common than changes in other parts of the DNA? Something other than selecting for better toxins one at a time must have been attracting variation to the high-mutation corner of the toxin DNA. If genetic variation is more likely to happen in one corner of the DNA than in another, mutation isn't random.

Before saying any more about this, I need to explain how the DNA that codes for the toxin can change without changing the toxin protein. Mutations in protein-coding DNA can occur without changing the protein itself because the genetic code is degenerate. In code language, *degenerate* means that there is more than one way of saying the same thing. Because more than one sequence of DNA can code for the same toxin protein, it is possible to change the sequence of letters in the DNA without changing the toxin protein at all.

A protein is born as a necklace, a string of amino acids. Amino acids are added to the string in the order specified in the genome. This order is specified by reading DNA in blocks of three letters, or *codons*, which is why the genetic code is called a triplet code. Each of the three letters in a codon can be any one of DNA's four letters, and thus there are $4 \times 4 \times 4 = 64$ possible codons.

The 20 letters shown across the top of the boxes in Figure 3-1 represent the 20 amino acids that form our proteins. They are shown once each in alphabetical order only for illustration. The number of times each amino

A	C	D	E	F	G	H	I	K	L	M
GCU	UGU	GAU	GAA	UUU	GGU	CAU	AUU	AAA	UUA	AUG
GCC	UGC	GAC	GAG	UUC	GGC	CAC	AUC	AAG	UUG	
GCA					GGA		AUA		CUU	
GCG					GGG				CUC	
									CUA	
									CUG	

N	P	Q	R	S	T	V	W	Y	stop
AUU	CCU	CAA	CGU	UCU	ACU	GUU	UGG	UAU	UAA
AAC	CCC	CAG	CGC	UCC	ACC	GUC		UAC	UAG
	CCA		CGA	UCA	ACA	GUA			UGA
	CCG		CGG	UCG	ACG	GUG			
			AGA	AGU					
			AGG	AGC					

Figure 3-1 The genetic code.

acid is used, and the order in which they are connected to each other, is what gives different proteins their different properties.

The triplets listed under each letter are the codons that can be used to encode each amino acid. For example, the codon GAG means "Add the amino acid E to the growing protein," and· GAC instructs the protein-assembling machinery to add a D. Because messenger RNA has an alphabet of four letters, G, C, A, and U (RNA uses U where DNA uses T), there is a total of 64 codons (including the "stop" codons used to mark the end of the protein). With only a few variations in meaning, these same codons are used by all life on Earth.

By choosing different combinations of the codons available to encode each letter, there are $4 \times 2 \times 2 \times 2 \times 2 \times 4 \times 2 \times 3 \times 2 \times 6 \times 1 \times 2 \times 4 \times 2 \times 6 \times 6 \times 4 \times 4 \times 1 \times 2$ or nearly 340 million ways to encode this particular string of 20 amino acids (times three ways to encode "stop").

There are 64 codons, but, typically, proteins are strung together from an ingredients list of no more than 20 amino acids. Thus, there are more than three times as many codons as there are amino acids; 64 codons specify 20 amino acids. More than one codon is available to encode each amino acid, allowing some flexibility in the use of language and enabling the code to be degenerate. Indeed, most (but not all) amino acids are encoded by more than one codon; some amino acids have as many as six codons. In other words, for some amino acids, the DNA can use any one of six codons to signify that this amino acid should be added to the growing protein. And if different codons can code for the same amino acid, then different strings of codons can code for the same protein: Either AGCGAAGAGGAT or

TCTGAGGAGGAC could encode the protein piece "SEED." Your DNA can say it either way.

If the cone-snail toxins did change just by random mutation followed by selection for the "winner" toxins, we would expect to see a lot of changes in the DNA that were not synonymous; we would expect to see changes that would change the amino acids, like changing the amino acid E to D by changing the codon for E, such as GAG, to a codon for D, such as GAC. We certainly wouldn't expect to see a lot of extra changes that only replaced a codon with its synonym in the toxin genes, such as changing a codon for D to another codon that still means D. Of course, there would be some synonymous changes just from random mutation, but the rate of change between these synonyms wouldn't, randomly, always be higher in the same corner of the toxin gene than they are somewhere else in the cone-snail genome.

What we would expect, assuming that mutation is random, is not what Olivera found. When he compared DNA from many different cone-snail toxins, he found a very high rate of change between codons, including a high rate of change between synonyms, in the region of DNA that codes for the toxins. He also found that this part of the gene often gains and loses patches of DNA. Selective pressure might favor changes in codons that change the amino acids to create new toxins, but why should there be *so many* changes, even between synonyms, in this small region of DNA?

Olivera wondered if a special variation-generating mechanism might somehow be directed to the little stretch of DNA that codes for toxin proteins.[4] Perhaps selection has favored not only snails that evolved a good new toxin, but, most significantly, snails that evolved a *strategy* of directing genetic change to the stretch of DNA that codes for the toxin. Rather than mutating and waiting for selection to assess each change letter by letter, some snails may have been favored by evolving mechanisms that focus mutation in this important corner of the toxin genes. Some of these changes would be synonyms, and so would not affect the protein; but many of these rapid changes that were directed to the toxin region would be changes in the toxin protein itself. This mechanism would guarantee that generation after generation, cone snails could retain a competitive edge by being able to try out new toxins rapidly.

The snails could, of course, evolve new toxins quickly simply by having a generally high mutation rate, and perhaps some now-lost cone snails used that strategy. But why mess up a lot of good genes when it is, generation after generation, specifically toxin diversity that you need in order to help ensure that some of your progeny will survive changes in predators, prey, and food? The progeny of cone snails with uniform, higher mutation rates would be weakened by errors in important housekeeping genes. (On the other hand, the progeny of cone snails with uniform, low mutation rates might not be able to defend themselves against a new competitor or a new predator, or they might miss the opportunity to catch a new species of fish if old food sources became scarce.) It is more likely that among the progeny of cone snails with a high mutation rate that was focused specifically on the toxin gene, there would be some progeny with new toxins that were useful when there was a change in their predators or prey, or in competition against other snails. The progeny of these snails would have an advantage and would survive.

It is a more efficient route of evolution, and a clever genetic strategy, to increase genetic exploration for a toxin and let the rest of the genome change more carefully. So perhaps there has been positive selection in the evolution of the cone-snail genome for a strategy that generates new toxins quickly. Other predators, too, from vipers to scorpions, seem to have special mechanisms to generate rapid variation in the very genes they need to attack their prey. Cone snails have many, many progeny. It is likely, but it has not yet been proven, that cone snails with a modulated mutation rate that is especially high in the toxin gene and lower elsewhere would be the winners, and thus would be the ones that we admire while we step gingerly around them on Pacific beaches.

We can step around the cone snails on the beaches and vipers on the trails, and shake scorpions out of our shoes in the morning, but there are other dangers that are harder to avoid. They cannot be avoided by staying home; they lurk on our cutting boards, grow in our sponges, attack from the air, travel quietly in unseen insects, hide in our food, and sneak across in a handshake. Many of these tiny predators, pathogens that are individually invisible to us without a microscope, evade our immune system by quickly changing the genes that encode their coats. They too appear to have come up with something better (from their point of view) than random muta-tion. Just when our immune response gets ready to kill anything wearing the pathogen's coat, many pathogens can put on a new coat.

Bacteria that look like the spiral that twists around a screw are called *spirochetes.* The spirochete that causes Lyme disease has a large selection of patterns for its coat. We can watch what happens by taking blood samples from mice infected with Lyme disease spirochetes. Each time the spiro-chete bacteria that cause Lyme disease are isolated from infected mice, a large patch on the spirochete's coat is different.[5] The spirochete keeps changing its coat by inserting new patches of DNA into its coat-protein gene; each new patch of DNA results in a different patch of amino acids in the coat protein, as if one day the back of the coat is red, the next day green, and the next day orange.

The mouse's immune system, which was alerted to grab anything wearing a coat with a red patch and then has to learn to grab anything in a coat with a green patch, and so on, can't keep up with the pathogen's wardrobe. The Lyme spirochete can thus continue to live within the mouse, surviving in spite of the mouse's stimulated, searching immune system.

The Lyme spirochete takes its many quick wardrobe changes from a large inventory of extra DNA pieces called plasmids. It can also mix and match pieces of the stored coat patches, making patchwork of the patches and giving them even greater variability. In fact, it is estimated that the spirochete has 10^{30} (1,000,000,000,000,000,000,000,000,000,000) different patch patterns.

If we examine the spirochete's coat carefully, we can see that surrounding the ever-changing patch in the spirochete coat protein, there is a completely conserved repeat of five amino acids, EGAIK. If we stop to examine the 15 letters of DNA that, using the triplet code, encode these five amino acids, we find something very unexpected. Because of the degeneracy of the genetic code, there are nearly 200 DNA sequences that could have been used to encode the five amino acids EGAIK. But the 15 DNA letters that encode EGAIK in the repeated patch in the spirochete coat always are part of an identical sequence of 17 letters, TGAGGGGGC TATTAAGG, that is found on both sides of the repeat and in all samples of spirochete DNA tested. We never see TGAAGGAGCAATAAAAG or TGAGGGCGCCATCAAGG or any of the nearly 200 other ways to encode the very same amino acids.

If these really are synonymous codons, why is it that time after time, spirochete after spirochete, it is always, always TGAGGGGGCTATTAAGG? The other 192 synonyms for EGAIK are not acting as synonyms should.

You and I could make a plan: If you say "I'll *call* you tonight," it means that you'll call me at 8 P.M., but if you say "I'll *phone* you tonight," it means that you'll call me at 9 P.M.. With two different ways of saying the same thing, we can create another code that sends more information underneath the message. People who didn't know about our code would hear you say, "I'll call you tonight," and think they knew the whole message. But you would have transmitted an additional message, with even the existence of the message remaining hidden from those who did not suspect it was there.

Might there be a secret message that attracts genetic variation to a patch of DNA? Some kind of message would in fact be needed to attract enzymes that cut out the DNA in between the spirochete's repeats and replace it with DNA that codes for a different patch of spirochete coat and is stored somewhere else in the spirochete's DNA. When you have an enzyme that cuts and pastes DNA floating around, you don't want it to cut just anywhere. It is safer to require strict recognition of a special sequence, an address, to direct the cut to the right place. In the Lyme spirochete, the cut could be placed precisely on either side of the ever-changing patch in the coat-protein DNA by a message hidden in the DNA.

This targeted cutting allows the Lyme spirochete to make its rapid wardrobe changes without waiting for random changes everywhere in the spirochete's DNA to make a lucky hit. If the DNA that encodes the amino acids EGAIK changed to any one of nearly 200 synonymous sequences, it still would encode the amino acids EGAIK, but the DNA recognition site would be damaged, the biochemical mechanism that exchanges pieces of DNA wouldn't work, and the spirochete couldn't keep changing its coat. Those spirochetes that tended to make what appear to be synonymous changes in the DNA that encodes EGAIK would in fact lose the ability to change their coats and could be caught by our immune response.

Perhaps codons that have been considered synonyms ever since the genetic code was cracked in the 1960s do not always behave as true synonyms. True, the codons are synonyms in that they code for the same amino acid. But what we thought were synonymous codons may have additional, distinct, content-dependent meanings for the proteins and enzymes that cut and paste DNA.

The spirochete coat protein has a telltale pattern: conserved patches surrounding a region of great variability. This pattern may point us to a broader biochemical strategy that the successful spirochete has evolved for protection from its most predictable challenge: the host immune system. In fact, if you look very closely at the spirochete's genome, you will find other stretches of absolutely conserved DNA around patches of changing protein.

We expected random codon choice, but codon choice is not random in the spirochete coat protein. Something unusual is afoot. There is extra information embedded in the stretch of DNA that encodes the amino acids EGAIK. The spirochete genome will call us at 9 P.M.; it has something else to say.

4

Mutation Is Not Monotonous

Rare is not a synonym for random.

—Lynn Ripley[1]

For all the reverence in which we hold it, DNA is just a molecule, composed of chemical pieces that we represent by the letters A, T, G, and C. The information encoded in one DNA double helix is different from the information encoded in another DNA double helix with a different sequence of As, Ts, Gs, and Cs. The different order of the pairs of letters on the strings makes each of us different, and it makes the DNA itself different, too.

Looking from one side of the double helix, there are four letter pairs: A on this strand paired with T on the other, T on this strand with A on the other, G on this strand with C on the other, and C on this strand with G on the other. Each of these pairs looks slightly different from the others. As DNA is run through the copying machinery, these differences in the DNA make some mistakes more likely to occur than others. The proteins that hold onto and copy DNA interact with it as one molecule with another molecule. Physical forces dictate their interactions.

The two strands of the long helices seem to breathe, spreading apart a little, then settling back together. How often each step in the helix breathes depends upon how tightly each pair of letters holds each step together. The strength of an A-T pair is different from the strength of a G-C pair; thus the A-T pair's tendency to separate slightly for an instant—the breathing of the helix—is different from the G-C pair's. The structure of DNA changes subtly, then, as we move along the helix. The differences in DNA sequence that carry the linear code also affect the amount of breathing. How much DNA opens up at one step depends not only upon the letters at that step, but also upon the letters nearby. A string of six A-T pairs, one on top of the other along the spiral staircase, will allow the DNA to breathe much more than a string of six G-C pairs.

Not only does the helix breathe, but, as in a badly constructed staircase, the rise and angle of the steps is not uniform.[2] When an A-T letter pair is one step up from a G-C letter pair, the twist and rise of the G-C step are slightly different from those found when a G-C letter pair is above a C-G step. Just as you may trip running up a badly constructed staircase, the copying machinery is affected by the differing rise and twist of the steps in the helix. Such subtle differences in shape affect the accuracy with which the DNA itself is copied, and which mistakes are most likely to be repaired. These changes may be small, but they are not without effect.

As the copying machine moves along a strand of the helix, it may pass along a GCAC or a GTGC. The physical structure of these sequences differs because of the way the letters "stack" on top of each other; some sequences are easier for an enzyme to copy than others. Variations in copying fidelity along the helix can be dramatic. Because of these shape changes, a particular mistake may be as much as 100,000 times more likely in one place in the genome than in another. Just as your jacket's zipper may keep catching on a small bend in a metal tooth, some steps in a DNA helix simply are not copied as accurately as others. Copying may even stall at these places requiring enzymes to come in to cut and unwind the tangle. These differences also affect the accuracy of the error-correcting machinery. Different copying machinery and different error-correcting machines trip up in different places.

Some mutations are so likely that they hardly seem random. Like accidents at a busy intersection without a stoplight, certain mutations keep happening. Some can be predicted, if you look closely. It is as if a local shopkeeper, watching the magic staircase on the plaza, could pick one particular step and say that, on the average, once a week or so, an apricot will slip in there next to the cobalt, instead of cobalt's usual partner gold, at that very place.

In her laboratory in New Jersey, molecular geneticist Lynn Ripley looks very closely, too.[3] For example, she looked at mutations over many generations of a virus called T4, which kills bacteria. A section of the two-stranded sequence of T4 DNA that Ripley has studied with particular interest looks like this:

TOP STRAND

ATGCTTCACGTTCGACGCTTCGACGGGAAGGGA

TACGAAGTGCAAGCTGCGAAGCTGCCCTTCCCT

BOTTOM STRAND

I'll focus on just the top strand to describe what happened to this sequence. (Of course, because of the pairing rule, if I say that an A changed to a T on the top strand, that means that a T will be changed to an A on the bottom strand.)

To a casual observer, it looks as if there were a variety of seemingly unrelated, random mutations in this region of the T4 DNA. In one mutated version of the T4 virus, the A in the 8th position had changed to a C. In another version, the 12th letter, T, had disappeared. In another mutant virus, a new A appeared between the 22nd and 23rd positions in the sequence. In yet another mutant, the G at position 26 was replaced by a T. No obvious pattern here; all very random, it seems. Yes, it seems random—except for one thing that Lynn Ripley noticed: She kept getting these same "random" mutations over and over again.

If this was random, Ripley asked, why did she keep seeing the A in the 8th position mutate to a C, or the T in the 12th position disappear? Why did an A keep appearing between the 22nd and 23rd positions? Why did the G at position 26 get replaced by a T so much of the time? Why wasn't it just as likely, she asked, for the C in the 7th position to mutate to a G or for an A to appear between the 20th and 21st positions? If this really was random mutation, why wasn't it, well, . . . *random*?

To visualize what might be happening, Lynn Ripley bent a representation of the sequence over in its middle, between the G at position 17 and the C at position 18, as illustrated in Figure 4-1. She could see that the letter pairs across two sides of the bent sequence matched correctly as if they were across from each other on two different strands of a DNA double helix, rather than both on one strand folded back on itself. When she bent the sequence of letters in the middle, the C at the fourth position was across from the G four positions from the other end. The T at the fifth position paired up with the A five positions from the other end; the T at the sixth position was paired with the A six positions from the other end. And so the pairing went up the center of the folded DNA sequence. It was almost perfect.

The pairing of letters across this imaginary bent helix was almost perfect, but it was not exactly perfect. In addition to a small loop in the mid-

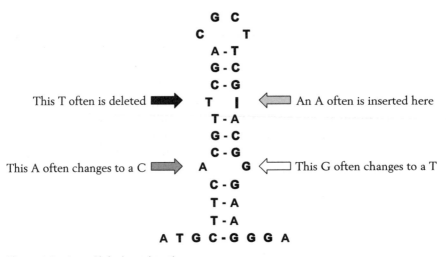

Figure 4-1 Lynn Ripley's explanation.

dle that was needed to allow the bending of the DNA like a hairpin and three letters that were unpaired at each end, there were a few mismatches. Lynn Ripley could see that the A at position 8 was mismatched—because there was a G, rather than the T needed to make an A-T pair, eight positions from the other end (at position 26). To allow the CGA starting at position 13 to match with a GCT 12 steps from the end (at positions 22 to 23), the T at position 12 would have to loop out so that the G would be across from a C rather than this T. Those few changes—a four-letter loop at the top, a single A to G mismatch, and a T looped out of the hairpin—were all that were needed to make a perfect hairpin; other than that, from position 4 counting from the beginning to position 4 counting from the end, there was a perfect little stretch of matched pairs.

It became very clear to Lynn Ripley that her folded hairpin model could explain the mutations she kept seeing, over and over and over again. The single mismatch would be eliminated if the A in position 8 mutated to a C or the G at position 26 was replaced by a T because these mutations would create either a C-G or an A-T pair, "perfecting" the hairpin palindrome. If the T at position 12 disappeared, changing the GTTCG that begins at position 10 to GTCG, there would be no need for the imperfection of a looped-out T. GTCG would be perfectly matched with the CGAC that was across the little bent double helix, at positions 21 to 24. Or, if an A appeared between the 22nd and 23rd positions, replacing the CGAC at positions 21 to 24 with CGAAC around the bent helix, the T at position

12 would now have a partner. This hairpin also explained why some of these mutations never happened at the same time. The A at position 8 might change to a C in the same mutant in which the T at position 12 disappeared, but she never saw an A appear between positions 22 and 23 in the same mutant in which the T at position 12 disappeared.

What Lynn Ripley realized was that during copying, somehow, something like the little hairpin actually could form. Then the copying and error-correcting mechanisms that swirl around when each strand of a DNA helix is copied somehow would try to "fix" the doubled-over little helix, "fixing" the A-G mismatch at positions 8 and 26 to A-T or C-G, and excising the looped-out T at position 12 or giving it a partner by inserting an A between positions 22 and 23. Lynn Ripley looked at a little, imperfect hairpin loop and watched it be "corrected" (by mutation) to a more perfect helix.

What had looked like random mutation was, upon very close inspection, not random at all. Or at least it wasn't happening at a random place in the DNA sequence. The likelihood of each mutation depended upon its sequence context, that is, what other As or Ts or Cs or Gs were nearby, and in what order. Some mutations were orders of magnitude more likely than others. Looking at other similar sequences, Lynn Ripley could predict where they might mutate. A mutation that is predictable is not random.

For this discussion, I have to separate two uses of the word *random*. It is clear, from work like Lynn Ripley's, that mutations do not occur at random places in the DNA. However, they might be at random places with respect to the biological effects of the mutation. Whether or not they are random with respect to biological effects (for example, they did not appear to be random with respect to biological effects in the cone-snail toxins) is an important issue that I will return to soon. For now, I am just talking about where mutations happen in the DNA.

Predictable mutations depend not only on the sequence of letters in the DNA, but also on which side of the double helix is being copied. Imagine that you are moving down the helical staircase, one railing on your left, the other on your right, just ahead of the machinery that is making a new copy of DNA. The "steps" that you are using to go down the center of the double helix are, of course, the letter pairs, A-T, T-A, G-C, and C-G. The railings of the staircase form the structural framework that links the two life-generating strings of letters. Each railing is a chain of the sugar deoxyribose, the D in DNA, and atoms that connect the sugars to each other. Because of the way the sugars are linked together, the railing has a pattern.

The pattern is the same on both railings, but it has a direction. It runs *down* the railing on one side of the helix, and *up* the railing on the other side of the helix. This pattern comes from the way the sugar backbones, the deoxyribose molecules that connect the letters, are hooked together. (When we talk about letters in DNA, like ATTCGG, we leave out the connecting sugars, but in real DNA, they are there between the letters, linking them to each other through hooks called *phosphates*.) If the sugar patterns on both of the double helix's two railings went in the same direction, they might be described as parallel patterns; because the patterns go in opposite directions, they are called antiparallel. These antiparallel patterns complicate the copying of DNA.

To follow along, you could draw two railings with antiparallel patterns, perhaps arrows running in opposite directions or something more creative. Now imagine separating the strands and copying each of them, as was illustrated in Figure 2.1. When DNA is copied, the strands separate, and a copy is made of each strand. Conceivably, this could have been done differently. It could have been that when DNA is copied, the result would be a completely new double helix, leaving the original double helix intact, but it doesn't work that way. The strands separate and are copied, and each copy remains with the strand that it was copied from, the strand that was its template. The two original template strands, each with its new partner strand, leave each other, giving us two half-new DNA double helices.

The enzyme machine that builds a new copy of DNA is designed to work in one direction, always building the pattern from left to right. But, here's a problem for the DNA copying machinery: Because of the antiparallel railing patterns on the original helix, when the double helix opens up at one end for copying, the copying machinery is at the right end of the pattern on one strand of the helix and at the left end of the pattern on the other strand. The railing pattern on a new strand built from left to right starting at one end of the original helix will have the required antiparallel pattern, right to left on the original strand and left to right on its new partner. The problem is on the other side of the helix, where the helix railing pattern runs left to right. If it too is copied from the left using the DNA copying machine, which builds a copy with a left-to-right pattern, the new railing patterns will be parallel, not antiparallel as they need to be.

This is how the problem is solved: To make a copy of the problem strand, the DNA copying enzyme machine slips a bit down the helix from the open end, then works its way back up, making a small piece of DNA called an Okazaki fragment after the husband and wife team that figured this out.[4] Then the copying machinery slips even further down the open helix and, moving up again, makes another small piece of DNA until it reaches the Okazaki fragment it made just before. This new fragment of

DNA is then attached to the first fragment, and so on down the helix. So, one strand is copied in this discontinuous, jumpy way. Because the machinery slips down a bit and copies up, the second strand of DNA can be copied with a backbone pattern that is antiparallel to the original, as it should be.

There is still another level of complication in DNA copying, because a piece of DNA cannot be built by starting in thin air. Like a seamstress using a needle threader, the machinery that copies DNA begins by making a piece of RNA (similar to DNA, but with a different sugar, making it ribonucleic acid instead of deoxyribonucleic acid); the new piece of DNA then begins to grow, attached to the RNA needle threader. Each piece of RNA later has to be replaced with DNA before the new DNA strand that was made backward in little pieces is stitched together. When a little fragment of RNA/DNA is waiting to be processed, and the DNA copying and repair machinery is swirling around, pulling the DNA through in two directions, some unusual things can happen. Among other things, the little hairpin loops that Lynn Ripley envisioned have a chance to form.

As you might expect, the types of errors made when DNA is copied tend to be different, depending upon whether the copy was made as one piece or in little pieces. On the leading strand, the strand that is copied straight through, the machinery is more likely to leave a mismatched letter as it rushes straight through. On the strand that was made in a discontinuous, jumpy way, the lagging strand, DNA sequences are likely to loop out and get lost.[5]

Thus many mutations are not random, at least with respect to their position in a DNA sequence. It clearly is not true that all mutations are equally likely, that any A in the DNA is just as likely to change to a G as any other. It is possible to assume that this is true and still do research if you study large numbers of sequences, in which the rare hot spots and cold spots may get buried in the noise of the average. But it really isn't correct to make the assumption that mutations are random in the sense that they are equally likely at every spot along the DNA. Some changes are more likely than others.

It is the other sense of *random* that I want to focus on now. This is the assumption that mutations are random with respect to their effect on the fitness of an organism. In other words, the assumption is that mutations that increase, that decrease, and that have absolutely no effect on fitness are all equally likely to happen. Once these mutations happen, natural selection will select the "fittest" from among these random mutations.

Generally biologists figure that since the organism's genome can't predict what challenges its offspring will confront, mutations have to be completely random with respect to whether or not they might increase fitness.

The rare, lucky child gets a mutation that will help when a food source dies out or a new predator appears that begins to eat its sisters and brothers. The question I would like to raise here—and then return to with concrete examples, such as the cone-snail toxin, throughout the book—is whether mutation always is completely random with respect to its effect on the organism. In other words, can we really assume that how likely it is that a particular spot in the genome will mutate has no connection to how the mutation will affect the organism? In my experience, questioning this assumption invites controversy, or even the accusation that we are turning our back on Darwin, who proposed that selection acts on natural variations.

Of course, Darwin died before he could learn about DNA, the genetic code, or even genes. But in the twentieth century, we learned much about genetic variation within a species and about mutations. We began to see what might underlie the variations in fitness that affect survival under natural selection. Once we learned about DNA, we saw that mistakes in copying generate mutations and so we've assumed that random mutation followed by selection underlies evolution.[6] However, I have come to the conclusion that using our current knowledge to expand on Darwin's insights does not require that all mutations be random with respect to their potential effects on biological function. We need to consider Darwin's arguments in light of what we now know about intrinsic variations in mutation from spot to spot along the DNA. Much as the descendants of a bird experience selection based on variation in the shape of their beaks, descendants of an organism can experience selection based on variations in the intrinsic likelihood of mutation from spot to spot in their genome.

Some types of changes are less risky than others. One single mutation may change the codon for one amino acid to that for a similar amino acid in a place in a protein where it makes absolutely no difference at all. Whether the amino acid at that spot is D or E, the protein still works just as well. But elsewhere in the protein there may be much less tolerance for change. There, changing even a single amino acid may damage or even destroy the protein's ability to function. If that protein had an important role—say carrying oxygen to our tissues or starting the growth of the heart in an embryo—the small change might prove fatal, and not just for that one embryo; if this mutation were to happen very frequently in forming the sperm and eggs of those that carry this genome, it might lead to the end of the line for the genome itself.

It is the survival of its children, and their children's great-grandchildren, that carries the genome forward in time. If a lot of important information in a genome's DNA tends to change, many children will not get that important information. If the children do not get that important information, they are likely to be at a disadvantage compared to the children of parents whose genomes did not store important information in such an insecure place. If a genome encodes copying machinery that tends to make risky changes, fewer of its children are likely to survive, compared to those of a genome with a copier that tends to make more creative changes. If fewer of a genome's children survive because an important piece of information keeps getting lost, the genome won't have as many descendants.

Diversity and exploration—and, indeed, mutation—are needed, but it clearly is better if these creative forces do not tend to damage information that is essential for life. If important information is encoded in more stable parts of the DNA, generation after generation, this important information will have a better chance to survive and pass into the future. Genomes that survive natural selection will be those that tend to keep important information out of, for example, large disappearing DNA loops.

The foibles of enzymes that repeatedly copy, move, and repair the sequence of letters in a DNA helix affect the evolution of that DNA sequence, and thus will fall under selective pressure. An example would be the alacrity with which enzymes correct the different "errors" in Lynn Ripley's hairpin. Thus, not only individual mutations but the probability that certain classes of mutations may occur can become a substrate for natural selection. Because the chance of error at each step along the DNA staircase affects survival, the copying machinery itself, which affects the chance of mutation at each type of step in the helix, feels the pressure of natural selection.

The locations, along a DNA helix, of accidental variations in the chance of a mutation can in this way be adjusted by selective pressure. Most differences in the probability of genetic change from position to position in the genome will be small, but some are large. In each genome, including each of ours, certain genetic changes are, simply put, orders of magnitude more likely to occur than other changes. Natural selection can act on intrinsic variations in the probability of distinct types of mutation along a DNA sequence just as it can act on all biological differences that have consequences for survival.

The theme that occurs over and over again in evolution is that variations that may start out as accidental can be put to use. Charles Darwin pointed out that "the mind cannot possibly grasp the full meaning of the term of a hundred million years; it cannot add up and perceive the full effects of many slight variations, accumulated during an almost infinite number of generations." He named "this principle, by which each slight variation, if useful, is preserved, . . . Natural Selection."

Just as a breeder selects the prettiest roses, or cows that give the most milk, Darwin argued,

> *Why . . . should nature fail in selecting variations useful, under chang-*
> *ing conditions of life, to her living products? What limit can be put to*
> *this power, acting during long ages and rigidly scrutinising the whole*
> *constitution, structure, and habits of each creature,—favouring the*
> *good and rejecting the bad? I can see no limit to this power, in slowly*
> *and beautifully adapting each form to the most complex relations of*
> *life. The theory of natural selection, even if we looked no further than*
> *this, seems to me to be in itself probable.*[7]

Now that we understand mutation at the molecular level, we should think again about this statement of Darwin's: "Why should we doubt that variations in any way useful to beings, under their excessively complex rela- tions of life, would be preserved, accumulated, and inherited?" As will be discussed in many chapters, the properties of a genome that lead to tiny, intrinsic variations in the probability of mutation along the DNA can be "in any way useful to beings" and thus become a substrate for natural selection.

5

What the Antibody Genes Tell Us

The structure of the genotype is perhaps the most challenging remaining problem of evolutionary biology.

—Ernst Mayr[1]

A vertebrate genome first emerged on this planet about half a billion years ago. It led to orangutans, rabbits, chickens, sharks and whales, beavers, bears and bats, dinosaurs and dogs, and to us—to every animal with a backbone. Bacteria, viruses, fungi, and parasites already were here to greet us.

To protect ourselves from the pathogens, we vertebrates emerged equipped with an innovative immune system. This chapter is devoted to the many levels of genomic creativity possessed by our immune systems. I am spending this much time on the vertebrate immune system because I deeply believe that for over 2 decades—ever since we discovered its "jumping genes" and its focused mutations—our immune system has been waving in our faces some important ideas about genome evolution.

The vertebrate immune response demonstrates how a creative genome can be structured to handle the unexpected, how it can integrate a variety of mechanisms for focused genetic change into one effective system. Like the Lyme spirochete, our immune system can move pieces of DNA around the genome in a targeted, strategic manner, but with even more complex choreography.

The DNA we inherit prepares us to resist repeated challenges by an extraordinary array of pathogens, but the information for making the antibodies and other molecules needed to respond to these infections is contained in our DNA only implicitly. Our DNA does not protect us by "knowing" in advance the identity of every bacterium, virus, or parasite we will encounter; rather, it protects us by providing a strategic genomic infrastructure. This infrastructure facilitates efficient evolution of an effective response each time we are infected by a pathogen. It must be creative, for the pathogens that challenged our ancestors have continued to evolve.

If we fail to respond, it is because the pathogen kills us too quickly, before our immune system can fight back, or because (as is the case with HIV) the pathogen damages the immune system itself, like a rogue gang that burns hospitals, ambulances, and pharmacies and kidnaps doctors and nurses. It doesn't kill anyone directly, but it destroys the infrastructure that fights serious illness.

Our bodies do have a few "canned" responses that evolved in our distant ancestors to handle common kinds of pathogens. For example, nine proteins in our blood, working together, can recognize and kill certain members of the gram-negative bacteria family. This family includes *Escherichia coli*, *Salmonella*, *Vibrio cholerae*, and other bacteria that can cause a wide range of diseases, from meningitis to pneumonia to food poisoning, especially when they build a capsule that protects them from our canned response against them. To get rid of bacteria that can resist our canned, predictable responses, we have an "adaptive" immune system. Our adaptive immune system is harder for a pathogen to evade because we keep changing, altering our DNA to create an effective response to the wide range of pathogens we encounter every day within each of our lifetimes.

The discussion of the immune system in this chapter focuses on the antibody-producing cells, or B cells, which exhibit an impressive repertoire of unusual genetic activity. These B cells are not the only important immune-system cells. T cells, which control much of the immune response and some of which can kill virus-infected cells, also play an essential role in protecting us, and employ many of the same genetic strategies used by B cells.

Even the simplest virus is made of many protein molecules plus DNA or RNA. An antibody is just a protein molecule, and is much, much smaller than a virus. For an antibody molecule to protect us, it is not enough for it to grab onto a virus or other pathogen (unless the antibody molecule has managed to cover up the very part of a pathogen's surface that the pathogen uses to stick to our cells). An antibody molecule sticking to a pathogen is just another protein molecule on the pathogen's surface: For a virus, the antibody would be fur on its coat when viewed in an electron microscope; for bacteria, which are whole cells and are much larger than a virus, a molecule of antibody by itself would be nothing to be feared, or might possibly be food.

Once an antibody has grabbed a pathogen, the antibody must trigger an *effector* response that ensures that the pathogen is destroyed. An antibody is a bit like a sentinel; it calls in the troops. For example, an antibody that has a pathogen in its grip can attach itself to a phagocytic cell, which can swallow them both and destroy the pathogen; or the pathogen-gripping antibody can trigger a whole complement of blood proteins that can poke holes in the pathogen's surface.

The design of antibodies, and therefore of the genes that encode them, has two somewhat opposed constraints, variation and conservation. On the one hand, the genome must provide a huge variety of antibodies in order to try out different ways of getting a good grip on an ever-changing landscape of pathogens. On the other hand, the genome must conserve those parts of the antibody molecules that are required for calling in the troops, whether that involves attaching to a phagocytic cell or fingering pathogens that use a capsule to hide themselves from aggressive blood proteins. A variable part of the antibody, then, is needed to grab whatever pathogen may come, to handle the unpredictable, while the conserved part is needed to carry out the more routine, yet essential, job of interacting with other cells and molecules to trigger one of the specific effector systems that our bodies have available to inactivate, destroy, and remove the pathogen.

The tools for these two types of jobs are encoded separately in the DNA that we receive from our parents.[2] The DNA that we received at conception did not come with intact antibody genes; the part of our genome responsible for our immune response came to us from our parents in pieces. It is as if our parents left the holiday gift in the box, unassembled, but with instructions, and went to bed. But don't feel bad. Many vertebrates' parents do that.

We inherit three types of things in the genomic antibody gift box: a large variety of potential pathogen-binding pieces, a few regions of DNA that encode the pathogen-destruction information, and creative DNA-moving mechanisms that enable us to recombine these pieces. This genomic kit enables us to create and to explore a huge variety of antibody genes very quickly, while conserving the pathogen-destroying machinery.

We have DNA encoding a large selection of potential pathogen-binding regions stored in our genomes, much as the Lyme spirochete stores a large selection of DNA that encodes different patches for its coat. Some of these variable, or V, regions will enable the antibody to get a grip on the mumps virus; some will enable it to grab onto the measles virus; some will help it grab, we collectively hope, pathogens that neither we nor our ancestors have ever seen before. Our antibody genes are assembled, during each of our lives, from this palette of potential pathogen-binding V regions, together with a small set of C regions, conserved pieces of DNA containing information that encodes a short menu of ways to destroy pathogens.

Before and soon after birth, temporarily protected by antibodies that our mother has given us through the placenta and in her milk, our immune system prepares for the inevitable onslaught of the many pathogens to come. Each B cell moves one of the bits of DNA that encode its hundreds of stored V regions next to a stretch of DNA that encodes C regions. (Actually, each B cell does this twice, as in each antibody molecule there are two kinds of protein chains, each with a variable region, that cooperate to hold onto a pathogen. The multiple possible combinations of these two chains generate further pathogen-binding diversity.)

In order to create a fully functional B cell, the antibody gene-assembly machinery must find where the patches of DNA that encode V regions are stored in the genome. If we looked for these stored patches, we could use their special signal sequences to locate them. The signal is made up of two "words" that are separated by one or two turns of the double helix. One word has seven letters (e.g., CACAGTG), and the other has nine letters (e.g., ACAAAAACC), and they are separated by a spacer (like this message: scissorgnirtsrecapsrighthere). Such a message is easier to read in DNA because the letters in between the seven- and nine-letter words face the other side of the helix; the message is connected in space as if it were a tapestry attached to the railings on one side of a spiral staircase.

Like tabs and inserts on paper dolls and their clothing, complementary DNA signals mark the borders of the C region where the moving V regions will land. Also separated by a spacer, these complementary signals are (written antiparallel, according to the A-T and G-C pairing rules, so that the first letter pairs with the last letter of the V signal in the previous paragraph) GGTTTTTGT and CACTGTG. As you can see, the two signals can pair with each other, a little like Lynn Ripley's hairpin. Assembly instructions direct that the DNA be broken and joined between two words that are separated by one turn and two words that are separated by two turns of the double helix. In other words, if the V-region signal has about 12 letters (about one turn of the DNA helix) between its 7- and 9-letter words, the DNA it will become attached to has about 23 letters between its 7- and 9-letter words.

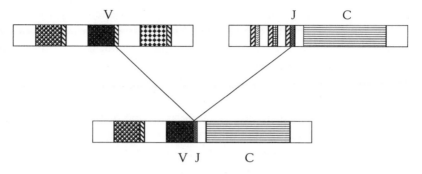

Figure 5-1 Moving the V region. A V (variable pathogen-binding) region is moved near the C (conserved effector) region. Variation is generated when one of a large selection of V regions is moved beside one of several J (joining) regions that sit beside the C region, identified by the signal sequences (indicated by stripes) to the right of the V region and to the left of the J regions.

This DNA moving (see Figure 5-1) creates our diverse repertoire of antibody molecules, each with a talent for grabbing onto something different. Like actors in a casting call, once the letters that encode the "auditioning" V regions have been moved from their storage place in the DNA we get from our parents to a place near the C-region DNA, they await the moment when their special talent is required. They await the pathogen that the antibody they encode is able to nab.

Our genome has additional tricks for creating variation among our antibody proteins: In the very act of attaching one piece of DNA to another, it can vary the precise site of attachment. When the DNA encoding a V region and that encoding a C region are about to be attached, in the order V-C, a cut is made to the right of the V-region DNA and to the left of the C-region DNA. The precise position of this cut can vary in two ways, each of which generates additional diversity in the antibody. The first source of variation comes from a selection of one of several short patches of DNA, called *joining*, or J, regions, that are found in the genome at the left of the DNA that encodes the antibody C region. The new antibody DNA will look like this: VJ-C. V and J together encode what is considered the variable pathogen-binding site in the antibody protein. Therefore, depending upon which joining-region DNA is attached to the V-region DNA, the antibody will have different amino acids in its pathogen-binding region.

There is yet an additional source of variation, which, again, focuses diversity right where it is needed, in the pathogen-binding site. This variation comes at the very site where the V and J regions are connected together. Suppose that the edge of the V region that is on the left side of the joint consists of the codon GAA, and the J region on the other edge, which will be on the right side of the joint, has the codon AGC. The assembly rule says that when the V-region and J-region DNA are attached, this connection can be made anywhere within or on either side of the three letters in each of these edge codons, as long as a total of three letters is chosen from the two codons at the edges of the V and J regions.

As illustrated in Figure 5-2, without any mutation, depending upon where the connection is made when these same two pieces of DNA are joined, you could encode any one of four different amino acids at the site of the joint.

It turns out that this very variable joint encodes a part of the antibody molecule that holds onto pathogens. It therefore creates a lot of extra variation; this extra variation further expands the range of pathogens that the antibody can bind beyond what is encoded explicitly in the genome through the repertoire of V regions. Of course, this extra variation at the joint is, in a way, also encoded in the genome, but not explicitly.

Our immune system DNA allows us to create yet more variation at this important place in the pathogen-binding pocket of the antibody. Right at this place, where variation will increase the range of possible pathogens that can be grabbed, patches of extra letters can be added at the joint in the DNA that encodes one of the antibody protein chains. This extra diversity

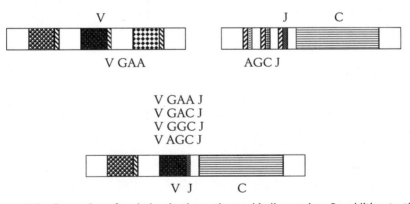

Figure 5-2 Generation of variation in the pathogen-binding region. In addition to the availability of many V regions and several J regions, variation is generated through the ability to form one of four different codons at the site of the splice between the V and J regions, each one encoding a different amino acid.

comes from small "diversity" regions, different from the V regions but also surrounded by the two words of seven and nine letters, with a spacer in between. One of these can be patched into the DNA near the C region along with the V region that is being moved. In this way, stretches of amino acids of various lengths can be added, which is a good thing, because different pathogens may have different "shoe sizes." What's more, while this variably sized diversity region is being attached, extra letters can also be added to the DNA by a creative enzyme that does not need to copy them from another strand. It can add a patch of "untemplated" letters; it appears to make things up.

So, encoded in our genome is a set of mechanisms that generates a tremendous amount of variation in the pathogen-binding region of our future antibody genes. V regions are moved, splice sites are varied, additional diverse pieces are patched in, and extra letters are added—all generating diversity at the very spot in the antibody molecule that must be prepared to defend us against all of the pathogenic variety that can emerge in our environment at any time. The more varied our antibodies are right at that pathogen-binding spot, the better the chance that we will have an antibody that will be able to grab onto whatever pathogen infects us. In other words, the amount and location of genetic variation in the DNA that encodes our antibodies is matched to the functional requirements of the antibody protein.

As big as the palette of V regions is, and as much as it may be enhanced by variation at the splice site, there is no guarantee that we have inherited a V region that can get a tight grip on any pathogen that might infect us; even if we have, a pathogen might mutate to elude the antibody's grip. But if we have an antibody that can hold the pathogen even weakly, it is possible that a few well-placed changes in this antibody will allow the pathogen-binding V region to tighten the grip. Indeed, beyond the variation generated by the mechanisms I have described, our immune system generates still more variation in the pathogen-binding region of antibodies through hypermutation. Just as the cone snail's toxin-encoding DNA seems to change more quickly than the rest of the snail genome, the part of our DNA that encodes the pathogen-binding part of our antibody genes can mutate much more quickly than the rest of our DNA. Mutation can tighten the antibody's grip on a pathogen.

The antibody genes begin to mutate after the V regions have moved into their new genomic context near the C regions. These mutations are specifically in the pathogen-binding variable region. Like Babe Ruth pointing to the precise place in the stands where he was about to hit a homer,[3] our immune system has evolved the ability to focus mutations. There is information in our genome that directs mutation to the pathogen-binding region of antibody DNA. This information is found in the DNA near, but outside of, the DNA that encodes the antibody's amino acid sequence. We know that this information is there because if you remove certain pieces of DNA that are near the rearranged variable region, you can stop the hypermutation. Or, if you replace the V region with a gene that normally does not hypermutate, say a piece of a hemoglobin gene, suddenly that gene will begin to hypermutate.[4]

This hypermutation is not spread evenly through the variable region, and that is a good thing. Mutation is more likely to happen in those very spots that create a pocket on the antibody's surface that holds onto the pathogen, and it tends to keep away from the part of the antibody protein that makes up the scaffolding that holds the pathogen-binding pocket in place.

One clue as to how mutation is focused may come from the way the antibody gene's DNA encodes the amino acid S. There are six codons for the amino acid S. Therefore, wherever an S is needed in the protein encoded by the DNA, we would expect to find any one of these six. For example, AGC and TCA are considered synonyms because they both code for the amino acid S. Therefore, if natural selection favors an S in the protein, it really shouldn't matter whether the S is encoded in the DNA by AGC or by TCA. But in the hypervariable part of the antibody gene, the amino acid S tends to be encoded using codons that begin with the letter A. In conserved places in the antibody gene, codons for S tend to begin with T. As our immune system tries out new pathogen-binding regions rapidly, the AGC S codons tend to change into codons that encode other amino acids, while the codons for S that begin with T tend to remain S codons. In the laboratory, you can change the odds that there will be a mutation in the V region just by changing the "synonymous" codon.[5]

As in cone-snail toxin DNA and Lyme spirochete DNA, codon synonyms behave as if they are not synonyms. Have we been missing something? There appears to be another message, "Make mistakes over here; we are trying new ways to combat a pathogen." The antibodies, too, may phone us at 9 P.M.

How hypermutation takes place is still a bit of a mystery, but it seems to be an active process, often focused, within the DNA encoding the V regions, on sequences with four letters in a special context. The first of the four letters can be G or A, the second is G, the third is T or C, and the fourth is A or T. As I write this, the evidence indicates that the process starts with a protein that targets a cut in the DNA to this spot.[6] These cuts can be repaired, probably by a "sloppy" polymerase (a DNA-copying enzyme) or by patching in pieces of DNA from other V regions. People may use a sloppy polymerase; chickens and rabbits tend to use the patch. If we knock out certain proteins needed for "recombination"—the process that puts in the patch—chicken B cells seem to turn to the sloppy polymerase too.[7] The details have not been worked out, but in fact a "sloppy" polymerase is turned on in immune-system cells.[8]

After all the gene moving and hypermutation needed in order to evolve, in real time, the right pathogen-binding region, our immune system is not done with its fancy footwork. Before I describe more genetic creativity, I want to mention, briefly, the cells in which all of this is taking place.

The cutting and pasting of antibody genes takes place in the cells that become our B cells. Like a merchant displaying its wares, each B cell displays on its surface—its interface with the rest of the world—many molecules of a unique antibody. It can manufacture this antibody using the information in the DNA that it has patched together from V and C regions and perhaps some extra DNA in between. If this antibody bumps into and holds onto a pathogen, this plus a signal from other immune-system cells can trigger the B cell to reproduce itself, creating many, many more cellular factories that can manufacture the same selected antibody. This increase in the number of factories that can make the selected antibody vastly increases the number of antibody molecules available to bind to this specific pathogen. The cells that serve as these extra factories survive for a long time, providing immunologic memory of the attack (or memory of a vaccine that looks like the pathogen) and leaving us well stocked and prepared to manufacture the right antibody, right away, to combat another attack by the same pathogen. Thus we are immune to this pathogen.

Once there is enough of the appropriate antibody, it must direct an effective attack on the pathogen, and to do this it must have options. Pathogens are not predictable, and they don't come with instructions. One pathogen may try to establish a foothold in the blood, another in our guts. One may be a virus, which commandeers the protein-making machinery of our own cells. Another may be a parasite, which attaches to us and feeds upon us. An antibody may have to travel out into tears to protect the surface of an eye, or circulate in the blood and attach the pathogen to phagocytic cells; it may need to cross the placenta or trigger the release of histamine. But before an antibody can direct any of these attacks, it has to grab onto the pathogen. And in order to do the appropriate thing once it does grab onto the pathogen, it must be attached to the appropriate effector region. As you might expect, in order to get the right binding site to the right effector region, the immune system undergoes still more genetic gymnastics.

The DNA that encodes the variable region that just has evolved by hypermutation to grab the pathogen from the B-cell surface can move yet again in the genome of our B cells and so become attached to DNA encoding any one of seven other distinct effector domains that can dispose of the pathogen. As the infection proceeds, our immune system will switch the pathogen-grabbing variable region from the first C region, which holds it onto the B-cell surface, to a different effector region. To move the pathogen-grabbing region to the new effector region, in precise genetic surgery, the DNA must be cut. The cut end near the pathogen-grabbing region must be joined to a cut end near the effector region that is appropriate to the task at hand. When we are under attack by parasites, for example, the ε effector region is likely to be most useful. Antibodies that protect us against *Staphylococcus*, to use another example, can go into our tears if they are attached to effector domain α, or they can go into our bloodstream if they are attached to effector domain γ. Antibody-producing cells cut their DNA in specific locations in response to a signal from other cells in the immune system. These other cells let the antibody-producing cell know which type of response is needed, and thus which effector region should be attached to the antibody.

Because it is a bit startling to think about making a regulated cut in the DNA of an active gene, I want to take a moment to describe how this might happen. The signal that triggers the DNA cut that switches the pathogen-binding region to a new effector region seems to start out like a typical signal from one cell in our bodies to another: A signaling protein, this one called a *cytokine*, travels from a cell that senses the type of invader to the antibody-producing cells. This cytokine attaches to the surface of the antibody-producing cell and, through a relay of protein signals that reach from the outside of the B cell into its chromosomes, turns on specific genes.

"Turning on" a gene means copying the gene into RNA, and that is what happens with the antibody genes. Like many of our genes, the antibody genes have *introns*, additional letters in the DNA between the letters that encode the V region of the protein and the letters that encode each effector region. Introns are copied into RNA, but they are spliced out of the RNA before it gets to the protein factories. When antibody genes are about to be cut in order to switch effector regions, something unusual happens. The machinery that copies information into RNA does not copy the protein-encoding part of the V-region DNA; rather, it starts copying in the intron, just after the letters that encode the pathogen-grabbing region, so that it copies through the place where the "switch region" DNA will be cut.[9]

With one strand of the DNA holding onto the RNA copy, the other DNA strand in the double helix can "loop out." This switch-region loop will be full of Gs. If it loops out and is left to its own devices, this G-rich strand can form a very unusual structure, with 4Gs in a plane instead of a helix, with these planes stacked on top of each other. As there is an enzyme that can cut DNA next to these unusual G structures, it may be that this enzyme makes the first focused cut in DNA[10] although the DNA in this region also is rich in palindromes, which may focus the cut.

Eight of our effector regions are near such switch-region DNA. When an RNA copy is made of the switch region appropriate to the pathogen at hand, that switch region DNA is cut. The V region is attached to the appropriate effector region by cutting the DNA between the switch region to the right of the pathogen-grabbing region and the switch region to the left of the appropriate effector region out of the genome, leaving the pathogen-grabbing region attached to an effector region that once was many letters further away. When the new antibody protein is made, the variable region that evolved the ability to grab the pathogen now is attached to a new effector region in one seamless protein chain.

It is clear that our immune system has a large repertoire of unusual genetic tools at hand. It can recognize specific sites in the DNA where it can cut, move, and attach pieces of DNA. It can focus variation on a small region of the DNA, and, within that region, on specific spots. These spots produce variation exactly where it is needed, in the pathogen-binding region of the antibody. Then our immune system cuts active genes to generate an appropriate pathogen-destroying effector response. Our immune system has integrated a range of creative tools for genetic exploration that generates effective responses to likely challenges. It faces, repeatedly, the need to hold onto any one of a huge number of potential types of pathogens, and then to dispose of them in one of a few well-defined ways.

The lesson that our immune system teaches us, dramatically, is that mutation can be focused at an appropriate site within a gene in a way that is regulated by signals in the cell's environment; whole regions of DNA can be moved around in a regulated, evolutionarily favored way; and DNA can encode information that attracts mechanisms that cut and paste together pieces, or modules, of DNA at specific places in the genome, creating hot spots of genetic variation. Hypermutability can be intrinsic to a specific DNA sequence placed in a specific genome sequence context.

While antibodies are selected one at a time for their ability to bind to a specific pathogen, the infrastructure that creates antibody genes was selected on a higher level for its ability to focus genetic mutation in the appropriate spots. What has emerged from natural selection is a genetic infrastructure that rapidly creates new binding sites, while conserving what it takes to be an antibody. Most important of all, the antibody DNA demonstrates that genetic hot spots of variation can evolve in appropriate locations, locations that are well matched to the actions required of the protein that is encoded by the gene. In the immune response, variation is focused at the pathogen-binding region, the region within a gene where variation is most likely to create useful new antibodies.

In evolution, only some variations are favored by natural selection. So, too, in the immune system, not every rearranged V region will be selected for by binding to a pathogen. However, it is an effective strategy for a genetic infrastructure to provide a diverse selection of V regions—all variations on a theme, with diverse pockets available to bind diverse pathogens—along with a menu of options that enable the immune system to get rid of different classes of pathogens. We are ready. This infrastructure gives us better odds, compared to random variation, that we will be able to protect ourselves against each pathogenic challenge that confronts us. Like the snails and spirochetes, our antibodies illustrate that biochemical tools can evolve that can make genetic variation, i.e., mutation, more efficient than random mutation in evolving useful new functions.

With all of these genetic tools lying around, available for focusing variation, it seems reasonable to suppose that they would have been picked up and used for other creative explorations in the genome. There is no reason to assume that the use of these tools is limited to battles between pathogens and their prey. Indeed, some of the proteins that move the antibody genes and generate variation are turned on in our germ cells as well, and, interestingly, in our brains. Perhaps the dramatic viper/snail, pathogen/prey battles are simply the ones that have drawn the attention of our research programs, just as the fires and murders draw the attention of the TV local news while the day-to-day work of educating children generally goes unreported.

I have been told that mutation must remain random with respect to function because a genome cannot predict the future. Can you and I predict the future? Even though we can't exactly predict the future, our actions are not completely random. We go about our lives each day, making informed guesses about what will happen next. We can do this because events in the world around us are not completely random. Certain types of challenges tend to confront us again and again. We discover, starting at a young age, that some types of responses to those recurrent challenges tend to work better than others.

A genome can "see" into the future the same way we do, on the basis of what it has experienced, and survived, in the past. But wait a second— aren't we different from genomes? We are conscious; we can learn; we are not strings of letters. Let's meet again for this discussion toward the end of the book. In the meantime, let's hold this thought: We excel when our brains capture information and learn, efficiently, from experience. Perhaps our genome has been structured, by natural selection, to be efficient at evolving.

6

Slippery DNA
and Tuning Knobs

*In a scientific context, the word spontaneous
is meaningless.*

—Barbara E. Wright[1]

Even if you were a highly evolved DNA copying machine, it would be easy for you to lose your place and miscount when you kept running across something like TTTTTTTTTTTTTT, at 80 to 500 letters per second, time after time, generation after generation. In some bacteria, each of these repetitive sequences increases or decreases in length about once every 10,000 times the DNA is copied; that means that among the descendants of an individual bacterium, which can divide in two every half hour, each of these sequences can slip many times each day. Each slip makes one sibling unlike another. Each slip generates diversity.

Copying and repair machinery also can miscount repetitive sequences such as CAGGGCAGGGCAGGGCAGGGCAGGG. The new strand can slip and partner up with the wrong CAGGG on the other strand. This kind of slip results in copies of the gene that have more or fewer CAGGGs in a row.

One of the most unstable places found so far in any DNA is a part of the mouse genome that can have from 200 to over 1000 repeats of CAGGG.[2] These CAGGG strings can change in length by more than 1000 letters between parent and child mouse. As the cells of an individual mouse divide to form the mouse's tissues, this string can slip so often that the mouse's DNA differs from tissue to tissue.

Remember the badly built staircase, with each rise and tilt being a little different, depending upon the DNA sequence. When you run up a flight of stairs, you are not thinking about raising your leg the right amount to reach the next stair; your body adjusts your steps subconsciously based on the first stair or two. So, if, in the middle of a staircase, a carpenter builds an individual stair, or a run of several stairs, with a different rise, angle, and depth, someone is likely to stumble. When a tilted DNA sequence repeats stair after stair, a whole stretch of DNA can have a very unusual shape, throwing the rapidly moving copying machine off of its game.

Some repetitive sequences even can fold back on themselves when the two DNA strands come apart and are being copied. A string of repeated CTGs tends to loop out into a hairpin in the DNA strand template that is copied backward. When that happens, if the hairpin is long enough and stable enough, all the CTGs in the loop will be missed as the copying machinery moves by, and the new generation will be missing copies of all the CTGs that were in the loop. On the other hand, if a loop bulges out in the new strand of DNA that is being built, then the copying apparatus may not know that these CTGs are there; and so some of the CTGs in the original template strand may be copied again. These progeny get extra CTGs.[3]

When short strings of repeats are miscounted, the mismatch repair system sometimes can fix the mistake, but if the repeats grow too long, the jumps become too big to be fixed by mismatch repair. As the repeats grow, the chance that they will get even longer becomes from 3 to 175 times greater than the chance that they will get shorter, and the size of each change increases. Once the repeat is long enough, it can increase by as many as 1000 letters in a single jump.

Long CGG and CTG triplet repeat sequences keep bending in the same direction, making loops that turn back on themselves every 81 letters (or 27 triplets) to form toroids, which are structures that look like a helix wrapped around a donut.

When the DNA strands come apart for copying, a string of GAAs can form triplexes, in which three strands line up: one of them the string of GAAs, one its original partner, a string of TTCs (read backward according to the antiparallel rule), and the third another string of GAAs copied from the partner. These three-strand structures are held together with their own new pairing rules: Two of the strands have an A or a G, the third strand a T or a C. When one stable triplex structure of this type was followed, researchers found it slipped so often that 96 percent of the children inherited a different number of repeats.

Some DNA sequences, such as strings of CGG, can even form fairly stable tetraplexes when they are opened for copying. In a tetraplex, two hairpins can form on the same strand and then stick to each other, breaking the usual A-T and G-C pairing rules. For example, two Gs from each step of one hairpin loop can stick to two Gs from each step of the neighboring hairpin loop.[4] If the repeated G-rich sequence is long enough, many tetraplexes will form along the DNA chain and stack together, forming hollow stems or cylinders.

Just when you think you have gotten to know it, DNA can begin to remind you of a seemingly conservative neighbor who one day invites you to a funky gallery on the fringes of SoHo to show you her mazelike floor-to-ceiling-to-walls installation of intertwined, multicolored string artforms. Especially in the midst of the action, when its strands come apart, and it is being copied in two directions at once, DNA can form unusual structures and behave in unexpected ways.

Once the normal copying structure is disrupted, DNA can become unstable, creating a gap—a slip between cup and lip—between this generation and the next. When the copying machinery slams into unusual structures, such as tetraplex cylinders, it stalls. Okazaki fragments, the bits of the new partner to the strand of the helix that is copied discontinuously, can fold back and not be trimmed properly. A repair system may cut the DNA at the stall, copy some sequence from another strand, bring in an error-prone enzyme that may stick in the wrong letters—and the result is a mutation "hot spot."

When the DNA copying machinery is idling and cannot move forward, this increases the likelihood that it will slip again and slip again, copying the same repeat over and over again at the edge of the block and increasing the length of a large repeated DNA sequence. If the tetraplex is built of repeats of CGGCGGCGGCGG, then the stalled DNA copying machinery may keep copying CGGCGGCGGCGG, inserting many extra copies before it is able to move on. These strings may increase in length many times within the space of only a few cell divisions.

CGGCGGCGGCGG's usual partner strand, with repeats of CCGCCGCCGCCG (again read backward), does not form these stable tetraplexes, so the copying machinery doesn't stall when it copies that strand; thus the new double helix that results from copying the other strand keeps the original number of repeats. This means that one of the two children gets the expanded string and the other doesn't, creating diverse children.

A very common slip occurs at repeats of triplets, such as CAG. Because the slip is exactly three letters, which, in the case of CAG, encode the amino acid glutamine (Q), the children inherit genes that code for proteins that are identical except for increased or decreased numbers of glutamines. Too many Qs in a row can make the proteins sticky and can do some damage.

Woody Guthrie[5] was born in a small frontier town in Oklahoma in 1912. The family was poor, his sister was killed when their house burned down, and his mother was stricken with a mysterious illness and institutionalized. Woody set to wandering, at the time of the Great Depression and the dust bowl, meeting many other poor and hungry migrants along the way. He spoke out—sung out, actually—for the cause of those who were oppressed. He hosted a radio show, and he wrote children's songs and songs such as "Union Maid" and what has been called America's second national anthem, "This Land Is Your Land." Constantly in motion, outspoken about what he believed in, standing up and fighting for the unfortunate, Woody Guthrie seemed like someone whom nothing could keep down. But something did knock Woody Guthrie down. He began to move and behave erratically. Some people thought he was suffering from schizophrenia or from alcoholism. By 1954, he had checked himself into a hospital, but he continued to deteriorate. In 1967, he died.

It turned out that Woody Guthrie, like his mother before him, had Huntington's disease, an inherited disorder. In 1993, 26 years after Woody Guthrie's death, through efforts spearheaded by Nancy Wexler, the daughter of a Huntington's disease victim, we learned that the tragedy of Huntington's disease is a legacy of the slipping of DNA when it is copied.[6] An expanded repeat of three letters, CAGCAGCAGCAGCAG, killed Woody Guthrie and, later, two of his eight children.

The first symptoms of Huntington's disease are subtle and easy to ignore—just some slight clumsiness or mild absentmindedness. But in a family that knows that it carries this disease, every dropped key and forgotten phone number can be cause for silent panic: Is it starting? Is it happening to me? Clumsiness and unsteadiness in walking lead to random involuntary movements, such as jerks, twitches, and flailing arms and legs. Speech becomes more and more slurred, and eventually the victim cannot walk, talk, or stand. What began as mild irritability, forgetfulness, or depression gives way to disorientation and dementia; and death in about 10 to 15 years.[7]

Although there have been Huntington's patients ranging in age from 2 to 80, the disease usually strikes in middle age, after its victim has had children. So patients and their families have to worry that the disease is lurking like a time bomb in the DNA of their young children. Huntington's is a dominant genetic disorder, which means that there is a 50/50 chance that a child has inherited it from an affected parent.

As if that's not cruel enough, the CAGs tend to keep expanding; so a child may well have inherited an even longer repeat, and thus the disease may strike this child at a younger age and be even more aggressive. In other words, Huntington's disease exhibits *anticipation:* The severity increases and the age of onset decreases in successive generations. As the length of the CAG repeat grows, so also do the size of the successive expansions and the likelihood of yet another jump in size. Expansion to more than 90 letters can occur in Huntington's disease patients, and this makes a string of more than 30 Qs in a row in the protein.

Families without any affected relatives have not necessarily dodged this bullet. A bad jump can bring Huntington's into a new family, as the length of the string of CAGs grows beyond the outer boundaries of unaffected. In the gene that slips in Huntington's disease, people with 28 repeats are fine; their DNA doesn't tend to slip. DNA with 38 repeats often slips. DNA with 60 repeats almost always slips. A string of 30 to 38 repeats is just at the boundary and is common; it is found in an estimated 1 in 50 people in the United States. In unaffected families, a string of CAG repeats is often interrupted by a CAA. If that CAA mutates to a CAG, there can suddenly be great instability.

This expanded gene seems to enter new families after something slips when the father is making a sperm. Scientists examined CAG repeats in over 3500 sperm[8] from men with repeats ranging from 37 to 62 CAGs, and found that there were slips in 82 percent of the sperm. Both the number of slips and the size of the jump increased as the number of repeats increased. For men with at least 50 repeats, 98 percent of their sperm had slipped. Individual sperm from each individual had different lengths of the expanded repeat.

Right now, Huntington's disease is rare—but not rare enough, of course—in the United States; about 25,000 people suffer from it. But in one small village on Lake Maracaibo in Venezuela, a large fraction of the people you are likely to meet will be struggling with the effects of Huntington's disease. They are the descendants of a woman whose DNA had slipped, perhaps in the one of her father's sperm that had fertilized her mother's egg.

Huntington's disease isn't the only serious disorder linked to expanding repeats in DNA. In fact, there are at least 14 such diseases that strike people.[9] Like Huntington's, eight of these other disorders resulting from slippery DNA involve expansion of the triplet CAG in different genes, thus encoding strings of Q repeats in distinct proteins. People born without the time bomb may have 5 to 30 CAGs, and thus 5 to 30 Qs, in the protein. But when the string of CAGs slips to make a protein with 40 to 100 Qs in a row, the proteins begin to stick together in long-lasting clumps and interfere with the normal on/off bumping and parting of proteins.

In four other time-bomb disorders, triplet repeats expanded in regions of DNA that are not actually translated into protein, but are copied into RNA. In myotonic dystrophy, for example, a string of repeating CTG triplets expands from a normal range of 5 to 40 repeats to a disease-causing range of 50 to 3000 and beyond, jamming up RNA handling systems and interfering with the translation of information in the RNA into proteins.[10]

We are not the only ones with slippery DNA. Bacteria too have repetitive DNA sequences, such as CAATCAATCAATCAAT, that often slip, growing and shrinking in size by multiples of the size of the repeat, in this case four letters. Because the genetic code is read in groups of three letters, a slip of four letters throws the message out of frame, mgitun in telligible-toth er ead er. In fact, repeated shortening and lengthening of the DNA by four letters disrupts, then restores, then disrupts again the function of many of the bacteria's genes. But, far from causing trouble for the bacteria, this bacterial slippery DNA causes problems, once again, for us.[11]

How does a bacterium like *Haemophilus influenzae* survive in our nose and throat, which are constantly bathed in protective antibodies? *H. influenzae* keeps changing its coat by turning genes off and on by slipping at repeats. Not only do these ever-changing coats keep the bacteria a step ahead of the immune response, but they even may find a coat that doesn't trigger the immune response.

These rapid changes enable the bacteria to avoid antibodies, but that is not the end of the trouble that they cause for us. *H. influenzae* has repeats of CAAT and *Neisseria meningitides* has repeats of CTCTT that both slip and change their surfaces. Not only does this help them to evade antibodies, but this changing of their coats may change the repertoire of tissues that the bacteria can invade during an infection. To invade, bacteria have to stick to us. They have evolved many specific surface structures that permit them to stick firmly to our "inside" skin, the skin that lines our gut, nose, ears, throat, etc. Because bacterial coats are stitched together from many fabrics, changes in several genes that encode the proteins that put together the coat allow the bacteria to mix and match patterns in different combinations. This combinatorial exploration of surfaces allows them to explore different ways of attaching to us.

Suppose, for example, that you had a palette of five possible decorations for a wall, each of which is available if a specific "decoration" gene is on, and is not available if that gene is off. Say one of the genes encoded information that created a circle with a hook to attach it to the wall, another created a triangle, another poured red paint into a can for use in painting the shape, another poured yellow paint, and the last encoded the ability to create ribbons and tie them to the wall. So, depending upon which genes are on, your wall could be decorated with a circle painted yellow with ribbons, red triangles streaming with red ribbons, orange ribbons, and so forth.

In the same way, by turning genes on and off, bacteria "decorate" their surfaces with different coats that allow them to hide from our immune system and to stick to different places within us. The bacteria get even more sophisticated than turning genes either on or off. DNA slips also can vary the amount that the genes are used. It is as if, when you are decorating the wall, you were to tinker with the amounts of red and yellow paint that you poured into the can. Rather than one evenly mixed orange color, you would have different gradations of orange depending upon the relative amounts of red and yellow that you used.

In order to use the information in a gene, we first have to find the gene. After all, DNA is just a very long string made up of four different letters. DNA encodes more information than just the order of amino acids in the protein. There is information in the DNA that is copied into RNA that does not become protein, but that helps the RNA get translated and determines how long it lasts before the message is destroyed.

There is other information in DNA that is not even copied into RNA. For example, there is information that tells the RNA copying machinery where a gene begins. The recognition signal for the start of a gene involves two specific groups of letters, which are found about 10 and 35 letters before the place where copying should begin. If these two groups of letters are the correct distance apart, this points the copying machinery to a gene.

What is the right distance apart? Actually, there is a little flexibility. There are optimal distances, but there also are longer and shorter distances that can work, although maybe not as well. Longer and shorter distances change how well the copying machinery fits, how efficiently it starts, and how often the information in the gene is turned into a protein. For example, in the DNA that encodes the *H. influenzae* surface structures that stick to us, a spacing of 16 letters results in the highest level of copying. If the spacing is just two letters shorter, 14 letters, the gene will not be copied. For *N. meningitidis*, spacers with a run of 11, 10, or 9 Gs between the telltale gene-marking groups result in high levels, medium levels, or no creation of messenger RNA, respectively.[12]

The length of a repeat not only turns a gene on and off as it slips from generation to generation, but also changes how sensitive the gene is to being turned on and off by molecules in the environment. In one example, how sensitive a gene was to being turned on and off by a specific compound in the environment depended on the length of a run of TTTTs.[13]

Slips that keep turning different sets of genes on and off generate diversity, the molecular equivalent of changing the availability of decorations for a wall. These slips generate a repertoire of variants from which the bacterial cells that are the fittest can be selected. In this case, "fittest" can mean the best at attacking us, avoiding our immune system, and sticking to and entering our tissues.

The infection process is a dynamic one. Variants that are fit at one place, say when they enter our throats, may not be well adapted for life in our bloodstream. *N. meningitides* builds a capsule around itself, which allows it to resist being killed by our immune system. But this protective capsule poses a dilemma for the bacteria, as it also interferes with its ability to attach to our throat. Most meningococci carried in people's upper respiratory tract are missing the capsule. However, during one outbreak of meningococcal disease studied closely by researchers, capsular forms predominated at the sites of invasion of tissues.[14] An insertion or a deletion of one C in a string of seven Cs, which happens about once in every 1000 bacterial cell divisions (possibly occurring a few times a day) stops the copying of the gene for the capsule. When the disease broke out and the immune system was called into action, the DNA had slipped back; isolates had exactly seven Cs in that string, and the deadly bacteria were encapsulated and protected from attack.

These bacteria are able to adapt their genes to generate variation depending upon their location inside us—a tremendous advantage. It is as if you could vary the bottom half of your body to optimize your experiences during a day in a lakeside village: The bottom half of your body would become wheels to get you down the road, then would be flippers when you entered the lake, and finally would turn into a lawn chair at the end of the day when you wanted to relax and watch the sun set over the water.

While short repeats, such as the seven Cs, seem to be mainly involved in turning genes on and off, bacteria also have longer repeats that can adjust properties of their proteins. For example, in a *Staphylococcus aureus* molecule that sticks to us, the variability of the numbers of repeats of the amino acid pair QS works like an adjustable stalk, almost like a jack raising a car, to allow the part of the protein that sticks to us to get up high enough above the bacterial surface.[15]

Because of their strategically slippery DNA, bacteria can keep generating diversity, allowing them to find the right approach to challenge our defenses and to move through the different microenvironments of our body.

These slippery DNA sequences are found in many bacterial genes, but are absent from many others. And these groups seem to be different kinds of genes. Genes in one group, which have been called *contingency* genes,[16] demand flexibility—for exploration, to respond to challenging circumstances, and to adjust to the environment. Different combinations of these genes are needed if the bacteria are to bind to our different tissues. These contingency genes appear to be different from *housekeeping* genes, which are needed to run the more predictable everyday business of turning starch into sugars and copying the information in DNA into proteins.

The ability to adjust their surfaces to explore new territory, to vary their coats to avoid capture by the immune system, and to enter and colonize new environments—all by selectively changing the most appropriate subset of their genes at a high rate, without waiting for mutation to damage the rest of the DNA—is an effective strategy for bacterial survival and evolution.

But is it only bacteria that have captured the value of slippery DNA? Walter Schaffner,[17] Director of the Institute of Molecular Biology at the University of Zurich, Switzerland, suggests that slippery DNA is important in other species as well, especially in genes that affect the extent that other genes are turned on and off. Evolution depends not just on the creation of new genes, but on changes in the activity of the genes we already have.

One example of the importance of slippery DNA to animals comes from fruit flies. Fruit flies may be little, but they are much more similar to us than bacteria are. Like us, fruit flies come from fertilized eggs and grow muscles, a gut, and a brain. It may be hard to recognize a sleepy fruit fly, but, again like us, fruit flies have biological clocks, 24-hour wake/sleep cycles. These cycles are managed by genes that are similar to the genes that manage our own wake/sleep cycles. Fruit flies do not maintain their body temperature, however, and so they have an additional challenge: to keep their biological clock running accurately at different temperatures.

In one of the clock genes of one kind of fruit fly, a string of the amino acids TG changes in length. At warmer temperatures, fitting its Mediterranean lifestyle, a variant with 17 TGs in a row can keep its clock running at close to 24 hours.[18] At colder temperatures, this variant's clock runs a bit too fast. Another variant, with 20 TGs, has a clock that works about the same at both temperatures; it runs a little fast, but it's more accurate than its Mediterranean cousin's clock in northern Europe, where this variant lives. These effects are marginal, but it is possible that a slippery gene coding for the amino acid pair TG gives a slight advantage to the fruit fly.

Ed Trifonov,[19] who runs the Genome Diversity Center in Haifa, Israel, and David King[20] of the University of Illinois have suggested that slippery sequences like TTTTTT or CTGCTGCTG would be useful to our genomes too. Trifonov and King independently began to use the metaphor that, because these sequences change in length so easily, they can act as "tuning knobs." The activity of genes might change frequently between generations, increasing and decreasing how often the information in the gene is copied into RNA as the number of repeats increases and decreases when the enzyme that copies DNA to DNA slips. Some slips will hurt, some slips will help, but each slip ensures that among the human family there is variation in the activity of certain genes. It generates diversity.

These slips may even be relevant to another observation of Darwin's, anticipation. "I could give a good many cases of variations (taking the word in the largest sense) which have supervened at an earlier age in the child than in the parent."[21] Perhaps anticipation allows a genome to try something out in adults first, then move it to younger and younger ages if it is a successful variation. We know that anticipation can occur by expansion of triplet repeats, as we saw with Huntington's disease. Finding out whether the expansion of repeats might be among the mechanisms responsible for the anticipation that Darwin observed will require the sequences of many more genomes. We do not know yet if this is true. If asked to bet, I would guess that it is.

The correct balance between fidelity to the text (careful copying of the genome) and variation (genetic exploration) emerges though natural selection. The correct balance does not have to evolve with an even, genome-wide, probability of change; it may be better to have different rates of change in different places. In some places, such as in contingency genes in bacteria, changes create variation that is adaptive. Genetic variation at each position in a genome becomes a conversation, across generations, between DNA and the enzymes that repair, copy, and move it.

And what about us?

Repetitive sequences occur in thousands of places throughout our genome. Strings of 1 to 5 letters may be repeated in tracts that are from 10 to 1000 letters long. Elsewhere, strings of 5 to 100 letters can be repeated in tracts that are from 400 to 30,000 letters long; these vary so much between people that they are used as genetic "fingerprints"[22] in paternity suits and criminal investigations.

While long strings of CAG cause tragedy, as in Huntington's disease, shorter strings of CAG are found in many genes. Perhaps variation in the string of Qs in the Huntington gene is good until the string gets too long. Many proteins with strings of Qs can turn on the copying of certain genes and block the copying of others. For example, there is a protein called the *androgen receptor* that detects the presence of testosterone and turns certain genes on or off when testosterone is present. The gene for the androgen receptor has a string of CAGs, and so the androgen receptor protein has a string of Qs. When this string gets longer, the androgen receptor is less effective at turning on some specific genes. The glucocorticoid receptor and many other proteins that are part of control systems that turn genes on and off also contain tracts of Q-rich regions. So far, we know that Q strings are present in more than 30 proteins involved in regulating the extent to which the information in particular pieces of DNA is transcribed into a messenger RNA.[23]

Strings of Qs often are involved in binding proteins to each other; in fact, they have been called a protein "zipper," linking two proteins together. It is very likely that the strings of Qs in the tragedy of diseases such as Huntington's are just too long and too sticky, but shorter, variable strings of Qs probably are very useful in adjusting binding.

Strings of CAGs in parts of the DNA that are not copied into protein certainly could have an adjustable, tuning-knob-like effect. When the gene is transcribed into RNA in preparation for making a protein, there can be a dramatic decrease in the amount of that RNA that gets translated into protein as the string gets longer.

Like the bacteria, we have probably captured value from slippery DNA. Our inheritable traits are not so discrete as "blue" eyes or "brown" eyes. We see subtle differences all around us that involve gradations, say of height or of facial features. It is likely that some genetic mechanism is generating a subtle range of diversity frequently. One way to generate diversity would be with a combinatorial mix of levels of the proteins encoded by different genes. Rather than being just a matter of turning genes on and off, variation can come from adjusting the levels of expression of the genes, like different tones of orange paint. Because of the interconnectedness of the systems that regulate our genes, mutations that alter the expression of one gene can change the expression of genes that have not mutated.[24]

This type of variation is bound to affect our fitness. It certainly does so in very special circumstances. The number of repeats next to an enzyme that is targeted in cancer treatment, for example, affects the amount of the target protein that the cancer cells contain, and recently was found to predict whether the treatment would work.[25]

Now that our genome is available, we will be able to connect these slippery DNA regions to their tuning-knob role, if they have one. But we will be able to do this only if we look into our genome with some respect, seeking to learn. We will not find them if we dismiss "boring" repetitive sequences as "junk DNA."

7

Everyone Has Something
to Teach Us

*We are a small, although important, part of this
wonderful world, the development of which is based
on deeply anchored interdependencies.*

—Werner Arber[1]

Whether it is poking and prodding our defenses as a pathogen or living
in the soil and competing for a new niche near a tree, a bacterium's
genome can mutate in many directions. Where should it begin?

Escherichia coli, a common bacterium in our gut that is widely used in
research, has a genome of 4.7 million Gs, Cs, As, and Ts, strung in a row.
When it faces the challenge of a changed environment, such as when it
infects a new person, *E. coli* has 14.1 million ways to change one single letter, to replace any one of its 4.7 million As, Gs, Cs, and Ts with one of the
other three. If each single choice of a letter change were a word in a book
about the same size as this one, the book would have over 140 volumes.
And what if 20 specific changes are needed for fitness in a new environment? Trying all combinations of 20 changes to get the helpful 20 would
require a mass of *E. coli* that would weigh more than 6,000,000,000,000,
000,000,000,000,000,000,000,000,000,000,000,000,000,000,000,00
0,000,000,000,000,000,000,000,000 Earths.

Because each letter in its genome can either stay the same or change to
any one of the other three letters, 4.7 million Gs, Cs, As, and Ts strung in a

row can create 1 followed by nearly 3 million zeros different possible genomes, not even counting times when letters are inserted or deleted. This list of options is so long that it is hard to describe. And what about our genetic options? Our human genome has more than 3 billion base pairs.

For a given *E. coli* to explore placing each of the three other bases at each position in its genome would require $10^{2.8}$ million (1 followed by 2.8 million zeros) genomes. *E. coli* can make copies of its genome very quickly, sometimes even three times an hour, one into two, then each into another two, then each into another two—eight new *E. coli* from each one every hour. Within 18 hours, a single well-fed *E. coli* could divide to be your size and shake your hand. From Friday dinner to Sunday brunch, the entire surface of the Earth would be knee-deep in the progeny of this single well-fed *E. coli*. If this *E. coli* had started dividing when Columbus got support for his voyage from Queen Isabella, there would have been the requisite $10^{2.8}$ million *E. coli* about the time the Bill of Rights was added to the U.S. Constitution 300 years later. But first, the bacteria would have run out of food. In fact, the problem is that if *E. coli* could divide, in health and without competition, from breakfast on Monday to dawn on Thursday, there would be more *E. coli* than all of the elementary particles in the universe.[2]

So *E. coli* cannot randomly try every possible change and then wait for selection to capture the very best ones. If *E. coli* got a little fitter each time it made one change that was on the route to a fitter genome, it might get there; but if a single change in the right direction didn't provide any particular advantage, this *E. coli*'s descendants might never reach the fitter bacterial genome. It is as if the bacterium faces a huge landscape full of alternative new genomes. Which ones should it approach?

Genomes that evolve efficient biochemical systems to navigate through the space of possible future genomes would have an advantage. They and their descendants would discover, more quickly, the direction to take, a way to adapt to an environmental challenge. These bacteria would race ahead of those that are wandering aimlessly around the genomic landscape, those for which evolutionary innovation awaits the results of purely random mutation.

The bacteria's repertoire of options is not limited to a high mutation rate, or even to a high mutation rate focused just in certain genes. Sometimes, even for a bacterium, it is more efficient simply to ask a neighbor for advice. Why reinvent the bacterial version of the wheel? Bacteria can capture genetic information, the gift of other genomes' experience, by getting DNA from the outside and pasting this DNA into their own genomes.

Our first hint that bacteria can learn from one another came from a mystery involving bacteria responsible for pneumonia. Some pneumococci bacteria were deadly, and some were harmless. When the deadly pneumococci were killed by heating them in the laboratory, not a single one survived, but somehow they were not fully dead. When harmless pneumococci were mixed with material from the heat-killed deadly bacteria that had been shaken in soapy liquid, the harmless bacteria became deadly. In addition, the once-harmless bacteria's progeny also were deadly, for generation after generation. How could generations of bacteria inherit information from dead bacteria?

Oswald Avery wanted to figure this out. At the Rockefeller Institute in New York City, Avery and his colleagues Colin McLeod and Maclyn McCarty worked to purify, from the many things in a soup of heat-killed, soap-shaken bacteria, the "transforming principle." They wanted to find what it was in that soup of pureed dead bacteria that could transform harmless pneumococci and their descendants into killers.

Year after year the Avery team grew the deadly bacteria, killed them, used a converted cream separator to separate the killed deadly bacteria from the fluid they grew in, and dissolved the killed deadly bacteria in soap. The soapy dead bacteria were then put through something like a carnival ride, a centrifuge, which spun them around at high speed, so that the heavier things flew to the outside end of the test tube. The transforming principle—whatever it was—remained dissolved in the liquid. The researchers then poured the liquid that held the transforming principle into another test tube and added ethanol. The ethanol caused the transforming principle, to crash out of solution into a pellet along with some, but not all, of the other molecules that were in the mixture.

The Avery team poured out and discarded the things that stayed in solution above this mysterious pellet; then they added salt water. This took the transforming activity back out of the pellet and into solution again. On and on they went, separating the molecular contents and testing pellet and soup to find where the transforming activity had gone. It was as if they were working with a bowl of alphabet soup with letters too tiny to be seen, trying to isolate the invisible letter P. After years of work, they had it.[3]

What Avery and his colleagues found was completely unexpected. To everyone's surprise, they found that the transforming principle that could come out of killed deadly bacteria and transform harmless bacteria into killers was DNA.[4] This was in 1944, and back then everyone assumed that DNA was a simple molecule, limited to some kind of scaffolding role in the chromosomes.

After all, DNA is made up of only four "letters": A, T, G, and C. Even simpler than that, the number of As always equals the number of Ts, and the number of Gs always equals the number of Cs.[5] So DNA was made of only two kinds of things, even amounts of A and T and of G and C, and yet now it seemed that it was acting as if it were the stuff that genes are made of—encoding information that is passed down from generation to generation! How could this simple molecule carry so much information? As Avery himself wrote to his brother Roy, "Who could have guessed it"?[6]

Many people still doubted that DNA could do this, even after Maclyn McCarty and Jacqueline Jonkowske showed that an enzyme that destroyed DNA also destroyed this transforming principle. This was treated as so incredible that there was no Nobel prize awarded to Avery and his team, even though these careful, thoughtful workers had made one of the major discoveries in human history: that the genetic material is made of DNA.

Avery and his colleagues were, of course, right. In fact, these very experiments with pneumococci were the first clear demonstration that genes are made of DNA. DNA, a chemical, a translucent, shimmering substance that can be spooled up out of a test tube onto a glass rod, could, by itself, transfer information from one bacterium to another, and this information could somehow be copied and transmitted to descendants.

The focus on DNA that followed led within a decade to the publication of Watson and Crick's famous model, based upon Chargaff's rules (A = T and G = C) and Rosalind Franklin's work with her student Raymond Gosling showing that DNA is a double helix with the letters next to each other. (Unknown to Franklin, Watson had peeked at, and essentially stolen, her data before she, a very deliberate worker, had a chance to present her interpretation of what it meant.[7])

The Avery team's discovery that DNA from deadly bacteria could transform harmless bacteria and their descendants into killers for generation after generation was a double surprise. First, there was the surprise that such a "simple" molecule as DNA could be the stuff of genes. Second, there was the inescapable conclusion that genes can pass not just from "parent" bacteria to "progeny" bacteria (vertically in a family tree), but between two bacteria in the same generation (horizontally on the family tree—as if, at least among bacteria, genetic material can pass from brother to brother to cousin to classmate to neighbor).

So the very discovery that DNA was the genetic material resulted from the ability of DNA to transfer information, not just between parent and child, but between two different bacteria. Bacteria could "learn" from their environment by swallowing pieces of DNA.

The ability to learn from its neighbors provides a tremendous leap forward for the bacterium that we left sitting at the edge of the mutation landscape with uncounted options before it, each of unknown value. The advantage that bacteria gain by sampling DNA sequences from other bacteria is demonstrated by their resistance to antibiotics. Indeed, information encoding resistance to nearly all commonly used antibiotics has been found to be strung together in a useful information packet—a sort of "how to" manual for antibiotic resistance that bacteria pass among themselves.

A newborn baby had trouble breathing and so was put on a respirator. He had an infection caused by *Staphylococcus aureus* bacteria, and he was given antibiotics. This baby was in the Netherlands, in the year 1998, but of course this sequence of events is not unusual; it happens to many babies in many places. But what happened next was, we hope, unusual. After being treated with antibiotics, the baby seemed to recover from the infection. But when the baby's infection came back, the antibiotic amoxicillin no longer worked. Before he was two months old, the baby was fighting a strain of *S. aureus* that had become resistant to amoxicillin. Fortunately, the baby recovered.

The medical staff was determined to figure out where the resistant bacteria had come from. The baby had not traveled. The nurses and doctors and other hospital staff were tested and did not carry these dangerous resistant bacteria. DNA from the baby's antibiotic-resistant *S. aureus* was compared to DNA from over 300 samples of amoxicillin-resistant bacteria from all over Europe. It was not any of them, but it did look familiar. In fact, the resistant *S. aureus* that infected the baby looked very familiar. It was the same *S. aureus* that had caused the baby's original infection—the same, that is, except for one small change: A patch of about 40,000 new letters had slipped into the *S. aureus* DNA.[8]

Amoxicillin, like other antibiotics in the penicillin family, kills bacteria by interfering with their ability to build their cell walls, an essential structure that surrounds each bacterial cell. The patch of new letters in the newly resistant *S. aureus* that infected this baby encode a protein that can keep building the bacteria's cell wall without being bothered by amoxicillin.

These 40,000 letters, and thus the information that allowed the bacteria to survive in the baby while swimming in antibiotic, must have come into *S. aureus* sideways from somewhere. In fact, they came from somewhere inside the baby. Also growing in the baby was a cousin of *S. aureus* called *S. epidermidis*. The cousin had this 40,000-letter patch in its DNA, and had passed it over to *S. aureus*.

Bacteria help one another resist antibiotics; they also can help one another resist our immune system. Much like the Lyme spirochete's system of moving patches into its coat protein, bacteria can share information encoding coat patches with one another, providing a greater repertoire than is available in any one strain; this happened in a recent epidemic of meningitis in West Africa, enabling bacteria to make rapid changes in their surface as they spread through the population.[9]

The *S. aureus* that infected the baby in the Netherlands already was a pathogen; what was new was that it had become resistant to antibiotics. But bacteria that are not pathogens, that normally live within us while causing no harm, can get new information from other bacteria and become pathogens. This is what happened to the harmless strain of pneumococci in Avery's laboratory, and it has happened to some *E. coli* on our farms.

E. coli lives with us, harmlessly, in our guts. It is so common, and so harmless, that a strain of this bacterium—coincidentally called K-12—is used in laboratories by inexperienced students for simple experiments as well as by professional researchers, in routine ways, every day. This tame, safe bacterium has been our reliable teacher. Without subjecting us to risk, it has shown us how DNA is copied, how the simple viruses that infect bacteria work, and many other things.

But suddenly, one day intense TV anchors were talking about our friend *E. coli*; it had killed people who ate hamburger at a picnic. Once cattle are infected with this aggressive form of *E. coli*, then everything from hamburger to unpasteurized milk, to fertilized fruit and vegetables, to ice cubes made from water contaminated by runoff from cattle pastures can make people very sick, and often kill them. In fact, we now know that *E. coli* sickens about 75,000 people in the United States alone every year. What had happened to our laboratory sidekick? It was as if coming home one day we saw our pet teacup poodle turn into an aggressive pit bull. It is hard to believe that the teacup poodle with the pink bow, and the snarling pit bull are members of the same species, although they both are called dogs.

Now that we can read the complete sequence of its genome, we can get a fairly thorough answer to the question of what happened to *E. coli*, an answer that would have been inconceivable in its detail a few years ago. Two complete *E. coli* genomes were compared: the genome of the standard-issue laboratory companion *E. coli*, which lives harmlessly in our guts, and that of the killer, a strain of *E. coli* called O157:H7 that sickened people who ate undercooked ground beef in 1982 in Michigan. The DNA sequence of O157:H7 was lined up, letter for letter, with the DNA sequence of the tame *E. coli*.[10] The comparison revealed not only how the two strains are different, but also how they became different.

Unlike our genome, which is arranged on two sets of 23 linear chromosomes, the *E. coli* genome is on one circular chromosome. Most of the way around, it was clear that both circles were *E. coli*: 4.1 million base pairs of the two *E. coli* genomes lined up well, like a common backbone, although a piece of the O157:H7 genome was flipped around so that it was backward. This is not to say that the 4.1 million base pairs were identical. We can compare you and your cousin and find that she has green eyes while your eyes are hazel, but your eyes and hers clearly are related structures. Out of *E. coli*'s 4.7 million letters, there were 75,168 individual changes from one letter to another. On the average, the same gene in the two strains was alike more than 98 percent of the time, although a few genes involved in interaction with the host (e.g., us) were only 34 percent identical. Most of these single-letter changes were between two codons that code for the same amino acid—i.e., between synonyms. These single-letter changes were not responsible for the dramatic change in the behavior of *E. coli*.

The variation introduced into the genome by these single-letter changes pales in comparison to the fact that over a million letters were found that had come into the genome sideways. Scattered around the circles of the two *E. coli* genomes were hundreds of patches of DNA that were found on only one of the circles, like islands of unrelated DNA in a sea of similar sequences. One of the islands on the deadly bacterium's genome, containing 106 new genes, came in two identical copies. In fact, there were a total of 1.34 million letter pairs, estimated to contain 1387 genes, that were clustered on islands found only in O157:H7, called "O islands." There were about half a million letters, with 528 genes, clustered on islands called "K islands" because they were only found in K-12.

While the O islands were not found in K-12, they were not completely unfamiliar. In fact, they include many genes known to be, or suspected of being, involved in diseases caused by other pathogenic bacteria. For example, some of the O islands encode proteins that help bacteria stick onto our tissues. Others encode toxins, including a toxin that harms our macrophages (cells that usually engulf and kill bacteria) and a "type III" secretion system that also is found in virulent strains of bacteria like *Salmonella* and *Shigella*, which use it to inject things into our cells.

These types of genes are nasty, invasive, and manipulative—and they lead to disease. Where did they come from? Some of them seem very similar to genes used by bacteria that get intimate in a friendlier way with the cells of organisms such as plants and animals. These helpful bacteria stick to plant roots; indeed, they invade root cells and stimulate their growth. They also take nitrogen out of the atmosphere and convert it to a chemical form that can be used by plants. All plants and animals depend for survival either directly or indirectly on these bacteria; the nitrogen that is converted, or "fixed," with the help of these bacteria is essential to them, and it turns up in their, and subsequently in our, proteins and DNA.[11]

Examining *E. coli* gives us a view of evolution that differs dramatically from the model of random letter-by-letter mutation followed by selection. Bacteria are not restricted to that unstructured approach. How do bacteria learn from their neighbors without the cream separator, centrifuge, and other tools used in the Avery lab? Bacteria have evolved, and no doubt have acquired, mechanisms that enable them to sample and adapt information that is available in their environment and, in a two-way exchange, to share information with neighboring bacteria by sending pieces of DNA outside. DNA uptake is not an accident. Originally, perhaps, a bacterium, exploring for food, with an ancient, molecular curiosity, had taken up a dead bacteria's DNA and discovered what it could do. Modern bacteria have multiple mechanisms that they can use to acquire DNA.

Among the gene-swapping tools used by bacteria are *integrons*, a genetic framework that carries genes and groups of genes in and out of bacterial genomes.[12] Integrons make it easy for a bacterium to pick up not just fragments of DNA that happen to be lying around, but entire genes, and indeed to pick up and broadcast whole sets of genes. New genes can pop in and out of integrons like cassettes. Unfortunately, these cassettes do not play beautiful music. Instead, they spread antibiotic resistance, pathogenicity, and other properties. Integrons also encode their own enzyme for inserting genes into and removing them from other DNA, and information that allows their genes to be turned on and copied into RNA messages to make proteins. Integrons have tremendous significance for the emergence of new pathogens. Some integrons carry information into willing bacteria that helps the bacteria to survive in the face of nearly all known antibiotics.

In fact, learning from their neighbors is so important to bacteria that they have many mechanisms available to them, not just one. Bacteria can swallow naked DNA, they can take up "packaged" DNA, and they can have sex.[13]

Bacteria can learn from other species. Indeed, rather than prospering by shoving out other strains in a competition for survival, bacteria may benefit when other strains live near them, inside us, for this adds to the diversity of DNA available to them. Bacteria can swallow naked DNA that happens to be in the soup around them, say from neighborhood bacteria that spilled their contents when they died.

The bacterium *Haemophilus influenzae* preferentially takes up DNA from other members of its own species. (Some strains of *H. influenzae* live harmlessly within us, but others can cause life-threatening infections, from respiratory distress to meningitis, especially in children.) The naked DNA is taken into a protected compartment at the bacteria's surface. Uptake of DNA into this compartment is facilitated by a "password." DNA passes easily between bacteria of this species because the DNA knows the password. In this case, the password is a nine-letter-pair sequence:

AAGTGCGGT

TTCACGCCA

If you looked for the password in the first strain of *H. influenzae* that was sequenced, called Rd, you could see that it is likely that any piece of *H. influenzae* Rd DNA that is floating by will carry the password, as there are 1465 copies of the password in each copy of the bacterium's single 1.8-million-letter-pair chromosome.[14]

Following its uptake, the DNA slowly moves out of the protective compartment into the cell itself. When it enters, one strand of the helix is completely chopped up, and the other strand is partially chopped up. This may seem like an inauspicious welcome, but Nobel laureate Werner Arber suggests[15] that perhaps it is safer for the cell to chop up the DNA into bite-sized pieces than to allow a whole genome to enter and take over. If a piece of DNA can find a good patch of matches on the host bacterium's DNA (matching by the A-T G-C pairing rule), the entering strand will push aside one of the host's DNA strands, recombining and sharing the information that it has. Bite-sized pieces binding similar sequences are most likely to vary a preexisting gene, making many changes at once. Since these changes come from a version of the gene that is functioning in the bacteria that sent the DNA, they contain valuable information that can guide the host cell through the mutation landscape. Something like this happens to our own genome when we form sperm or eggs, as is discussed further on in the book.

Passwords make information sharing more likely within one species of bacteria, but bacteria share DNA with other species, too. New genes can be made this way. In one bacterial genome, the gene encoding an enzyme that digests a carbohydrate was pieced together out of DNA from two different species;[16] the part that sticks to the carbohydrate came from one species, and the part that cuts carbohydrates from another. So, with help from their neighbors, bacteria can learn to digest new food sources.

While *H. influenzae* often swallows DNA, other bacteria more often exchange genes through extra pieces of DNA called "plasmids," using sex, or via bacterial viruses. Not likely to find its way onto the screens of movie theaters in red-light districts, bacterial sex usually occurs in settings that are outwardly more innocuous, such as an idle food processor.[17] A bacterium can build structures that facilitate the transfer of a copy of its DNA into an attached bacterium. Bacterial sex may increase under stress, which turns on genes that create the environment that allows the DNA transferring system to be built and to function. Another way in which bacteria can get new genes is with the help of viruses.[18] One type of bacteria, which can grow in both insects and plants and which damages citrus trees, got at least 83 of its approximately 2900 genes, making up 7 percent of its genome, from viruses; many of these genes are responsible for the bacteria's virulence.[19] Another type of bacteria can become virulent and cause cholera when it gains a cluster of genes by horizontal gene transfer and also from a bacterial virus.[20] Viruses are pieces of genetic material wrapped in protein. There are viruses that invade and kill bacteria—(known as bacterial viruses), just as there are viruses that specialize in harming us. But many viruses do no immediate harm when they put their package of DNA into a bacterium, even when they insert their DNA into the bacteria's chromosome. They may do nothing until the bacterium is stressed, such as with DNA-damaging ultraviolet light, when these viruses emerge again, spreading the genes they carry among other stressed bacteria.

Often, the edges of DNA islands have patches of DNA sequences that look like bacterial viruses and encode machinery that can move DNA horizontally from one bacterium to another. These patches also have a different "color," or dialect—(the relative use of A-T and G-C letter pairs), which indicates that they probably came in sideways from other species. Toxin genes are hooked up to the bacteria virus system in such a way that when stress—such as from certain antibiotics—induces the viruses to leave, the toxins may be expressed too. This is why it sometimes is dangerous to treat a bacterial infection with antibiotics; when the toxin is turned on, it may kill us. On the other hand, not treating an infection also can kill us.

Salmonella makes major use of viruses, which provide it with "a transferable repertoire of pathogenic determinants."[21] *Salmonella*'s ability to infect different hosts depends on the viruses that have infected it. One tiny virus protects *Salmonella* from attack by an oxidative burst by phagocytic cells. If we remove this gene from the virus, the phagocytes[22] can kill these bacteria. The different symptoms of *Salmonella* infection also depend on the viruses that have infected the bacterium.

Macrophages ("big eaters") defend us against infection. They wrap themselves around bacteria, forming a *phagosome* ("eaten body") inside of them, where the bacteria are isolated. Then they move a vessel full of digestive enzymes and hydrogen peroxide-generating systems into the phagosome to kill and digest the bacteria.

So, the last place a bacterium would want to live, it would seem, would be in a phagosome, where it risks a bath of peroxide and other deadly concoctions. Yet some bacteria seem to live very happily in phagosomes.[23] Of course, natural selection would favor the bacteria that came up with a mechanism to block the macrophage's poison cocktail. This would let them live within a macrophage, hidden from the immune system's surveillance.

Bacteria can pick up, from other bacteria, instructions that enable them to live inside a macrophage; these instructions come packaged on *pathogenicity islands*. A pathogenicity island picked up by some *Salmonella typhimurium* prevents the peroxide-generating systems from ever getting into the phagosome where the bacteria were taken after they were swallowed by the macrophage. These bacteria have a type III protein secretion system, which lets them inject some of their own proteins into the macrophage after they are swallowed, interfering with the biochemical machinery that would otherwise kill them.

Avery and his colleagues' discovery that we can change the genes of bacteria by feeding them DNA eventually transformed genetics research. This discovery was the first seed that, within four decades, became genetic engineering. If we need large amounts of human insulin to treat diabetics, we can put the gene for human insulin into bacteria and let the bacteria divide and copy the genes; the bacteria and their progeny will make human insulin for us. Like living, growing, dividing factories, the bacteria construct more and more of the protein that interests us, mixed in with their own. We separate the factory product that we want, in this case insulin, from the others. If we want to learn how to block the growth of a deadly virus without risking our lives by growing the virus itself, we can put a gene that is essential for the growth of the virus into bacteria under careful constraints, get the bacteria to churn out large amounts of viral protein, and use the manufactured protein to study how to block the biochemical action of that isolated protein—safely, away from the deadly virus—in order to kill the virus.[24] We can even chop up the human genome, put it into bacteria, and have the bacteria grow extra copies of it for us to study; indeed, that is how we were able, bit by bit, to determine our genome's sequence of 3 billion letters.

So Avery and his colleagues' experiments with DNA and pneumonia were the seeds of a revolution in research that led, later in the century, to the ability to manipulate, study, and sequence genomes. But, surprisingly, the implications of these experiments for evolution were not really incorporated into evolutionary theory. Where, after all, did we get the bio-chemical tools that we use in laboratories for genetic engineering? From bacteria. From ancient bacteria that grow in hot springs at Yellowstone; from bacteria that grow in our guts. From bacteria, companies that supply our laboratories have put together, and sell, whole catalogues of molecular scissors that cut DNA in precise ways, molecular paste that links DNA in precise ways, and molecular machines, polymerases, that copy genetic material over and over again. We are not the first genetic engineers.[25] That title belongs to the tiny microbes. So, what were the microbes doing with all these tiny tools?

Few people asked.[26] In spite of the Avery experiments, evolution continued to be viewed in purely vertical, parent/progeny terms. Now that we can look at complete genomes, as we read along a bacterial chromosome, suddenly we find a whole block of DNA that looks different, out of place; it doesn't fit—there is a cobalt patch on a turquoise string. The relative amounts of A-T and G-C along the helix seem to change suddenly, as if it's talking a different dialect. A block of genes seems to be very closely related in sequence to the same block of genes in a very different bacterium, encoded by a cobalt string. These genes seem to have come into the more turquoise genome sideways.

In spite of the way DNA's role was discovered, it wasn't until we had sequenced entire genomes that the prominent role of horizontal gene transfer was incorporated, deeply, into our understanding of evolution. The genomes are shouting at us; we can't ignore them now. Patches of DNA—genes—have come from somewhere else.

Perhaps we didn't visualize this bacterial networking before because we can't truly see what we don't understand. We can't get the right answer if we can't imagine how to ask the right question. Perhaps only now that *we* are networked and internetworked can we see that bacterial genomes are networked too. Just as we post and download recipes from the Internet, bacteria broadcast and receive information on how to destroy or otherwise get rid of an antibiotic, or of all known antibiotics. They have been on the planet a very long time, and they are masters at what they do.

Whole organisms have come together in many creative ways to build a new form of life that can do more than any one of these organisms could do alone. It even is possible to evolve, in the laboratory, an amoeba that is completely dependent upon being infected by a specific bacteria in order to survive; after an initial devastating infection that killed many amoeba, the bacteria and the amoeba learned to work together; they became a team.[27]

And we, too, live in partnership with other genomes. I want to reflect here on a group of bacteria, cousins to each other, that chose to head down different paths in their relationship with us. Both live within us. One cousin gave up its ability to be free in exchange for a steady supply of amino acids and other foods from us. In order to survive, it must live within our cells. It is spread from person to person by lice; this cousin, typhus, helped tremendously by war, killed tens of millions of people in the twentieth century, including Anneliesse Frank.[28]

The other cousin chose to team up with an ancient cell; it came to stay. It too lives within us, not as an enemy, but as a partner; in fact, we cannot live without it. The "good" cousin became our cells' energy factory, our mitochondria.[29] We rely on the energy it gives us every time we move an arm or think a thought, and every time our heart beats. For this teamwork, eukaryotes take the good cousin wherever they go on the planet. The good cousin thrives in the sunlight; it is not limited to struggles in disease, war, and famine.

Cooperation provides options for moving beyond barriers; it is much more efficient than random change. An infrastructure that facilitates cooperation lets two genomes combine the benefit of what they have learned in their separate experiences. It predates the successful adaptation of cooperation in human society; each of us separately does not have to figure out how to build an airplane when we want to fly. Bacteria do not each have to figure out, separately, how to combat a new antibiotic. It is evolution's clear message that the fittest is likely to be the most cooperative.

8

The Genome Sends an SOS

*Some people in the crowd wake up . . . they emerge
according to much broader laws. They carry strange
customs with them. . . . The future speaks ruthlessly
through them.*

—Rainer Maria Rilke

In 1967, Evelyn Witkin, a geneticist then working in Brooklyn, New York,
wrote two papers that at the time seemed to be on different subjects.[1]
Both were based on what happened when she gave *Escherichia coli* a bit of
a sunburn. The first paper examined how ultraviolet (UV) light affected the
behavior of the bacteria, and of a virus that had inserted itself into *E. coli*'s
genome and was quietly passing from generation to generation along with
the bacteria's DNA. When the bacteria were sunburned, they began to
grow in long threads rather than separately, and the dormant virus was
"induced": It started to reproduce and spread through the colony of bacteria. Witkin reasoned that damage from the ultraviolet light generated a signal within the bacteria that had a variety of effects, including changing their
growth behavior and awakening the dormant virus.

Witkin's seemingly unrelated work in the second paper was about mutations. Usually, ultraviolet light causes many mutations. However, when she
shone UV light on bacteria that already had a mutation in a place in their
DNA called LexA, she didn't find these UV-caused mutations. Previously,
as Witkin put it, "the prevailing notion . . . was that mutations were instan-
taneous events . . . the mutagen went 'zap!' and that was that."[2] In contrast,
Witkin's data suggested that to cause these mutations, UV light actually

needs the help of the bacteria themselves, in particular of LexA. Witkin suggested that LexA's role was to provide a way for bacteria to copy their UV-damaged DNA. While the bacteria without LexA couldn't copy their damaged DNA and died, the bacteria with LexA could copy their DNA, but this copying was error-prone and so caused mutations. The survivors Witkin found that did not have UV-induced mutations were the progeny of bacteria that either had managed to repair their DNA without error before attempting to copy it or had escaped UV damage in the first place.

So, here is the situation. Suppose you are the captain of a ship, and you have on board a well-trained engineer who can, with a box of precise tools, perform routine maintenance on the ship, patching occasional damage so well that no one who inspected the ship could see that it had been patched. Also on board is a group of very enthusiastic and inventive do-it-yourselfers who can fix just about anything, but who leave rough edges and loose ends—in general, a bit of a mess. Whom would you rely on?

Well, there's one more piece of important information. The exacting engineer has a personality quirk: If the damage is so severe that, working with these precision tools, a perfect repair cannot be made, this engineer will refuse to touch the spot. Now suppose that your ship bangs into a rock, and a three-foot gash is opened just at the water line. The engineer backs away in horror. Will the ship go down, the damage unrepaired? In rushes the team of do-it-yourselfers. A metal plate, some rags, a carton of Krazy Glue that someone found in cargo—whatever it takes, the ocean is kept out and the ship is saved. It may not be the same sleek ship it was before it hit the rock, but it will be able to continue its journey.

So, too, for DNA. The precise DNA copying machinery demands an exactly matched pair of letters, A and T or G and C, before it can go on. If this machinery puts in the wrong letter, it cuts this mismatched letter right out. It cannot, except ever so rarely and only accidentally, extend misshapen DNA. We depend upon this personality quirk, for this fussiness is the basis of our ability to copy our 3-billion-letter genome accurately, time and time again. This machinery is intrinsically unable to be sloppy.

Missing or unrecognizably damaged letters must be replaced before DNA is copied, or the copying machinery may stall or fall off. Will the cell die? Perhaps many cells did die under such circumstances; they have no descendants among us today. Miroslav Radman, the son of a fisherman and currently a molecular geneticist working in Paris, recognized the nature of this emergency.[3] Radman recognized that cells would evolve a response that would save their life—that would keep the ship from going down—when DNA copying stalls, and he named this the SOS response.

So it turns out that Evelyn Witkin's two papers were very much related to each other. In response to DNA damage, the sunburned bacteria turned on the SOS response. This had systemic effects on the bacteria—on the way they grew, on the behavior of the viruses that were asleep in their genome, and also on their ability to copy damaged DNA.

A central player in the SOS response is a protein called RecA. When the copying machinery falls off, RecA sticks to the separated single ribbon of the DNA helix. What RecA does next determines how the damage is fixed. If a photocopy came out smudged in one spot, you could look back at the original to read the correct letter. Or, if a spot of water smudged the original, you could find the information on the unsmudged photocopy. You could use the same approach if you were a repair system sent in to fix damage to DNA, and this is what RecA does. Sometimes RecA can get the damage repaired by recombination with another DNA molecule, perhaps the very DNA molecule that contains the damaged strand's recent partner, before copying.

But if RecA, holding onto the piece of damaged DNA, cannot quickly find a good match to repair the damaged region, it will send out the alarm:[4] The copying machinery fell off, the cell could die—Save Our Ship. As the first signal in the alarm, RecA shoves another protein, causing it to cut itself;[5] this other protein turns out to be none other than LexA. We now know that LexA is a repressor protein, something that sticks to genes and keeps them turned off. It is as if LexA were a climber holding onto a cliff and RecA were banging on its fingers. LexA loses its grip and falls off, allowing about 20 to 30 genes that it had repressed to turn on.

Among the genes that are turned on when LexA's repressive grip is released are genes that encode enzymes that can copy damaged DNA. Because DNA is made up of a string of letters, it, like nylon, is a polymer of repeating units. The ending -ase refers to its role as an enzyme. Thus, an enzyme that makes a polymer is a polymerase, and an enzyme that makes DNA is a DNA polymerase. These polymerases can be activated and directed to the damage by RecA.[6]

In fact, there isn't just one enthusiastic do-it-yourselfer polymerase. In E. coli, we know of five, each of which has slightly different skills.[7] One of these can copy DNA that is so badly damaged that its letters are unrecognizable. It can even copy DNA at spots where a letter is missing—it makes things up, it plays the odds. One enzyme simply adds a C across from a place where the DNA is missing a letter. If the DNA is still a bit misshapen after only one letter is added, this enzyme can add another C. This gets us past the damage[8]—it saves the ship—but it does not make an accurate copy. In other words, it causes mutations. Working together, these polymerases can fill in the hole where the DNA was damaged and extend the chain past the damaged spot so that the careful polymerase can step back in to complete its job.

This is what happens in bacteria like *E. coli*, but what happens in us? Much of the important biochemical machinery in our cells, including DNA itself, emerged in an ancient organism that was an ancestor both of us and of the bacteria alive today. Therefore, it is fairly standard in biology to develop hypotheses about what might be happening in our own cells based on the biochemistry of bacteria. These hypotheses need to be tested, of course, often first in yeast or in little animals like fruit flies and worms. But now that we have whole genome sequences, we can actually peek inside to see whether there are enzymes encoded in our own genome that look like the bacteria's unusual polymerases. There are.[9]

When one of our own versions of these SOS polymerases copies undamaged DNA in the laboratory, it makes a mistake about once in every 200 letters it copies.[10] That would be more than 10 million mistakes every time it copies our several-billion-letter genome. Clearly, copying undamaged DNA is not this enzyme's day job.

Our DNA is not kept in an impenetrable protected vault. It moves through life with us every day. If you are reading this book on the beach, I am sorry to bring this up, but ultraviolet light tends to tie together two Ts that are next to each other on the same side of the helix—a T dimer; this jams up the DNA copying machinery. UV light from the sun struck the first DNA on the surface of the Earth. We have been living with UV light for so long that we are not passive in the face of this T tying. We have enzymes that spot and cut out T dimers. If the dimer has not been cut out by the time the DNA is copied, the standard polymerase cannot copy it. Fortunately, we have another enzyme that can put two As in the new strand of DNA across from the funny misshapen piece of DNA with the two Ts tied together. This is more than a good guess. A T dimer comes from two Ts, which means that an accurate copy of the DNA as it was before the damage should have two As on the new partner strand. The enzyme that can copy T dimers does this reliably, much as the standard enzyme recognizes the normal Ts one at a time. However, if this enzyme is let loose on normal DNA, it makes a lot of mistakes, getting about one letter wrong for every 18 to 380 letters copied.[11] And it can't proofread.

There are other ways of getting past a T dimer, but they cause mutations. People who are missing the enzyme that can repair T dimers are likely to get skin cancer from UV radiation,[12] for however their DNA-copying systems may deal with the T dimer, they do not reliably insert two As across from the damage. Even when the T-dimer-fixing enzymes are intact, different sequences of DNA letters near the dimer can affect how well the enzyme can get in and fix it. On the other hand, as Evelyn Witkin observed in her sunburned bacteria, some mutations actually decrease the amount of DNA damage that we see among surviving progeny. If a particular polymerase that copies damaged DNA is inactivated in human cells in the laboratory, little or no DNA damage will be induced by UV light, but these cells will be slightly more likely to die. In other words, knocking out this polymerase may protect against cancer because the cells will die rather than mutate.[13]

Even aside from UV light, mutation is a constant threat. Genomes have a natural tendency to fall apart. As a whole, DNA is stable, but, truth be told, it is not as stable as your living room chair. It constantly is dropping things and constantly being repaired by ever-vigilant proteins. DNA is a high-maintenance material. Every day in every cell in each of our human bodies, 5000 As and Gs fall off the DNA backbone just from bouncing around at the warmth of body temperature.[14] Fortunately, these missing letters can be replaced accurately, using the information in the complementary strand in the helix. Then there is the problem of restless letters. Like a cat stretching, every now and then the bonds between the atoms that make up the letter C can shift around a bit, so that just for a split second the C looks like a T. C stretches occur so often that in a genome with nearly a billion Cs, as many as 100,000 of them could happen to be stretching into Ts as the copying machinery rushes by. This stretching is so quick that as soon as the copying "mistake" is made, the C is back to itself. Proofreading then cuts out the A that had been inserted to pair with the momentary T, which now is inappropriately across from a C, and puts in C's partner G, and the polymerase moves on before the C stretches again.

But stretching occasionally to look like a T isn't the only way that the letter C can change into a letter that pairs with A rather than G; C also tends to lose a piece entirely, turning into the letter U. There is an enzyme that is on the lookout for Us in DNA, but if the broken C is not replaced before it is copied, the new DNA strand will get an A at that spot, not a G. Then, if the A is copied, it will bring in its partner, a T. This removes all trace of the original C, as if "lace" had been changed to "late." Is this mutation rare? Every day, in each of our cells, about 100 of the Cs lose this piece and become Us. Cs have been losing pieces and turning into Us since the very first DNA molecules appeared. A repair system has evolved that spots Us and cuts them out of DNA, also chewing off a few letters on either side to make room for the DNA copying machinery. The copying machinery sees the C's original G partner across the double helix and fills in the gap, putting the C back where it belongs.

DNA is a molecule that is touched by all of the effects of its environment. C is not the only letter that gets damaged from day to day. Groups of atoms can fall off of other letters too, and extra atoms can get stuck onto letters. There are about 20 enzymes that recognize different common types of damage to DNA and fix it. Between letters that fall off and enzymes that cut off damaged letters, it is estimated that in each of our cells every day, about 9000 places in the DNA backbone are missing letters.[15] Each cell is kept busy patching its genomic dike. The number of places in the DNA that are missing letters at any moment varies from one cell to another by over an order of magnitude. Since whether these mutations are fixed depends upon the activity of enzymes, how much they are fixed can be different at different places in a genome. Whether or not this is the explanation, it is true that in our genome, some regions are richer in As and Ts, and some in Gs and Cs.

Mutations can happen even where letters haven't fallen off, if the exacting polymerase errs as it rushes past. A mismatch between the template strand and the new strand most likely will be caught by the polymerase's proofreading activity as DNA is being copied. The proofreader assumes that the information in the template is correct. If there is a G-T mismatch and the G is on the template strand, the T will be cut off and replaced with G's proper partner, a C. Even if proofreading misses an error, mutations can be avoided by the action of a repair system that follows the polymerase along the double helix. But how can the repair system identify which is the template strand? If it notes that a G is paired with a T, or that a few letters are unpaired and looped out, which is right? Which strand was the original? Should the G-T pair be fixed to a G-C pair or to an A-T pair? Should unpaired letters be copied or cut out? Which strand is wrong?

One way to keep track of which strand came from the original helix is to mark both strands of the original DNA helix before copying them, like painting a patch of purple on every apricot step of the magic staircase in the plaza. When the strands of the "marked" DNA double helix separate and are copied, one strand of each new double helix will have come from the original helix; that strand will be the one with the purple mark. While *E. coli* doesn't have a can of purple paint and a tiny paintbrush handy, it does have a way to tag the original double helix. It marks the DNA by attaching a specific chemical label to certain letters. This molecular equivalent of purple paint, a carbon atom bound to three hydrogen atoms, called a methyl group, guides this bacterial repair machinery: This strand is the original.[16]

In addition to a "purple paintbrush" enzyme, many proteins are needed to spot and repair mismatches in DNA. One of these proteins binds to a place on the double helix with a funny shape, whether that shape is a mismatched letter or a place where extra letters were stuck in or letters were lost, so that one strand is longer than the other and a loop sticks out. Another protein finds the marks on the original template strand. Then yet another protein notes the proteins that mark the mismatch and the template strand, and cuts the new strand on the left side of a specific sequence of letters nearby (in *E. coli*, on the left of a nearby GATC). Yet another mismatch repair protein starts from the cut and chews in past the mutation, leaving behind a stretch where the double helix is missing one of its strands. Finally, a polymerase fills in the missing letters, restoring the double helix using information from the original template strand.

When *Meningococcus* is missing the "purple paintbrush" enzyme it uses to guide mismatch repair, its coat changes more quickly.[17] If the mismatch repair system isn't working, one strand may end up with an extra copy of some letters. If the polymerase fell off and got back on in the wrong place, there might even be extra copies of one or more entire genes. When a mismatched double helix is copied, two different double helices may be sent on to the next generation. Bacteria that are missing mismatch repair are called *mutators*. Evelyn Witkin found mutators when mutations knocked out the brakes on the SOS system, leaving its unusual polymerases stuck "on." Is it dangerous to be a mutator?

Mutation can be seen as a generally harmful random attack on a well-adjusted genome. After all, any species that is alive today has been selected to handle life in the range of habitats it typically encounters. But when an organism gets out of its comfort zone and is stressed to its limit, its progeny need to evolve in order to survive. If a bacterium is struggling, extra copies of some genes that it already has may help it survive until another mutation solves the problem.[18] It has to mutate. In fact, compared to pampered laboratory strains of *E. coli*, samples of "wild" *E. coli*, which have to handle repeated stresses, whether within people or elsewhere out in the environment, contain bacteria that tend to have a higher mutation rate.[19] Radman suggests that turning on SOS mutation is the genetic equivalent of joining with your extended family in a lottery pool, increasing the chances that one of the many progeny could have the lottery ticket to the future.[20] While mutators are at a disadvantage under comfortable circumstances, they can have more surviving progeny under challenging circumstances.[21]

We have more genes than we use at any one time, as a back-up, to handle the range of fluctuations in the environment in which we can live. The ability to sense and to respond to stress has evolved, enabling cells to adjust, for example, to changes in available nutrients. Bacteria that are fed the sugar lactose will draw on information in their DNA that encodes proteins that absorb and digest this sugar—unless the more readily usable sugar glucose is abundant. If glucose is abundant, why waste energy making the extra proteins needed for digesting lactose?

But for every organism, there will be a point beyond which it cannot survive unless its genome mutates. As we go up above sea level, our body adapts to the decreasing oxygen in the air by making more red blood cells. But we cannot go above a certain altitude, which varies for different individuals, without a pressurized cabin (or a spacesuit). So, too, bacteria may find themselves in a challenging environment. Perhaps a droplet containing bacteria from a mouse landed in your nose. If a mouse bacterium can mutate to expand its progeny's territory to include the human species, those progeny could live in all those places that are low on mice but full of people; maybe someday they could even fly across the world in one of those pressurized cabins.

Biological systems are constantly regulating and adjusting themselves in response to changing circumstances. Because of the bacteria's own role in mutation, from the care of their polymerases to the action of mismatch repair, selective pressure acts on mutations. Increased activity of unusual polymerases and decreased activity of mismatch repair are examples of changes that can increase the chance that there will be many additional mutations. Changes in the activity of genes also can lead to greater acceptance of DNA that comes in from the outside.

A successful genome evolves an optimal balance between the competing needs to be stable and to change, between genetic fidelity and genetic exploration. But what is optimal is not the same for all genes in all circumstances. As a biochemist, looking at the sequence of an organism's genome, I could wire things up to increase SOS polymerases and decrease mismatch repair under stress. I could do this, but to what extent has natural selection done this? Right now people disagree strongly about whether or not certain experiments show that it has, but eventually this question will be answered by careful analysis of the wiring of genomes.

While it may seem strange to consider the idea that mutation could be adjustable, at first glance the ability to adjust the mutation rate under stress does sound useful. An efficient pathogen might increase its genetic variation during the first hours when it infects a new host and is trying to get a foothold.[22] But on the other hand, when the mutation rate is increased, it can damage a lot of genes that the bacteria need if they are to remain viable. It would be much better, from a pathogen's point of view— (or worse, from ours), if mutations became more likely in just those spots in the pathogen genome where variation is least likely to harm the pathogen and most likely to help it adapt to us. We know that there are such spots, such as slippery DNA.

Indeed, distinct types of mutation can become relatively more or less likely when different proteins are present in the cell. Changes in the type and extent of mutation do not have to be randomly distributed throughout the genome. When mismatch repair is damaged, some mutations tend to increase more than others, and which mutations increase more can differ depending upon which mismatch repair proteins are inactive.[23] Without mismatch repair, changes in the length of slippery DNA become more frequent. In yeast with damaged mismatch repair, changes in the length of a particular TTT became one-third of all mutations detected in one gene, whereas normally only 1 in 20 mutations detected were slips at that TTT.[24] So, too, when the activity of a polymerase that doesn't proofread was increased in mouse cells, mutations in undamaged DNA increased tenfold.[25] One-third of these mutations were slips, turning the "tuning knobs" faster.

Not all slips are strategic. There was nothing obviously strategic about the TTT slips. While there are many places in a genome made up of slippery and other more mutable DNA sequences,[26] the *E. coli* genes that encode proteins that respond to stress appear to have more than their share of distinct classes of more mutable DNA.[27] These more mutable genes include those that repair mismatches and those that repair damaged letters. The DNA encoding mismatch repair gene seems to experience a lot of cutting and pasting,[28] for its sequence varies between bacteria in a very patchy way.

Mutations in DNA within the genes needed for mismatch repair result in an increase in uncorrected slips and other mutations elsewhere in the genome. In challenging circumstances, selection may favor bacteria that are less efficient at mismatch repair. [29] If mutations overcome the problem and relieve the stress, those among their progeny that regain the ability to repair mismatches are likely to do better. Patchiness may be a footprint of repeated cycles of losing and regaining, through recombination, of active repair genes as the optimal mutation rate rises and falls. This patchiness might result from recombination at closely spaced repeats. Such repeats are more prevalent in these genes than you would expect by chance.[30] It appears that distinct types of DNA sequence, with different stabilities, can tend to be selected for where they provide an advantage.

Among the strategic places where slippery DNA can be found are locations that vary the bacteria's surface, speeding its exploration of how best to get a foothold in its environment. For a pathogen, that environment would be us.

Richard Moxon and his team in England have shown very clearly that, for the bacteria they have examined, a particular kind of slippery site, repeats of four letters, is found in the genome at places where these bacteria tend to focus exploration on genes that contact and manipulate the host. These genes enable a pathogen to figure out how to bind to our tissues, how to get across barriers, how to gain entry to our cells, how to stay ahead of our immune system, and how to overcome other roadblocks to the pathogen's success. A pathogen that makes all these creative, genome-altering strategic changes while leaving its internal housekeeping genes relatively unchanged and undamaged clearly is at an advantage. Slips in these genes facilitate exploring the ability to bind to us, to poke and prod our defenses. Sometimes they break through.

Aside from causing back-and-forth variation of genes that already are inside the bacteria, mutations can affect how much DNA from the outside the bacteria will patch into its own genome. Perhaps some of the neighbors of a bacterium that is stressed by the environment have solved the local problem and so can pass along some helpful genes, such as how to destroy an antibiotic or how to digest a new food source. Because extra pieces of DNA in bacteria, called plasmids, can carry genes between bacteria, genetic changes on plasmids that prove favorable are positioned to spread especially rapidly from bacterium to bacterium.[31] One of the SOS polymerases can cause about a 1000-fold increase in mutations in plasmids.

The bacterium *Enterococcus* lives in our guts. Though it is often harmless, it is a major cause of hospital-acquired infections, some of which, including heart inflammation, are very serious. When stressed, *Enterococcus* can ask its neighbors for help using the molecular equivalent of a note in the form of a string of eight amino acids. A specific plasmid responds to the note by providing the information needed to build the apparatus that enables the plasmid to transfer to the cell that requested its help. Whether the plasmid responds, and also how many extra copies of the plasmid are made in the bacterium, depends upon the number of repeats in the plasmid of the letters TAGTARRR (where each R can be either an A or a G).[32] Because repeats can be slippery, information sharing may turn on more quickly when mismatch repair is not working.

When bacteria are crowded and starving, they conserve their resources, often not even copying their DNA. How do they get out of this fix if they cannot make mutations? Bacteria even can survive by eating DNA,[33] but once inside the bacteria, the DNA may have something to say, too. Enzymes cut up incoming DNA. This protects bacteria from being taken over by other genomes, particularly viruses. In this way, bacteria can try out new information in bite-sized pieces[34] without letting the incoming DNA call the shots.

In *H. influenzae* in our upper respiratory tract, DNA encoding a gene that looks like it affects whether incoming DNA is chopped up contains a string of 40 repeats of AGTC.[35] Since amino acids are encoded by groups of three letters, a slip of four letters throws this protein out of frame and may even create a codon that says, "Stop reading this message." In addition to this slippery section of DNA, another section of the gene has a lot of changes; variation in this latter section may change where the enzyme cuts DNA[36] so that different individuals in a population of bacteria cut incoming DNA differently, generating additional diversity. If DNA encoding DNA-cutting enzymes tends to vary, not all the bacteria in the population will cut the incoming DNA in the same place. This can protect any useful information that is encoded at that spot and will increase the diversity of progeny.

The DNA strands of starving bacteria may break.[37] Bacteria can "repair" breaks in their DNA either with information from other pieces of DNA or with an error-prone polymerase. In repair by recombination, pieces of DNA can be cut from one helix and pasted into another. The helix that contributes information to the broken DNA may be from the original genome, or it may have been swallowed, perhaps from the same species or perhaps, broken into bite-sized pieces, from another genome. It is a reasonable guess that it was under such stress that two pieces of DNA got together to create the carbohydrate-digesting protein described in Chapter 7. While the mismatch detectors generally enforce the requirement that only very similar sequences can recombine, when mismatch repair is damaged, more diverse sequences are able to be patched into the genome.[38]

Repair of damaged and lost letters is likely to decrease when cells are starving and struggling. If a missing letter is not replaced, and the polymerase stalls, this leftover damage could trigger the SOS response.[39] If the polymerase stalls only momentarily, it is likely to slip, or even fall off. If it slips, genes may be duplicated,[40] and repeats can expand or contract. Slips in repeats that are stimulated by breaks in DNA are very relevant to the human genome too. For example, the DNA in children whose parents lived in the shadow of Chernobyl's radiation had slipped significantly more often when being passed on to them from their parents than the DNA of children in England.[41]

Whatever happens in the environment, the extent of the mutation experienced by a genome is affected by the activity of the proteins that copy and repair DNA. Genome-wide increases in mutation can be risky. However, looking closely at mutators that are less effective at mismatch repair or that have sloppy polymerases stuck on shows us that distinct proteins can affect the tendency to mutate in different ways. As the activity of these distinct proteins varies, increased mutation is not distributed completely randomly across the genome, and natural selection acts on the progeny. Clearly, in a population of starving bacteria, we can see that the bacteria are not thriving. Most are likely to be dying. It isn't easy. But the range of options for random mutation is so vast that any focus that has emerged from repeated cycles of pressure and survival could increase the chance that some might survive again, and that with their survival, a once-fortuitous alignment of the tendency to slip and its biological effect also would survive. This alignment could increase variation in genes that encode mismatch repair proteins and pathogen proteins that stick to the surface of our cells, which may prove useful again to the bacteria in the future. When sequences emerge, such as slippery DNA, which enables reversible changes in the genome, the repertoire of the genome's progeny is enhanced beyond that which is encoded explicitly in the genome itself. Other changes are more permanent, such as those caused by polymerase "errors" or those that increase acceptance of DNA from outside the genome.

The realm of "normal" genome behavior seems to include slides back and forth in genes that have the effect of increasing and decreasing certain classes of mutations, allowing some flexibility around an evolved genome-wide optimum balance between fidelity and exploration. As certain types of diversity are generated among progeny, these progeny may come to find the environment not stressful at all. With so much time to learn to handle extreme challenges, some genomes evolved layer upon layer of strategies for finding the exits, the ways out of the extreme stress. Others didn't, their ship went under, and they died.

9

Journeys through Space and Time

When opportunity arises, Life shall be waiting.

—Rachel Carson

We think of bacteria as individual creatures, lonely killers, but they, no less than we, often live in communities, dependent upon one another for the future existence of their species. Like all members of a community, they send signals to one another that affect their behavior, and that they rely upon for their survival.[1] For example, bacteria can become more open to swallowing DNA from their surroundings when they receive the signal that they are among other bacteria, especially those of the same species, that might send over some recipes. In a sense, bacteria get new ideas at meetings. But how do bacteria, without eyes or a memory for names, know whether they are alone? They use what are in fact called quorum-sensing signals, small molecules that float around them. The intensity of these signals is determined by the number of other bacteria around and how close they are to one another.

Quorum sensing involves turning genes on and off depending upon how many neighbors are around.[2] Quorum-sensing bacteria produce and release chemical signal molecules, and there are more of these signals around if there are more bacteria releasing them. It's as if each person returning to your neighborhood after work began tossing paper airplanes with messages until they were piled up a foot deep at your door, and you saw them through the window. When bacteria detect more than a threshold amount of such a signal, they change which genes are turned on. Among genes that are turned on by a quorum are those needed for bacteria to interact with others, genes involved in virulence, in the ability to send out and to swallow DNA, to make antibiotics, to move, to build filmlike communities, and to form spores. Bacteria can talk to their own species, and to other species. This communication allows bacteria to behave as a community.

If there are no potentially helpful neighbors around, a bacterium that is stressed to the max may go into suspended animation, form a spore, and wait for the wind and water to carry it to more favorable circumstances. Of course, forming a spore has its risks. Still, with the organism's genome more comfortable in its package, no doubt, than my grandparents were probably in steerage, spores are an effective vehicle for travel in space and time.

Spores can travel across oceans on the wind, protected from ultraviolet (UV) light by the shade of their own dust clouds.[3] Like the great ocean liners, it takes around 5 to 7 days for a spore to travel from Africa to the Americas. African dust can be detected over about a third of the United States; about half of the dust lands on Florida. Given their food preferences, about a quarter of the microbes that might be blown in dust from a drought-ridden field will thrive if their journey takes them to elm trees or crops such as peaches, cotton, and rice.

If spores can move that far in space, how far can they move in time? Bacteria can be very patient. Anthrax spores can wait in the soil for over 100 years.[4] In an underground cave, in a crystal of salt, bacteria may have been waiting as long as 250 million years—until the scientist evolved who would revive them in a laboratory. The bacteria found deep in the cave are members of the spore-forming genus *Bacillus*, named by the researchers *Bacillus* strain 2-9-3. *Bacillus* are widespread in the soil, in water, and in dust in the air. Some live naturally with us in our intestines, but others, such as *Bacillus anthracis* (which causes anthrax), can be deadly. The bacteria found in the cave appear to be so closely related[5] to a modern species of halophile (salt-loving) bacteria, that some people suspect these bacteria leaked into the salt cave more recently, through channels so tiny that they cannot be seen under the light microscope. Therefore, the age of these bacteria is not settled.[6] Still, if other scientists confirm that the bacteria were in their crystal case for 250 million years, they slept through quite a show on the Earth above.

While the bacteria slept, protected in brine within a rock, the first dinosaurs appeared. They grew to dominate the Earth, but the bacteria were undisturbed by the sound of *Tyrannosaurus rex*. The plants on the Earth first began to create flowers, but through all of this, the bacteria remained in their brine in its rock. An asteroid hit and the large dinosaurs disappeared, and still the bacteria remained within their rock. The tiny mammals diversified and grew. About 50 million years ago, some took to the sea, becoming whales. Then the genome shared by mammals evolved the primate line. The bacteria waited while *Homo sapiens* appeared, developed agriculture, spread around the Earth, built cities, and invented a microscope. The bacteria remained in their rock in their cave while *Homo sapiens* built laboratories, learned about DNA, and first began to think about what might be there, within the ancient rocks.

Then came a day, between one sunrise and sunset—after over 91,000,000,000 sunrises and sunsets—when a tool brought by a hand reached down, chipped off a piece of the salt crystal, and carried the rock with its tiny passengers to a place beyond the imagination of the tiny reptiles who had once crawled by, near where the rock first formed around the bacteria. The rock was brought from what now is Carlsbad, New Mexico, to a laboratory in Pennsylvania. In this new place, the rock crystal, carefully protected from twentieth-century contamination, was split open. A nutrient-rich broth was provided, and the bacteria stirred from their very long sleep and began to copy their genome and to pass it on to their twenty-first-century progeny. We don't know for certain that they had slept as spores, but we do know that when things begin to get too salty, these bacteria do rush toward becoming spores.

A very lucky human might see 36,000 sunrises and sunsets—each of them, if the human took the time to pause and look up, a show-stopper, each one precious. Within the rocks, ancient bacteria are patiently waiting for something, whatever it may be, that is different.

It is hard for a biochemist to believe that bacteria really could have waited for a better environment, for as long as 250 million years. After all, DNA depends upon enzyme after enzyme in the cell to protect it; letters lose pieces and fall off, although storage in salt could protect it from some kinds of damage. Stepping into suspended animation as a spore—taking a chance on time, not knowing how long that time might be—seems risky. Over that long a time, I would expect breaks in the DNA and loss of too many of the life-defining code letters. I would think it would be a lethal wait.

And yet my biochemist's certainty that bacteria could not possibly survive the DNA damage accumulated over millennia of millennia is shaken by the example of the hardy bacterium *Deinococcus radiodurans*. *D. radiodurans* can live through blasts of gamma radiation 12,000 times as strong as would kill people. It can live through a drought so difficult that its DNA crumbles into 100 pieces. *D. radiodurans* was first noticed growing happily in an irradiated can of meat. Since then it has been found around the world in places where other bacteria cannot thrive, including on freeze-dried rocks in Antarctica and on sterilized medical instruments. It can resist DNA damage from x-rays and UV radiation, and from hydrogen peroxide. If its DNA double helix is severed, broken across both strands in hundreds of places, by 1.75 Mrads in a little over 24 hours, no problem. Most cells of *D. radiodurans* can patch up their genome without the rearrangements or even increased mutation frequency that we would expect.

D. *radiodurans* has ways of protecting itself against such severe damage.[7] First, it keeps extra copies of its DNA around; growing cells have 4 to 10 copies of their genome. The odds are that with two strands in each helix and 4 to 10 helices, there should be one strand that remains undamaged at each spot. *D. radiodurans* also is very efficient at repairing double-strand breaks in its DNA by getting information from an intact double helix through a process called recombination. During recombination, an intact strand of DNA can leave its double helix and partner with one strand of the damaged helix. Once there, a section might be cut out of the intact helix and pasted into the damaged one, or its information might be copied into the damaged helix by using the intact strand as a template to attract letters in the right order, replacing the damaged section.

We can guess that for each point in the DNA, at least one of the copies in at least one of the bacteria in the colony would have survived the DNA-damaging experience intact, and could be used as a reference. But *D. radiodurans* does not depend on redundancy alone. In addition to its main chromosome, *D. radiodurans* has two large extra pieces of DNA that seem to be specialized for survival in adverse conditions. Genes on these two pieces of DNA are turned on during periods of stress. Also, each bacterium is not alone. Not only might it turn to its neighbors to rescue information that was damaged, but it has very efficient systems for using all of the DNA building blocks and carbohydrates washing around it from the cells that don't survive. *D. radiodurans* also keeps a full bacterial DNA repair kit, along with, most probably, some things that we do not yet know anything about. Its full genome repair kit includes ways to recognize, cut out, and replace damaged letters, and to repair mismatches. It kicks damaged letters out of the cell before they get patched into the DNA. It is difficult to imagine how the repair kit itself could survive the damaging treatment, but, of course, *D. radiodurans* brings along extra copies of its repair kit, too. It is hard to believe, but the fact is that these amazing bacteria do survive.

D. radiodurans may be a particular champ at enduring radiation. Still, when even the most ordinary bacteria cast themselves into the future, protected as spores, they too prepare for uncertainty and package DNA repair kits into the spore. This is an evolved strategy for bacteria. The spores of one species of *Bacillus* was shown to be nearly 100 times more resistant to radiation damage than the bacteria themselves. A bacterium can diversify its genome, or it can wait for its environment to diversify itself.

If *D. radiodurans* can survive through treatments that would seem to mean certain death, perhaps the salt-loving bacteria could indeed have survived for 250 million years in their cold cave. An extraordinary observation has to be repeated in order to be believed, of course, but as scientists we do have to have some humility in the face of data. To help myself imagine how bacteria might survive so long in a cave, I did some calculating that is not accurate, but that gives me some perspective on how to understand this. Here is the calculation that helps me: If everyday bacteria can survive radiation 100 times better as spores than as metabolizing day-to-day bacteria, suppose that means that they can survive 100 times longer than I can imagine a suspended bacterium might survive. If 100 times better really does translate into 100 times longer, then this repair kit carried by the spore, turning a day in the lab to the distances of time, would make 250 million years seem like 2.5 million years. This is still too long a time, but it brings them closer to us (we were already walking upright by then).

The lab study in which spores were so much more hardy than bacteria used UV radiation, not drying in salt, and we have to figure out what might protect the proteins in the repair kit itself. There are proteins, called chaperones, that help to stabilize the structure of other proteins, and that are found in spores.[8] Do they help? All these musings suggest that if there are a few more biochemical repair tricks in the many undeciphered proteins in bacterial genomes, one or two of the bacteria may be able to crawl to the finish line after all. Just a small number of viable bacteria, out of the trillions upon trillions that may once have been present, have to survive to carry the genome, and with it the species, forward in time. And the survivors do not have to be museum pieces. They can have some genetic changes; they just have to be able to copy their DNA and to divide, to set out on the road of selection in their new environment. So if bacteria that were harvested indeed had survived 250 million years, they may well have had some tricks, too, things that we have not yet learned about by studying bacteria in their comfortable day-to-day lives in our laboratory broths.

Bacteria are not the only organisms that package themselves in capsules and trust to the wind, the water, and time. Little animals, like worms, have spores. Worms, fungi, seeds, bacteria, and even some crustaceans can survive desiccation. They seem to form a sort of glass around themselves by stringing together certain sugars or other linkable molecular blocks.[9] Plants package themselves for the future too, of course,[10] waiting within their seeds. A sacred lotus seed brought from China was radiocarbon-dated as 1450 years old; it flowered when it was planted in California. Seeds wait patiently on the forest floor until a forest fire sweeps through. They wait until a large tree lives out its life and falls, creating an opening for light. At that moment, their shoots spring up into the sunshine of the future.

10

Strategies as Targets, Round One: The Pathogens

There's no better way to locate the soft underbelly of a pathogen than through its genome.

—Elizabeth Pennisi[1]

Evolution is not just for the "good guys," for breeding corn from an ancient grass, for the ones we would pick for our team. Evolution also happens to the species that we might propose for an expendable species list[2]—our challengers, the genomes that harm us.

Through strategic mutation followed by selection, each of our individual immune systems evolves an impressive repertoire of antibodies during our lifetimes to combat genomes that threaten to damage us. But the genomes that attack us also can evolve. Unfortunately for us, when natural selection acts on tumor and pathogen genomes, it favors those that grow well within us. Bacterial genes change—they slide by decreased mismatch repair; they move patches in and out. Bacteria also pass genes around to one another. Tumors evolve and become more aggressive and harder to deal with. Our ability to combat the spread of antibiotic resistance, the emergence of new pathogens, and the growth, spread, and indeed evolution of each tumor all are affected by strategies for evolution that emerge in genomes that threaten us.

As entire genomes are sequenced, and as our blindfolds are thus removed, we can begin to comprehend the strategies of our challengers; we can fight back consciously. We can, of course, search[3] for those parts of surface proteins that are essential for infection, those that bacteria can't change without losing their ability to infect us, and target them with vaccines. With the complete sequences of genomes to examine, with computers to calculate and laboratories to test our ideas, we also can set to work to decode strategies. We are not stopping with the genome either; labs are hard at work trying to find all of the proteins, how they are modified, and where in the cell they are located; this information may be implicit in the genome, but it can be made explicit more quickly by looking at the proteins themselves.

Rather than chase after bacteria antibiotic by antibiotic, can we stop the passing around of genes that encode antibiotic resistance without destroying the bacterial information sharing that keeps our planet alive? Can we stop the variation in the coats of bacteria and viruses and parasites so that they cannot run away from our immune systems and so turn our vaccines into yesterday's news? Can we stop the evolution of tumors within us, stop the selection of tumors that grow better—the ones that spread and evade our immune system, the ones that ignore signals from within our bodies, and even from within the cells themselves, that sense their unregulated behavior and tell them to die?

The HIV genome uses a very high mutation rate to keep eluding our immune system. With as many as 10 billion new progeny each day swarming through its unwilling host, HIV can be creative; it can take risks, make millions or even billions of fatal errors, and still have many progeny survive. Fast genetic changes help HIV race to outstrip our hard work in the laboratory, where we in turn race to create new anti-HIV drugs. HIV has evolved a mutation rate that is fast enough to stay ahead of the immune system, but slow enough to avoid a molecular amnesia of what it is and how it grows. If we can change HIV's mutation rate, we may throw it off its game.

To find drugs that kill HIV, we look for things that block its ability to stick to our cells, or we figure out, by knocking them out in the laboratory, which enzymes it cannot live without.[4] Once we know its weak spots, we take its essential enzymes—reverse transcriptase, protease, and integrase—and our chemists work overtime making molecules in order to find one that will block each of these enzymes. But if we use the resulting drugs one by one, resistance develops. We must use mixtures of drugs, for the odds are that an individual virus will not be so lucky as to mutate and evolve resistance to all three drugs simultaneously and thus survive.

A drug that decreases the high HIV mutation rate—in effect, tying HIV's genetic hands—should decrease the development of resistance and improve the immune system's chances of combating HIV, and apparently it does.[5] The drug ddC blocks the ability of HIV's reverse transcriptase to copy its own genome. If HIV has to live in a person who is taking ddC, it has to change its reverse transcriptase so that it is not blocked by ddC. The changes that HIV has to make in its reverse transcriptase in order to avoid ddC also happen to increase the fidelity with which the reverse transcriptase copies its genome. The more carefully HIV copies its genome (the more stable it is), the less it is a moving target. But the difference in fidelity caused by ddC is not enough to make it a cure for AIDS. We can try to search for chemicals that block any possible active mutant of the enzyme. We also can look for chemicals that increase the fidelity of reverse transcriptase dramatically.

HIV is the latest in a long line of pathogens that have devastated the human family. New ones emerge from time to time, so we must be vigilant, to spot new threats, to head off what Laurie Garrett calls the coming plague.[6] In his book *The Forgotten Plague*, in a chapter entitled "The Reign of Terror," Frank Ryan reintroduces us to "one of the most dangerous epidemics in human history," tuberculosis.[7] We know that at least one person who died as long ago as 4000 B.C. was infected with TB. In the nineteenth and twentieth centuries, in some places TB killed one in three adults, a total of about a billion people in those two centuries alone; its impenetrable reign was not ended until the development of one of the first antibiotics, streptomycin. But we still have something to fear from TB. It remains with us, always opportunistic, always pushing back. In the early 1990s it reemerged in a form that was resistant to all antibiotics, threatening enough so that in 1993, the World Health Organization declared a global emergency.

More than 7 million people were estimated to be newly infected with active TB in 1998 [8] (many of them with bacteria that were resistant to our current treatments); that year, TB killed 3 million people around the world. TB lives in about 1 billion people, kept in check by their defenses, dormant but not dead.[9] For this reason, the TB genome was one of the first chosen for sequencing.[10] It has just over 4.4 million letter pairs. How does knowing this string of 4.4 million As, Ts, Gs, and Cs help us? The genes don't have labels. So far, the guess is that there are about 4000 genes, and about 4 in 10 of these genes don't look familiar.

Our first line of attack is to look for individual genes that may be essential for TB's growth, but that are not related to any genes found in humans. If a gene that is unique to TB encodes an enzyme that is essential for TB's survival, we might be able to block that gene, and stop TB, while leaving ourselves unharmed. This is the standard approach to drug discovery: Find a target that is essential to the pathogen's life. This standard approach has now moved into the genome, where we find many more potential targets than we had before.

But the bacteria always fight back; they mutate and develop resistance to our drugs. A strategic approach to drug discovery would be to find drugs that target the strategies that bacteria use to hide within our cells and to generate variation. This could be the subject of a whole book in itself, but the outlines are clear. Here are some examples.

Richard Moxon and his colleagues at Oxford University wanted to find, from among the 1,830,000 letter pairs of the genome of the bacterium *Haemophilus influenzae* strain Rd,[11] the right genes to target. They wanted to focus their bacteria-combating efforts on precisely those genes. How do we recognize the genes that are important for virulence? How do we discover which ones are important for enabling *H. influenzae* to interact with our tissues? Moxon and his team developed a hypothesis regarding how we might predict, before we know what most of the genes do, which genes would be important in helping a pathogen to settle into a host.

The Moxon team decided to look for genes that contained simple repeats of four letters—slippery DNA. They reasoned that looking for DNA sequences that tend to slip would lead them to genes that were relevant to microbe-host interactions because they had seen such repeats before, in genes that were important for virulence, for adjusting to life in the host. When they asked the computer to look through the genome for these repeats, it focused attention on nine spots that had repeats of four letters ranging from 6 to 36 repeats in length. As an initial test of their hypothesis that these repeats would lead them to genes that are important for virulence, they mutated, in the lab, an enzyme encoded by the DNA at one of these places; as they predicted, knocking out this gene with slippery DNA made the bacteria less virulent.

H. influenzae has additional strategies for surviving in our nose and throat, which are constantly bathed in antibodies. Rather than competing with one another, distinct strains of *H. influenzae* live together cooperatively; this makes it easier for them to get a broad selection of new DNA sequences from their diverse neighbors.

We need to learn how to block DNA uptake in specific bacteria. We should not assume that all bacteria, and all DNA uptake, are bad and try to block them all. Many bacteria live with us peacefully, competing with others that seek to invade; other bacteria build our environment. We do not want to harm them.

In addition to bacteria, there are parasites. The human race has a grudge match with the malaria genome that extends far back in history. Malaria has a complex "bicoastal" lifestyle: It lives both in people and in mosquitoes. When an infected mosquito bites us, malaria travels around; it gets into our liver, then, in a changed form, into our red blood cells, then out into the blood, where it is sipped up again by another mosquito. Malaria can hide out in our red blood cells, eating our hemoglobin, the protein we need to carry oxygen to our tissues, and making an adhesion protein that sticks red blood cells to blood vessel walls. One particularly deadly form of the malaria parasite, *Plasmodium falciparum*, can switch among various adhesion proteins that it puts on the surface of the red blood cell; this keeps it somewhat ahead of the immune system. As the adhesion proteins vary, the red cells carrying the malaria parasites will stick inside different organs, from our lungs to our liver to our brain, with different clinical consequences.

We know only a little bit about how *P. falciparum* malaria switches among adhesion proteins. We do know that for most adhesion proteins, the promoter that attracts the machinery that copies their DNA into RNA is hidden in fold upon fold of chromosome structure as the long DNA is packaged with protein within a cell; when the DNA is unwrapped to be copied, some information in an intron can cause a regulated switch that exposes one of the many hidden promoters and changes the deadly malaria's coat.[12] If we understood this better, we could stop this dangerous switch. Malaria was one of the first genomes to be attacked by the genome sequencers. To be sure that we figure out how to outflank it, we're working on the mosquito genome too.

Many pathogens get into a mammal when an insect, perhaps a mosquito or a tick, bites the mammal. These pathogens use a range of strategies to vary their coats.[13] In order to be captured by another insect and spread to a new host, they need to linger in the host's bloodstream. But our immune system keeps looking very carefully for anything unusual in our blood, anything that is not our "self." To survive in our blood, these insect-borne pathogens have evolved mechanisms that vary their coats; these mechanisms are as central to their lives as the beating of our heart is to ours. They turn different genes on and off by fooling around with the promoters that attract the RNA copying apparatus; they paste patches of new letters into genes, they hypermutate, they rearrange their DNA. Now, we can learn to attack each of these mechanisms used to generate pathogen-coat variation. Pathogens can hide from our antibodies, but not from our brains. They will be vulnerable.

For Lyme disease, the machinery that moves information that encodes new surface patches into the coat protein gene is an obvious example of a strategic target. A clue to another strategic target comes from growing

Lyme spirochetes in the lab. When they adapt to a well-cared-for life in the lab, Lyme spirochetes may lose specific plasmids, extra pieces of DNA, and when they lose the information in those plasmids, they lose their ability to infect us. To keep the plasmids, they must rely on proteins that guarantee that the plasmids are copied when their chromosomes are copied in preparation for cell division. If we target the mechanisms that coordinate replication of the plasmids and the chromosomes, we may be able to destroy Lyme's ability to remain an effective pathogen. It's worth testing.

Drugs that block the spread of DNA among bacteria, that block the insertion of integrons, should decrease the spread of antibiotic resistance. Similarly, as we understand how microbes sense stress, such as the stress of exposure to an antibiotic, we can learn to block the mechanisms that trigger increased mutation by blocking, for example, the SOS response,[14] so that the microbial ship sinks rather than survives. Blocking the SOS response also would block the production of certain deadly toxins that are "turned on" in some bacteria that are treated with antibiotics.

I have called the microbes "strategic targets, round one" and cancer "strategic targets, round two" because, in the second half of the twentieth century, many of us thought of microbes as vanquished, whereas a diagnosis of cancer was terrifying. In fact, I believe that the microbes will continue to be a challenge long after we have figured out how to beat cancer. The microbes are so varied and are evolving in every place throughout the world, finding new niches in the new structures we build. For example, *Legionella*, which can live inside amoebae, has moved into our spas, hospital plumbing systems, and air conditioning towers—and into our macrophages.[15]

The microbes themselves would be enough of a threat, but it is of course worse than that. Until the human heart abandons thoughts of killing other members of our species, we must be vigilant, and imaginative, to detect swiftly and to combat microbes that have been redesigned to be weapons[16]—a terrifying twist on the phrase "the enemy within."

11

Strategies as Targets, Round Two: Cancer

Nothing in life is to be feared. It is only to be understood.

—Maria Sklodowska-Curie

Why is it so hard to cure cancer? Of course, it is easy to kill a cancer cell—just pour bleach on it, fry it in oil, or poison it with cyanide. But we can't do any of that with tumors; they live deep within us, and they hold the rest of our body as a hostage. To cure cancer, we have to find a special sensitivity in these deranged cells, a target that allows us to kill them while sparing all of our other cells. It is so hard to cure cancer because cancer is part of us; it uses our own genome in an antisocial way. To cure cancer, we have to understand how our own cells make decisions: what signals they listen to, what makes them change their behavior, and when and how they decide to grow or die.

Every time you pick up the paper, it seems that a research team has discovered another mutation in tumor cells, with the hope of a cure if we could just fix it. It might be that in the tumor, genes that produce both a growth factor and the growth factor's receptor are stuck in the "on" position, so that the growth factor keeps triggering growth through its receptor, misusing a normal cell signal. Or it might be that a mutation in the gene encoding the growth factor receptor itself creates a receptor stuck in the "on" position, so that the cell keeps dividing and the tumor keeps growing even when the growth factor is not there. In other tumors, a protein that blocks cell death pathways might be turned on at a high level, interfering with all signals that tell the cell to die. Most cancer research laboratories are focusing on one or two of these broken proteins, thinking that if we could just undo that damage or block its action, we could discover a treatment and "cure" cancer.

A form of leukemia called *chronic myelogenous leukemia*, or *CML*, is driven by a very precise genetic change. DNA is cut and then pasted together wrong, so that the gene for an enzyme, a particular kinase, gets attached to the wrong spot in the genome, away from its normal neighboring DNA. The new protein that is created is a troublemaker; the kinase is stuck "on" in the wrong place at the wrong time in certain blood-forming cells. This new kinase triggers these cells to divide, and since it is stuck "on," the cells keep dividing and become a tumor. Since the loss of control of this one enzyme is responsible for the cell's uncontrolled growth, the idea was to find a drug that would block just this enzyme, to turn it off.

That drug worked! It was exciting and inspiring, and it brought us hope. It was the first of a new wave of cancer drugs, made possible by our growing ability to look under the hood. We were no longer limited to rampaging through cells, hitting their DNA with radiation and DNA-damaging drugs, and jamming their cell division machinery; we could target a drug to exactly what was wrong with that particular cancer cell.[1]

This drug generally worked well, but its effects did not always last.[2] There were patients whose tumor cells had been growing, without the normal controls, long enough for their genomes to have become unstable; their genomes had mutated a lot as the tumor cells divided. In some of these people, many new copies of the kinase gene appeared, with each copy generating enough kinase protein to signal the cell to divide. While it might be rare for the inhibitor to fall off any one molecule of the kinase protein at any given moment, with all of these extra copies of the kinase gene producing kinase molecules in the cell, the odds were that the inhibitor would fall off enough of them to leave enough of the kinase molecules free to send a signal to the cells to keep dividing.

In some other people, when their tumors grew back, it was clear that the kinase had mutated in such a way that the inhibitor could not block it. At least this told us that the kinase gene was the right target. We just needed to find a drug that would block all possible active mutants of the kinase and would hold on tight enough so that it would not be so easy for extra copies to slip away from the drug's grip momentarily. But this may just be whistling in the dark. For some advanced cancers, just blocking the problem that started the cancer may not be enough to stop it.

Where does cancer come from? People who are born with mutations that keep them from fixing damage to their DNA have a greatly increased risk of getting cancer. Some people can't cut damaged letters out of their DNA. Others[3] are missing a polymerase that accurately fills in gaps in DNA that result from cuts around damaged letters. Other people have problems repairing mismatches. The genome becomes unstable when genes that encode the proteins needed for DNA mismatch repair are not working; if such people's DNA slips when it is being copied, it is not repaired. These mutations often lead to cancer. In one study in the United States and Japan, 108 of 790 colon and stomach tumors had problems with mismatch repair. Some people are born with these mutations, and so colon cancer runs in their families; in others, the mutations happen later.

Tumors that have problems with mismatch repair were more than 15 times more likely than normal cells to become resistant to the drug methotrexate. Their speedy development of resistance was mostly due to their having extra copies of the gene that encodes the enzyme that methotrexate is trying to block.[4] This suggests that one strategy we should take is to search for drugs that block or reverse gene amplification.[5]

Tumors that cannot repair slips well accumulate hundreds of thousands of mutations in simple repeated sequences such as GGGGGGGG. In these tumor cells, insertions and deletions of one repeated unit are not repaired; letters are added and removed at each cell division at least 100 times more often than in cells with intact mismatch repair. These slips are risky, for they may damage systems that are needed for growth control.

Bcl proteins block cell death; they keep cells alive. Although they are a normal and important part of our lives, Bcl proteins were first discovered in a tumor, a lymphoma (a B-cell lymphoma). In this lymphoma, there was too much of a Bcl protein, so the cells wouldn't die and the tumor grew. In contrast, Bax is a protein that tells cells to die. One of its roles is to work in partnership—(or perhaps hand-to-hand combat would be a better way of putting it) with Bcl proteins. The balance of cell life and death can be regulated by a balance between Bax's death signals and Bcl's life signals. As in any even fight, with all else equal, if there is more Bax than Bcl, the cell will tend to die; and if there is more Bcl than Bax, the cell will tend to live. If there is too much Bcl or too little Bax, Bcl can outcompete Bax and keep the cells alive.

The amount of Bax and Bcl in a cell is balanced by a network of signaling systems that sense growth factors, DNA damage, and other information that determines a cell's fate. Through the relative amounts of these proteins, their ratio, a decision emerges: cell life or cell death. We can manipulate this balance. For example, certain anti-inflammatory drugs decrease the amount of a Bcl in colon cancer cells, raising the amount of Bax relative to this Bcl. Bax then gets the upper hand and is able to out-maneuver Bcl and kill the cells.

But in cancer cells in which mismatch repair is damaged, you can't count on this anti-inflammatory Bcl-lowering trick to give Bax the upper hand for long. There is an eight-letter-long string of Gs in the Bax gene. In the laboratory, when an anti-inflammatory drug was used to lower Bcl, in cells where mismatch repair wasn't working well, the string of eight letters in Bax either grew or shrank on *both* copies of the chromosome that encodes Bax (the copy inherited from the patient's mother *and* the copy inherited from the patient's father). In 42 of the 60 colon cancer cell lines tested,[6] this threw the reading of the Bax gene out of frame, so that a fnctionalB axp roteinn ol ongerw asm ade. More than half of colon and gastric cancers with mismatch repair problems have slips in this very string of eight Gs in Bax. These slips inactivate the Bax protein;[7] the sentinel is taken out. Without active Bax there to listen for them, these cancer cells may be able to escape from signals telling the cell to die. Patients who still had intact Bax in their colorectal or gastric cancer cells were about twice as likely to survive for 5 years than those with slips in the string of eight Gs in their Bax gene.

Normally, our genome is carefully checked. Ever vigilant, a cell will not divide if it has even one double-strand break between any two of the 3 billion letters in the genome. DNA damage is sensed at "checkpoints" that keep cells from dividing until the damage can be fixed. This is so important to genome integrity that the proteins that run these checkpoints have been conserved during evolution; they are similar in organisms from yeast to humans.

Humans who are missing one of the mismatch repair proteins are susceptible to colon cancer; their slippery DNA keeps slipping and is not repaired. Some of the mismatch repair proteins prevent chromosome rearrangements by blocking recombination between similar but inappropriate DNA sequences. Gene duplications increase significantly without these proteins. Some of these proteins recognize damage to a cell's DNA caused by cancer chemotherapy drugs such as cisplatin and trigger cell death. When these mismatch repair proteins are missing, the cells may resist being killed by these drugs.[8]

A protein called p53 is activated when cells are stressed or damaged; DNA damage, even a single break, is one of the alarms that wake up p53. Some cancer chemotherapy drugs also can kick-start p53. p53 can shut down the division of stressed cells and may even cause the death of cells that are too badly damaged to be repaired before division. But the p53 protein does not function properly in most human cancers;[9] this is especially true of cancers that resist treatment.[10] The protein p53 may be damaged by mutation. or it may become ineffective if the genes that encode proteins that work with it are damaged. When p53 is not able to do its job, cells, like naughty children when their parents aren't looking, can misbehave and divide when they shouldn't, without fixing the damage. When they are not held in check, cells can get away with being sloppy enough to become cancers.

A protein called BRCA1 that is involved in DNA repair helps to maintain genome stability.[11] It can respond to DNA damage, suppress growth, and help trigger cell death. This is important; fruit flies have a similar protein. Many families with inherited *br*east (and ovarian) *ca*ncers have mutations in BRCA1. Pieces of chromosomes are two to three times more likely to be misplaced in breast tumors of people who were born with BRCA1 mutations than in breast tumors of people who were not born with these mutations.

Another particularly bad place for a mutation is in a gene called ras, which encodes a protein that helps to control cell division. Ras is part of a switching system that receives and transmits signals telling a cell to divide. Mutated ras that is stuck in the "on" position has been found in cancers of the pancreas, colon, lung, thyroid, skin, bladder, and kidney, in melanomas and endometrial adenomas, and in certain leukemias. In a majority of these tumors, ras is stuck in the "on" position because of a change at the same place, the second G of a GG doublet in the ras gene.

Part of the reason that we find ras mutated at that spot so often is selection. If ras mutated in a way that did not drive the cells to keep dividing, we would not have noticed the mutation. However, mutations at the first G of this GG doublet, though rare, also promote cell division. When this first G is mutated in a laboratory, the mutated ras protein is just as effective at sticking ras in the "on" position as a ras protein with the mutation at the second G. So there must be a reason why ras tends to mutate precisely at the second G in this GG doublet, and that is because there is a "hot spot" there in the genome. There is an increased chance that a T, instead of a C, will be added across from the G and that the error will not be fixed.[12] These errors still are relatively rare; the letter C was correctly put opposite the G 1000 to 10,000 times more efficiently than the incorrect letter T. But this error remains too common for comfort. A tumor has orders of magnitude more than 10,000 dividing cells. It's an accident waiting to happen.

I am going into some detail about this ras mutation, not just because ras is an important protein, but because it gives us an example of how, as a cell evolves into a cancer cell, it begins to lose some of its normal balances. Things go (from our point of view) from bad to much worse. Here is an example of what can happen: As a cancer cell's metabolism moves out of balance, the amounts of A, T, G, and C that are available for copying DNA can get out of balance, too. An early misstep in this evolving metabolic mess may decrease the amount of C and thus increase the ratio of T to C. T then becomes much more likely than C to float in opposite the G at the hot spot in the ras gene when DNA is being copied, tempting the copying apparatus even further to stick the T into this hot spot.[13] Normally, the p53 gene might sense such a metabolic imbalance and prevent division until and unless the imbalance is solved,[14] but if p53 is not working, trouble is likely.

Now things can go from bad to worse to even worse. An imbalance in the normal ratio of T and C increases the chance of a mutation in ras. Mutated ras, in turn, leads to growth that is not properly regulated. Beyond just driving the cells to keep dividing, ras further affects the integrity of the genome; even in the very first cell division after ras mutates,[15] we can see chromosome abnormalities, including fragments of chromosomes.

Before a pilot starts a takeoff roll, he or she must complete a careful checklist. So, too, each of the cells in our body completes a careful checklist, each time, before it proceeds to divide into two new cells. One of the very important items on the checklist is to make sure that each of the two "daughter" cells is about to get a full set of chromosomes—in our case, the correct set of 46, with each chromosome carrying its special piece of the human genome. Metabolic abnormalities that damage chromosome choreography lead to genome instability and to tumors.[16] Normally, before a cell divides, the chromosomes are copied and attached to a fibrous spindle. The spindle is needed to pull each pair of matched chromosomes apart as the cell divides so that one of each pair goes to each new cell. If a chromosome were to fall off the spindle, it could get lost and wind up in the wrong cell. Then one daughter cell might get both copies, and the other neither copy.

Before cell division, a protein called MAD2 alerts the central checkpoint control system and stops the cell from dividing if there is a single lagging chromosome that is not attached to the spindle.[17] But if MAD2 is missing, or even if there is too little MAD2 in the cell, its usual frantic message to stop division may not reach the checkpoint control system in time. The cell may divide—the plane may take off—without meeting the requirements of the checklist.

MAD2 provides one example of how having too little of a single protein can make the cell's DNA unstable; from generation to generation, the cells don't necessarily get the DNA that they should. Once cells stop passing their DNA reliably to the next generation of cells, variation is generated at every cell division. When variation keeps being generated, natural selection can act; evolution happens. For a tumor, selection favors those that grow out of control within us, that draw upon our resources, construct blood vessels, and eat our stores. Of course, this is a short-lived selection, but there have been many irrational conquerors in history. The tumor doesn't know that if it kills us, it kills itself, too.

Tumor cells may have the wrong number of chromosomes; they may have rearranged chromosomes; a piece of one chromosome might become stuck onto another. Some of these cells with odd numbers of chromosomes may be damaged in ways that make them unable to do much. Often, those cells just die. Other damaged cells may be relatively healthy, except that they have lost the genes that "socialize" them to live at peace within us; they've lost the genes that tell them to stop dividing when things are getting out of hand, and to stay put. They divide more aggressively, and spread. Over time, it is likely that the tumor will lose more and more of the proteins that work together to stop cells from dividing when they shouldn't divide; if this happens, the tumor cell will begin to divide with less and less restraint, spiraling out of control as its genome passes from generation to generation of cells in the growing tumor mass.

Of course, as tumors grow we are trying to kill them, from both inside and out. They evolve ways to evade our immune system. Many tumor genomes carry extra copies of genes that encode tiny molecular pumps that get rid of the drugs that we use to try to kill them. We can try to find drugs that block these pumps; more generally, we can try to find drugs that block the mechanisms that make extra copies of genes.

Once a part of a chromosome is amplified, it can become unstable and tend to rearrange itself, even breaking off from the chromosome.[18] p53 usually guards against freelancing extra little pieces of DNA that set up shop independently of the regular chromosomes. These little pieces may keep getting copied, but they are likely to be lost in little blebs at the cell membrane during the choreography of cell division. However, if the freelancing DNA encodes extra copies of the proteins that provide a growth advantage, selection will favor those cells that hit upon a way for the pieces to be retained in the tumor[19] and amplified. Biopsies of human tumors find that most often, many extra copies of genes that drive cell growth can be found on these extra bits of chromosomes.

When p53 is missing, freelancing DNA can be found even in normal human cells. Defects in the ability of p53 to control genome integrity create a permissive environment that allows cells to get the wrong number of chromosomes. We should learn how to look for drugs that eliminate these extra pieces of chromosomes, although this won't be easy, as selection will keep pushing the process the other way.

And, as things continue to spiral from bad to worse, suppose one of the proteins that is amplified is a protein that will, if there is too much of it around, tend to mess up the number of chromosomes. Extra copies of this protein will actively generate the wrong number of chromosomes, compounding the problem once the controls that spot mistakes in the number of chromosomes are lost. Too much of this protein, which generates extra chromosomes, was found in more than 1 in 10 primary breast tumors.[20] Chromosomes mis-segregate in these cells, making a misshapen genome get worse at every division.

When a group of neurosurgeons took biopsies of 11 human brain cancers (glioblastomas), they found many extra copies of a growth factor receptor gene on extra little pieces of DNA in four of them. When they treated these brain tumor cells with a chemical that got rid of the extra pieces of DNA, the extra copies of the receptor gene were gone too.[21] Here is a strategic target. This drug is not useful for therapy yet, but perhaps we can find other drugs that will help a faltering genome keep its chromosomes straight. When these bits of DNA were eliminated, the cells regained sensitivity to other drugs as well, and were better-behaved citizens of the body. If we could find chemicals that are good at kicking out these little bits of DNA, we could begin to discover new types of anticancer drugs. These drugs might be less toxic, because our cells normally don't have all of these extra bits of DNA.

Tumor cells divide even when their DNA is damaged; this lack of attention to the integrity of the genome accelerates the genetic mess. As the carefully balanced signaling systems, and the genes for the proteins themselves, begin to take additional hits—as a cell plunges, losing its controls, down the path to a more aggressive cancer and the regulators of cell death pathways lose their grip—sicker and sicker cells can survive, invade, and destroy, spiraling further and further out of our range to call them back.

I do not mean to say that what I have outlined here is precisely the route taken by every cancer cell as it plunges into chaos. There is more than one route down the hill and over the cliff, but they all pass through loss of control, genome variation, and selection for behavior that accelerates growth. Once on this slippery slope of increasingly rapid generation of tumor-cell diversity, there are many mistakes that facilitate the emergence and selection of increasingly aggressive cells. The tumor cells start to ignore signals that should make them stay put; they spread, stick, and grow in the wrong places. They respond to growth signals meant for others, and they ignore death signals meant for them.

The fundamental problem with tumors is that they can keep generating variation. As their regulation breaks down, they can become increasingly aggressive. Tumor cells have more mutations than can be explained by typical cellular mutation rates. Just as muscle cells are set up to make muscle proteins, and beta cells in the pancreas are good at making insulin, dangerous tumors develop a specialized "mutator" behavior.[22] Tumors lose genes that tell them to stop. They make extra copies of genes that drive their division; they even can copy whole chromosomes and wayward bits of chromosomes many times, rushing ahead in unregulated chaos.

A tumor is an evolving system, selected for the ability to continue to divide and to grow and to spread. Like a section of society that grows out of control and takes more than its share of resources, tumor cells will thrive and further improve their ability to thrive until they destroy the infrastructure that supports them, the life in which they grow. Successful, aggressive, destructive tumors, in a sense, evolve a strategy of variation. Many cells in a tumor will make mistakes, lose genes that are needed for survival, and die. By damaging their DNA with chemotherapy and radiation, we will kill many additional tumor cells. But variation will take other cells in the tumor to a better error, and they will thrive. If dangerous tumors emerge on a foundation of generating variation, perhaps our strategy should be to learn how to decrease genetic variation.

This is not easy, at least not today. There is a lot of focus on "fixing" p53 or blocking ras, and these may be good targets. We need to pay more attention to the mechanisms that generate variation rather than trying to control each variation individually, with each lab looking under a different lamppost, each wonder drug focused on one variation, while the tumor is a variation-generation machine. For, really, there are two stages of cancer, the first exploding into the second.

At first, the tumor's survival may rest on a single lesion that can be combated by drugs targeted to control a kinase or two or some other specific growth target, or to patch up a checkpoint. Or there may be, right at the start, a mutation that generates many more mutations. The problem becomes more difficult when a cancer becomes an evolving system that is out of control, where one and then more and more variation-generating mechanisms establish themselves and must be blocked if we are to have any hope to catch the tumor in its race to thrive.

And, first do no harm. These strategic considerations raise flags of caution. Radiation and chemotherapy cause DNA damage. DNA damage triggers the death of tumor cells through programmed cell death pathways, but tumor cells can develop defects in their cell death pathways. Perhaps it is a mistake to use radiation and mutagenic chemotherapy after tumor cells have developed defects in cell death pathways—after the DNA damage that these agents create no longer kills the tumor cells at doses where it does not kill most of the normal cells too. At least, it could be a mistake to use these therapies until we figure out how to overcome what is blocking the death of the tumor cells.

By damaging tumor DNA, we diversify the tumor genome; we may risk speeding the emergence of more aggressive tumor cells. By damaging DNA, we might increase the rate at which cells within the tumor lose mismatch repair, or cell death pathways, or chromosome checks, or any number of other systems that restrain the tumor. A tumor that has only a few errors that could perhaps be fixed with targeted therapy could be turned into a much more serious disease by our current DNA-damaging treatments. Of course, many people have been saved by these aggressive, DNA-damaging treatments. But for others, we may be winning a battle—killing off much of the tumor—but still losing the war. We are now developing the technology to look into every single tumor and see which genes are on, which proteins are present, what forms each protein is in, and where in the cell each protein is. Tumors are mixtures of cell types, which doesn't make it easy, but with this new technology we have more chances than before. For each tumor, we can work to discover where we can remove the barriers to cell death and find the surviving control points—the places where we can strike the strategic blows that will bring these deranged tumor cells down.

For the tumors and pathogens that threaten us, we can begin to pull back from hand-to-hand combat. We have, or will soon be getting, the battle plans of our skilled opponents. We have broken their simplest codes, and now we must focus on understanding their strategies—what keeps them going, what will make them turn left instead of right, climb the mountain instead of dig a bunker.

After a friend of mine had his first brain surgery, I learned that he had a glioblastoma. When discussing treatment options, my reaction was, "What! The doctors didn't look for the p53 status, they didn't keep a sample to check which genes are turned on, which are amplified, what drugs the tumor is resistant to? How can we figure out what to do if we don't know what's going on???" My view may have been unrealistic then, in 1998, as the analysis infrastructure that will enable us to understand each tumor was not yet in place. Gary's battle was lost before the new millennium arrived.

12

Theme and Variations

Leverage everything. All resources have multiple uses.
Learn from your own experience.

—Alan Khazei[1]

Suppose that you have in your hand a piece of DNA that contains the design specifications for a protein that can capture energy from red light. This piece of DNA also specifies that the protein should be made only in those cone cells within our eyes that have the job of signaling our brain when something is red. The protein encoded by your piece of DNA doesn't just float around in the cone cell, either. It sticks to the surface of the cell, clutching a light-detecting pigment, on the lookout for any red light that appears in the tiny part of the world that it sees. When the pigment is struck by red light, the protein changes its shape; when it changes its shape, it pushes something inside the cone cell, creating a signal that says, "I see red." Other molecules in the cone cell take it from there, passing the signal on to our consciousness, through a relay of brain cells that integrate "red" with other information: a rose. If you have a gene that encodes such a self-assembling red-light detector in your hand, you have in your hand DNA that encodes a pretty sophisticated protein.

If you wanted to build a protein that detects green light, where would you begin? Why start from scratch? I'd tinker with the DNA that encodes the red-detecting protein, wouldn't you? This would be the most efficient way to design a green-detecting protein that is made in the eye, goes to the cell surface, and signals a cone cell. Perhaps we can get the protein to see green just by fiddling a little with the parts of the protein that interact with the pigment. Before I did any tinkering, of course, I would make a copy of the red gene. I may want to see green, but I still want to see red too.

In fact, in our own genomes, there is a section of our X chromosomes that encodes light-sensing proteins. It usually encodes one red-sensing protein and one to three green-sensing proteins. About 98 percent of the DNA letters in these proteins are the same, clearly related by copying.

Of course, evolution does not know that it wants to see light of another color. In fact, each organism misses a lot that is going on around it in the world. For example, unlike bees, we do not see ultraviolet light. Our eyes have proteins that detect red, green, and blue light, but a protein that was on the lookout for red light would be wasted effort for the coelacanth. If you have ever taken a picture underwater with film that is sensitive to all the colors that we humans see above in the sunshine, it is clear that the red light is gone, absorbed by the vibrations of water molecules. The world looks blue, and it gets darker and bluer as you go down. The Comoran coelacanth is an ancient fish that lives 200 meters (600 feet) below the surface of the water. Its world is blue, and so the coelacanth's two visual pigment proteins absorb only light that is blue.[2] This may seem narrow to us, but take a moment to imagine a world of deep violets, indigos, and blues—a different palette, perhaps, but very beautiful. Picasso's blue period?

A natural tendency to tinker with light-detector genes may enrich your world. Over the course of evolution, genomes have, in fact, "learned" that they do not have to reinvent the wheel. Useful information, such as the genes for antibiotic resistance that are swallowed by bacteria, may be available in the environment, but it may not even be necessary for a genome to look outside for helpful information. Often, all that is needed is a minor adjustment to a gene that is already being used for another purpose, just as changing a red-light-detecting gene can expand the spectrum of your vision. The genome may find useful information that can be adapted to a new role simply by rummaging around in the genome itself. A genome that has a way to copy and vary genes that it already has would be favored by natural selection.

In fact, having extra copies of a gene may in itself be useful, even without variation. Suppose you were a bacterium that was swimming in a sublethal dose of the antibiotic tetracycline. Making copy after copy of a protein that destroys tetracycline or that kicks tetracycline molecules out of you will help you to survive as the amount of tetracycline in your environment slowly rises.[3] Thus, evolving a system for making extra copies of genes can be favored under the right circumstances.

But suppose you are a bit sloppy in copying your genes, so that the new, inexact copy will do something similar to what the original did—but not exactly the same. Is this slightly new function useful?

Genomes have several mechanisms that make and retain[4] an extra copy of a gene from time to time. With the copy in hand, they can explore variations around a framework that has already proved useful. Genomes that can start up near the finish line in this way, with something that already is useful, have a strong selective advantage over populations that begin with random strings of letters and/or test every mutation and every insertion site.

We were not the first to discover the evolutionary power that can be gained by copying genes and varying them. Tiny life forms were ahead of us. As different as we are from anemones or eagles, we are built from many of the same interchangeable parts. This makes the biosphere's tremendous diversity, with its extensive underlying biochemical similarities, more comprehensible. Many of the genetic concepts that are used to go from worm egg to worm are also used to go from human egg to human.

In your second gene evolution project, suppose that you are handed the gene for an enzyme called a serine protease. This protein uses the amino acid serine (S) to cut the connection between two amino acids in another protein—sort of like a molecular scissors. Which other protein it cuts is determined by other amino acids in a "specificity site" on the serine protease; these specificity-site amino acids are in a position to grab and hold the cuttee, or substrate, up against the active-site serine, which does the actual cutting.

It is useful to have more than one serine protease. If you made a random, inexact copy of the DNA that encodes a serine protease, you might lose the serine or other amino acids that work very closely with the serine, and thus have an inactive protein on your hands. Alternatively, you might change some amino acids in the specificity site, the place that determines what protein the serine protease is going to cut; if this happened, your mutated serine protease would keep its ability to cut a protein, but now it might grab and cut a different protein. If cutting this new protein proves useful, selection may favor this change. If the change is destructive, it is likely to be crossed out, or erased, by selection. Such copy/vary mechanisms involving serine proteases—a theme and variations on that theme—built the pathway that allows our blood to clot. (See Figure 12-1.)

When we cut ourselves, the bleeding soon stops; unless the wound is too deep and large, it seems to seal itself. Most of us learned to take this molecular marvel for granted when we were small children and injured ourselves while we were playing. For our blood to clot, we rely on a cascade of proteins that cut other proteins. Serine proteases are enzymes. Enzymes are catalysts, usually proteins, that bind a molecule, change it, let it go, bind another copy of the first molecule, change it, let it go, each time very rapidly—a molecule-altering factory. The molecules that enter the factory are called the enzyme's *substrates*. Because each enzyme molecule can cut molecule after molecule of its substrate, each enzyme molecule amplifies the signal that activates it. Our blood clots by using an amplifying network of serine proteases.

One evening, molecules were being washed out of a blood vessel in my calf and forming a stain on my sock; the molecules were unable to do anything—other than perhaps attract the attention of the red receptors of my eyes—about the cut back at the calf, which had been sliced neatly and painlessly by the blade of an ice skate. In fact, my eyes and my attention were occupied with wondering how I came to be not standing up, getting me up off of the cold ice, and then trying the turn again. I did not notice the stained sock for another hour or so. By then, through a routine miracle, the bleeding had stopped.

Somewhere inside, at the edge of the cut, a molecule must have noticed that I was bleeding, that it and the blood it traveled in was flowing out. It must have noticed this quickly, before it was outside, diffusing away from the cut through the sock and beyond. But if a molecule notices that the blood vessel in which it is traveling is cut and leaking, then what? How can a molecule plug a chasm that is huge compared to the molecule itself; how can a molecule that notices the cut scream for help?

The major protein in a blood clot forms long, stringy fibers and is called fibrin. Fibrin fills our blood; it exists anywhere that blood flows, anywhere that a blood vessel may be torn and need to clot. But there is a dilemma here: We want to have this long, stringy protein handy everywhere in the blood, just in case a cut needs to be sealed; on the other hand, we *don't* want

G	Y	K	P	D	E	G	K	R	G	D	A	C	E	G	D	S	G	G	P	F	V	M	K
G	Y				D	T	K	Q	E	D	A	C	Q	G	D	S	G	G	P	H	V	T	R

Figure 12-1 Two members of a gene family. A short stretch of amino acid sequence from two serine proteases involved in blood coagulation. (The full sequences are hundreds of amino acids long.) The high conservation surrounding the active site serine (symbolized by S in GDSGGP) can be contrasted with variation at other positions. (To highlight the matching areas better when we look at the sequences, researchers introduced a gap in the sequence at the bottom, but in the protein itself the amino acid Y connects directly to the amino acid D.)

this stringy protein loose everywhere in the blood, forming long, stringy clots all the time and plugging up blood vessels that should be flowing. We need to keep on hand a good supply of fibrin that is tied up and unable to form its clotty strings, but at the same time handy, ready to be unwrapped quickly at the right moment, to string together with other unwrapping fibrin molecules.

In fact, the fibrin in our blood is inactive, tied up as something called fibrinogen. Fibrinogen is everywhere the blood flows. As soon as a vessel is torn and a clot is needed, the fibrin is freed to do its work quickly. Fibrin is cut out of fibrinogen by an enzyme called thrombin, which also is present everywhere in blood. Thrombin uses the amino acid serine to cut fibrin's chains; it is a serine protease. Each molecule of thrombin generates a flotilla of fibrin molecules. Like a molecular Paul Revere sounding the alarm in every Middlesex village and farm, thrombin grabs fibrinogen molecule after fibrinogen molecule as they come by, freeing fibrin molecule after fibrin molecule to rush onto the growing clot. Because each thrombin molecule frees so many fibrin molecules, the result is a huge amplification of the news that the blood vessel is torn. For each thrombin that "knew" that the vessel was breached, hundreds of fibrins are "told."

However, we still have the same dilemma. If the blood is full of thrombin and fibrinogen, we need a way to guarantee that thrombin frees fibrin only when a blood vessel is torn. Thrombin, too, needs to be tied up, bound and gagged, to be released only when it is needed—and it is. Another serine protease releases molecule after molecule of thrombin when the blood vessel is cut. Therefore, that enzyme too has to be tied up unless a blood vessel is cut. And so yet another enzyme frees molecule after molecule of this enzyme, and so on. Thus blood clotting is begun with a huge emergency phone tree, in which one enzyme, noting, in its molecular way, the torn blood vessel, spreads the signal to thousands of other molecules. In less than 15 seconds, the amount of active thrombin in our blood increases a millionfold.

At the very beginning, setting off the emergency phone tree, is a blood enzyme that is able to cut another protein when either it or a blood platelet touches the protein collagen. Collagen is found only *outside* of blood vessels. If the blood can touch collagen, the blood vessel must have been cut. Another molecule, which comes out of damaged tissues, can turn on the blood coagulation in a similar way. So, the emergency blood clotting phone tree is started by torn vessels or crushed tissues. A molecule appears to be reasoning: If I can touch collagen, I must start the emergency phone tree.

This molecular wound-sealing, phone-tree signaling system did not evolve by random mutation from random pieces of DNA. Thrombin and the other enzymes in the cascade have similar structures. Each contains the same molecular protein-cutting tools (including the active-site serine) to free the next enzyme in the cascade. The major difference among the enzymes in this cascade is not in what they do, but what they do it to. They all cut proteins, but they cut different proteins. There is a theme and variations. The theme is a common structure that includes protein-cutting tools, and the variations are the unique parts of each enzyme that stick to, or "recognize," the specific protein that the enzyme will cut and the specific protein that will cut it.

Some ancient genome evolved a protein structure that could cut another protein, and in so doing it evolved something far more important than a single protein, A, that could cut another single protein, B. It now had in its repertoire a genetic concept of how to build a protein-cutting protein—something that was much more valuable than the protein encoded by the gene itself. The concept could be conserved and leveraged.

Once it had the concept of how to build a protein-cutting protein, this genome could, relatively quickly, evolve yet another protein-cutting protein by making a copy of the first one and tinkering with it. If it could do that, it would be way ahead of a genome that had to rely on random mutation of random DNA to make more protein-cutting proteins. The tinkering genome had in its possession the root of a large family of related genes that encode protein-cutting proteins.

Genomic knowledge can be leveraged over and over again. The enzymes of the blood coagulation cascade have evolved this way: copy, vary; copy, vary—theme and variations. Blood-clotting proteins are related not only to one another, but also to members of a much larger family of protein-cutting proteins, all of which use the amino acid serine (S) as a molecular sword to cut through other proteins. All proteins in this family share the concept of using serine to cut into other proteins.

We don't reinvent the wheel; we use what we know about wheels to design different variations on wheels, from water wheels to the landing gear on space shuttles. Genomes too, during evolution and selection, build up a repertoire of tools and skills. They use interchangeable parts, adapting information that is already in the genome to meet new challenges most efficiently. Genomes that evolved efficient ways to tinker with useful information that already was inside them were bound to be favored in evolution.[5]

13

Family Heirlooms:
A Framework for Evolution

Nothing in biology makes sense, except in the light of evolution.

—Theodosius Dobzhansky[1]

A gene family can be like hats. Some people talk about the genome as a library, but wandering around in your genome might remind you more of a large department store. In the hat department, there is a big, wide-brimmed Stetson. There is a cloche in a purple fabric that hugs the head and holds some purple feathers and a veil. There is a rain hat made of waterproof fabric, simple, with a wide brim. There is a winter hat of fake fur that extends over the ears and the nape of the neck. There also is a bright yellow straw summer hat.

We don't get the hats mixed up with the shoes; there is an original concept of "hat." Whatever other frills they may have, the hats are the things with a head-shaped space in the center, and the shoes are the things with a foot-shaped space. In the department store, we find families of these receptors for heads and feet, and for many other parts of the human anatomy. There are pants on another floor; there also is a department full of dresses. Perhaps our department store has 1000 dresses, each a variant on the dress framework. And there's the jacket department, and departments for gloves, and socks. Whether they are made of silk or denim, with metal snaps or fabric-covered buttons, the jackets share an underlying concept that is different from that of the socks.

Evolution works this way. When it hits on a useful pattern, that pattern's a keeper. We have a closet full of very useful hand-me-down genes. The design concepts of almost all of our genes arose a long time ago, in tiny, crawly, creepy things, and even before that, in bacteria. The little crawly ancestors may have just had vests. We took the pattern from them and, by copying and varying it, added the sleeves, buttons, pockets, and other pieces that we now use in shirts, jackets, coats, and dresses. A fly descended from the same tinier ancestor might have added an intricate series of ruffles to the shirt, making it something that *we* of course would never wear, but that might be useful to the fly.

Genomes have made a lot of use of duplication and variation. This has led to the emergence of large "families" of genes that share a common "parent" gene many generations back. A gene family can consist of as many as 1000 genes, all related by duplication and variation.

New proteins most often evolve by revising copies of genes or by combining pieces of genes that already are on hand, rather than by starting from scratch. Nearly half of the proteins in yeast resemble proteins that we also have. About 1 in 10 of our proteins looks similar not only to proteins in gorillas, or worms, or flies, but also to proteins that have been on this planet at least as far back as our last common ancestor with yeast.[2] These more-than-billion-year-old protein designs generally are involved in the basic "housekeeping" functions that all life shares, such as metabolism, copying and repairing DNA, and the protein-making machinery.

For example, we all need nutrients in order to live. One example of an ancient gene family, which we share with bacteria, encodes the ABC transporter family of proteins. These genes code for parts of proteins that resemble little portable motors, using energy to drive diverse cell activities. The biggest department in the *Escherichia coli* genomic department store is made up of these ABC transporters. Various ABC transporters allow *E. coli*, which lacks hands and a mouth, to "eat" a diverse range of nutrients; they bring in nutrients like sugars from outside the cell. We use them too, for transporting things in and out of our cells.[3]

There are many proteins and pieces of proteins that we share with plants. Plants, too, must copy and repair their DNA, turn genes on and off, metabolize, and grow. More than 1 in 20 of the mustard weed's genes encode proteins that turn other mustard weed genes on and off. About half of these genes, and the proteins that they encode, are shared with animals and yeast.[4]

Some protein pieces and some proteins have been found only in animals so far, such as the EGF module; it has this name because it was first found in a receptor for a growth factor protein that tells epidermal cells to grow. There appear to be about 1200 groups of proteins that are found in humans, flies, and worms, but not in yeast.[5] More than 90 percent of the functional protein pieces, called *domains*, that can be identified in humans also are found in fruit flies and worms. These domains are needed for life as a multicellular animal; they include receptor signaling proteins and signaling kinases.

The people who got the first peek at our human genome list 1278 families of genes that they found there. At most, only 70 of our gene families and only 24 of our domain families are unique to vertebrates. The other 1184 gene families may also be found in anything from fruit flies to worms to starfish to roses, to yeast, or even bacteria; some are found in all of these. When we and yeast have similar needs, we are likely to use similar proteins.

What do vertebrates need to do that yeast, worms, and flies don't, other than to build a backbone? These vertebrate-only domains and proteins are mostly involved in our vertebrate defenses and unique immune system, and in our nervous systems and brains. Of course, flies and worms have their own versions of these systems—we added some new defenses and mental skills. When the human genome was sequenced, a protein turned up that we had not known was in our genome, but that we knew was involved in fish memory.

We share these special vertebrate proteins with one another—with orangutans, dogs, and parrots. And, as anyone who has gingerly eaten a poorly filleted fish knows all too well, fish also have backbones; that is, they are vertebrates. We share these 94 families with fish, too, and we swallow them when we swallow fish. As yet, I do not know of a single human-only gene family, and, indeed, I would be surprised to find one.

Our attention often is drawn to the apparent differences between us—the tall red-headed woman with the curly hair, the short bald man, the African, the Swede. But we are, overwhelmingly, similar, and not just to each other. A fertilized hummingbird egg, no less than a human egg, must divide and become an organism with a head, two eyes, four limbs, a mouth in the front, waste disposal toward the other end, and a heart inside.

Amongst the most venerable families of genes are those that encode proteins that turn genes on and off. Proteins that turn genes on and off allow an organism to adjust to changes in the environment within its lifetime. To turn genes on and off, there must be a protein that can attach to a few letters next to the gene that is going to be turned on or off, and that also can bring the RNA copying machinery to that place and get it started.

Usually the "regulatory" letters that this protein recognizes come before the first letter in the part of the gene that will be translated into protein, to the "left" of the gene in the DNA.

An early innovation was a protein domain that looks like a finger; it recognizes three letters in the DNA, say GCG, and holds on. Any string of three selected from the four letters A, T, G, and C occurs very frequently in our 3 billion letter genome, but these "finger" domains can be built up to enable more stringent recognition of the letters next to one gene. For example, three fingers combined in one protein might recognize, specifically, GCGTCGAGC. As more and more finger domains are included in a protein, the sequence of letters that the protein recognizes will be more and more rare in a genome, so that the protein will affect the activity of a specific group of genes. Many amino acids in the finger domain are involved in maintaining the finger framework, but a few hold onto DNA and from their properties define the specific letters that the finger will hook onto. For example, one finger with the amino acids R, E, and R at positions 13, 16, and 19 from the end of the finger binds to the DNA letters GCG. When the E at position 16 was replaced by the amino acid H, the finger changed its specificity and bound the DNA letters GGG.[6]

Whether in a protein domain that binds to DNA, a light-detector protein that is sensitive to a new color, a serine protease that cuts a new substrate, or a protein that performs any one of many thousands of other tasks, it has proved useful over and over again in evolution to create additional proteins that are similar to a functional protein, but with the protein's function directed to a new target. In other words, it has proved useful over and over again in evolution to create additional gene family members with a conserved framework that have changes focused in very specific regions.

These large gene families evolve by duplicating and varying genes. But is the variation random? As you tinker with the eye color receptor's DNA, or with the clotting protein, you want to avoid changing the part of the color receptor that gets it to the cell surface or the serine that makes the protein cut. A concept of where variation is most likely to be successful is encoded in our antibody genes. The pathogen-binding site is most likely to vary, and that variation is most likely to be helpful in discovering how to bind a new pathogen. The antibody genes actually are part of a family that also includes recognition genes that are active in T cells. The gene regions that code for different parts of antibodies, and for recognition systems on T cells, share mechanisms for the generation of focused diversity. Presumably, information that focuses diversity was copied when the genes were copied to build this family of pathogen-recognizing proteins.

The antibody family focuses DNA rearrangements and genetic variation where they are most likely to help. With all of these creative genetic tools available for focusing variation, it makes sense to consider the possibility that natural selection would have captured this capacity for regulated and/or focused genetic variation in other places where it would provide a selective advantage. There is nothing that would limit focused variation to genes that are involved in host/pathogen or predator/prey struggles. Efficiency also is needed for natural selection in the face of many other environmental challenges.

For variation in copies of genes that are not antibodies, it generally is assumed that mutation is random.[7] Randomly trying out mutations in each copy of each of many thousands[8] of gene families could mean eons spent wandering lost through the broad mutation landscape, in spite of the fact that information could be available to help guide the journey. Still, most people assume that mutations happen randomly throughout the duplicated genes, and that natural selection picks those that lead to a useful new function.

But for most genes, much as for the antibodies, the correct answer would be to vary the binding site, not the framework—to attach new domains on the edges of a domain, not in the middle where it will disrupt the function. To keep rediscovering by accident that the most likely way to create a new serine protease is to mutate the binding site and leave the serine alone would be to keep reinventing the genomic wheel. Those organisms that keep knocking out what is needed to be a functioning member of a gene family—the serine, for example, in a serine protease—will lose the race. The advantage goes to the genome that tends to change in the right places for exploration. In fact, Steve Grand, the designer of the computer game Creatures,[9] designed the creatures' genome in just this way, so that important things don't mutate as quickly as some exploratory things.

Like the wheel or a set of gears, certain protein structures are widely useful. If a gene family is large, with many members and many adaptable functions, this suggests that the protein sequence encoded by members of that gene family provides a structural framework that has a generally useful function, such as signaling the presence of another molecule or cutting another protein. The fact that a gene family is large suggests, at least to me, that the underlying DNA sequence that the genes in this family share may provide a successful genomic framework for the evolution of additional useful family members. An efficient genomic framework would evolve a tendency to be copied, and to focus variation where variation generates potential new members of the family, while avoiding variation that destroys the family's functional framework.

I am convinced that there is information in a gene that, for example, increases the tendency for sequence exploration at the binding site or decreases the tendency to change at places that are absolutely essential if the gene family member is to carry out the activity common to members of that gene family. This information can be conserved when gene family members are duplicated, and thus become a feature of a gene family or superfamily, much as it has for the antibody genes.[10]

The idea I have proposed, that variation-targeting mechanisms might be a general property of gene families, makes a lot of sense, but it is very controversial. It still is controversial to propose that specific molecular mechanisms have evolved that "assist the process of evolutionary change" because, it has been said, "selection lacks foresight, and no one has described a plausible way to provide it."[11] It would be hard to disagree with this objection if the challenges that confronted genomes were unprecedented and completely random. But challenges and opportunities are not random. Certain classes of challenges and opportunities tend to recur over and over again. If it is valuable to evolve new gene family members, there is pressure to evolve a mechanism to duplicate these genes. The need to avoid destroying the activity of the new copies as gene families grow is itself a challenge that recurs each time the gene is duplicated. Because certain classes of challenges and opportunities tend to recur, a response that is better than random can be favored by natural selection.

Genomes that evolve successful responses to challenges that they confront over and over again are at an advantage in evolution. Certainly a tendency to focus mutation is among the successful responses that genomes can evolve. It is not unreasonable to imagine that both special mechanisms that duplicate gene family members and mechanisms that tend to direct variation to the binding site at a low but nonrandom frequency would experience positive selection in evolution. When I suggest this, I attract a lot of controversy, but it is clear that careful tinkering with useful pieces of DNA is much more efficient than starting with random DNA and randomly mutating.

There is evidence that variation can focus on one region of a gene. This certainly is true for antibodies, for the Lyme parasite, and is likely to prove true for cone-snail toxins too. But it may also be true for our mammalian serine proteases. In serine proteases, there are more changes in some places than in others. At the binding site of the serine protease kallikrein, there is a high rate of change from one amino acid to another. The assumption is that this is due to selection for new amino acids there and selection against new amino acids elsewhere, such as at the active-site serine. But again, as we saw with the cone-snail toxins, this high rate of change includes changes among synonymous codons. Therefore, this focused change cannot be explained by random mutation followed by selection, since, when a synonymous codon changes to another, there is no change in the amino acid that selection supposedly acts on. Tomoko Ohta and Christopher Basten have proposed that this high rate of change that is focused in one region of the kallikrein gene results from sequence insertion by gene conversion.[12] Gene conversion involves the insertion into a gene of a patch of sequence from somewhere else in the genome. This generates variation in the pathogen-binding region of chicken and rabbit antibodies, and, it seems, also in mammalian kallikreins.

Where might those patches of sequence come from? They might come from genes encoding other gene family members, or from other genes. But we also should take another look at all that "junk" in the genome. Rather than assume that the genome would be better off if it could clean house, perhaps we should look at "junk" DNA with the patience of time. As molecular biologist Sidney Brenner likes to point out, you throw away garbage, but junk—like that old wood crate you might use someday to make bookshelves—you keep. The old wooden crate parts of the genome, little bits of what look like decaying genes scattered about, are called *false genes*. False genes comprise patches of DNA that look like known genes but are full of "stop codons" that would interrupt translation of any RNA encoded by this DNA into proteins. Most genes have one stop codon, demarking the end of the protein-coding region, but false genes are full of them. False genes appear to be left over fragments used by a former genome. But I speculate that in our genome, false genes may be put to use in gene families as a possible source of once-active sequences to patch into "real" genes; or, they might be sites of new types of regulation, perhaps involving RNA copies (introduced in Chapter 16) which we do not yet know about.

It seems probable that certain sequences within the protein-encoding DNA do increase the frequency of gene conversion, much as with coat changes in the Lyme disease parasite; such sequences might flank sites of increased variability, such as the binding sites that define the specificity of individual gene family members. As we peer into our genomes, it is very likely that evolutionary theory will begin to step away from depending on purely random mutation. Genomes that have evolved a toolbox of frameworks that allow efficient exploration of new properties would have a dramatic selective advantage compared to simple genetic sloppiness. These genomes would be the winners, and thus would be among us today. Indeed, we would be among them.

14

Interchangeable Parts

*One of my primary objectives is to form the tools so
that the tools themselves shall fashion the work.*

—Eli Whitney

Interchangeable parts enabled our industrial revolution. Gears that fit and
work together reliably can be used to turn the hands of a clock or to turn
the wheels of a car. Some combination of available gears of different sizes
can do the job, even if it's a new job that hasn't been done before.

Our genomes were using interchangeable parts long before Eli Whitney
introduced them to us. Combining and tinkering with useful bits of DNA
is an efficient way to discover something else that is useful. These bits of
DNA can be genes, or they can be useful fragments of genes. Some of these
bits of DNA may not be part of genes at all, but rather may be short strings
of letters that are near genes and that determine whether a gene will be
turned on or off. A genome that can link interchangeable genetic pieces
in different combinations has an efficient way to evolve an enormous range
of new combinations of functions, to explore their potential value. Combinations generate a huge range of possibilities, an artist's nuanced palette
from primary colors.

Comparing four proteins can be like comparing a bicycle, a limousine,
an ox cart, and a subway train. All four have parts that are descendants of
an ancient wheel module. The wheel module is recognizable by its structure—its round shape, its central axle—and also by its common function of
rolling. However, the bicycle, train, limousine, and ox cart have different
numbers of wheel modules, use different steering mechanisms, and draw on
different power sources (petroleum products, grass, or trail mix).

Different add-ons adapt modules to more specific roles. To get to mid-town Manhattan at 5 P.M., when the streets are snarled with suburban com-muters trying to get through the bottlenecks at various tunnels and bridges, I'd suggest traveling beneath the streets—take the subway train. If you need to be picked up at your front door, along with several heavy and poorly bal-anced luggage modules, at a prescheduled time and brought to the airport, the limousine may be a good adaptation. To move bricks for your home across rutted fields far from a transportation infrastructure, pick the ox cart. For a quiet solo day trip along the canal towpath from Washington, D.C. to Harper's Ferry, I was glad to be on a bicycle.

What is the kernel of evolution? We think of evolution acting on necks and beaks, wings and feathers. Or perhaps, if we've studied biochemistry, we think of evolution as favoring one sequence of amino acids in a protein over others. But if we really step back and look at genomes without pre-conceived ideas, without looking for eyes and fingers and bones, without blocking the genomes out into proteins—if we just look for patterns, we will suddenly find that it is the interchangeable parts that jump out at us. The same sequence of DNA is used to encode part of a receptor that snatches cholesterol from the blood and part of a receptor that tells cells to divide in response to a growth factor.[1]

Protein chemists use different words for different types of protein pieces. There are protein *domains*, which are independently folding units. A domain can fold in three dimensions all by itself and still carry out some independent activity even after it is cut off of a protein, much like a loose wheel. A serine protease, for example, can become a domain of another, larger, protein that has additional domains and other pieces added on. In a similar manner, the pathogen-binding variable region of antibodies is a separate domain. It is thus very easy to see how domains can be stitched together in order to form a larger protein that incorpo-rates all their properties.

Mitiko Go, a computational structural biologist in Nagoya, Japan, uses the term *modules* for shorter pieces of a protein that have a specific role that is universally useful, such as binding to the backbone of DNA. The way she uses *module* comes from a different tradition from the use of the term *genome module*, although we may find that protein modules can be genome modules too. Another term that protein chemists use is *motif*. The amino acids in a motif might be bunched together in one place in a protein, such as GSSD, or they could be far apart in the protein, but come together when the amino acid string folds up in three dimensions. Another example of a motif is 38 letters long, DD (a string of 35 amino acids in between) E;

proteins with this amino acid motif are centrally involved in the action of enzymes like HIV integrase that paste pieces of DNA into other pieces of DNA. Motifs are patterns; we recognize them, and molecules do too. In the rest of this book, I'll generally use *module* to mean any functional unit in the genome. Protein modules can transport, bind, catalyze, regulate, signal, and form scaffolds and other structures.[2]

Pasting modules together to form more complex proteins is made much easier by the structure of our genome. Most of our genes are, as Nobel laureate Walter Gilbert put it, "in pieces." Blocks of protein-coding letters in the DNA double helix are separated from one another by blocks of other letters. Therefore, after the information in a gene is copied into a string of RNA, some surgery is needed. The pieces that *express* the information in the protein-coding parts (exons) are stitched together, and all of the RNA *in* between (introns) is cut out.

This cutting and pasting seems very complicated; it takes extra energy and requires extra time between when the gene is turned on and when the protein actually is made. Bacteria don't do this; their genes are all exon with no intron. So why do our genomes bother with all these introns, or, as Gilbert asked, "*Why* genes in pieces?" Colin Blake, a molecular biophysicist at Oxford, had pointed out that the pieces might code for separate domains.[3] Mitiko Go found that protein modules, such as different sections of the hemoglobin molecule, did in fact tend to be encoded on separate exons.[4] So, why genes in pieces? Gilbert had a good answer to his own question.[5] He emphasized that this arrangement makes it easier for blocks of DNA that encode protein modules to be moved about and attached to one another in different combinations. By providing introns as favored sites of recombination, where one DNA double helix can be cut and attached to another double helix, this infrastructure facilitates cutting and pasting between, rather than within, modules—enriching, rather than disrupting, the protein function. Thus it will facilitate evolution.

We will not fully know whether most introns surround modules that have independent functions until we understand the function of the majority of the DNA sequences we have found in the genome. However, this idea clearly is true much of the time—for example, for antibodies. The variable pathogen-binding region is on a separate exon. The "class switch" to a new effector region takes place through mechanisms that target cuts inside two introns, one to the right of the variable and one to the left of the new effector region, and then move these two protein domains together.

Typically, just under 1500 letters are used to encode a protein; this is true both for our proteins and for those of worms and flies. Yet many human genes are more than 100,000 letters long, So far as we know now, the largest human gene is one that is damaged in muscular dystrophy; it is 2.4 million letters long.[6] Little of that information turns up in a protein.

One way in which we are different from the worm and the fly is that our genes appear to have much, much longer introns. While our typical intron may be around 90 letters, or 1.5 times the length of theirs, some of our introns seem to be as long as 3300 letters. And genes can have more than one intron. Another human muscle gene, elastic springy titin, has the largest number of introns found so far: nearly 180. In fact, one estimate is that while about one-third of our genome is copied into RNA that contains some protein-coding information, most of this RNA is in fact in introns, and thus gets cut out before it gets to the protein factory;[7] the guess is that only 15 out of every 1000 letters in our genome actually encode the amino acids in our proteins. All of this extra stuff makes it tricky to find some of our genes when we are staring at our genomes.

As protein domains get pasted together, new functions get built up. Several serine proteases, which make our blood clot, stick to the surface of our platelets. They are held there because, in addition to the serine protease domain, they also have a platelet-binding module—which, by the way, works only if you eat your green leafy vegetables, as vitamin K is needed to outfit it with its molecular hooks. The platelet surface is a good place for proteins that make the blood clot to stick, since platelets are likely to be sticking around the edges of a torn blood vessel. These proteins are made in liver cells and travel in the blood to find the platelets. One part of a protein steers another part of the protein through our bodies.

One piece of a protein can drag the other parts of the protein to different places within a cell, as a new friend may take you to a new country. If the protein contains a piece that I'll call N, it is brought to the nucleus; if it contains piece M, it is brought to the cell membrane. If different "address" modules are attached, the same protein can be sent to work in different parts of the cell, or even sent outside, into the bloodstream.

One protein module may have the amino acid tools to insert itself into the cell membrane, which forms the border between the cell and the rest of the world. When this protein module is attached to a module that binds to a particular sugar, and also to another module that can move it back through the cell membrane, the resulting protein can carry that sugar from the outside of the cell across the membrane to the inside of the cell. Dinner time.

Adding certain domains leads to communication within and between proteins. In a multidomain protein, the ability of one domain to signal may be conditional upon signals received by other domains of the same protein molecule. For example, a domain called a *regulatory subunit* may stop an enzyme from working. If that enzyme was at all useful, this subunit that blocks its action would seem to be a bit of an evolutionary dead end. However, the regulatory subunit adds something creative. Like a parent who says that you cannot eat until you have set the table, the regulatory subunit's stranglehold on the enzyme may be conditional. That is, it may release its block under certain conditions. For example, the regulatory subunit may block the enzyme until and unless a lot of another specific chemical—say calcium—is present inside the cell.

These blocked enzymes can be in place throughout the cell, waiting, not working, and then be turned on by the sudden appearance in the cell of a lot of calcium. If a lot of enzymes scattered across the cell have this calcium-sensitive regulatory subunit module attached, they all will start working together the instant that calcium floods the cell, as if a switch were flipped to light a room.

Where would the calcium come from? A protein that acts as a relay in a signaling system may also be hooked up to a gate in the cell membrane that will open when a signal comes in from outside the cell, thus releasing a flood of calcium. The effect of the message from outside the cell, perhaps from another cell, is to turn on thousands of actions at once, each action performed by an enzyme with a calcium-sensitive regulatory subunit module. When the calcium "light switch" is turned on, proteins are triggered to act together in time even if they are separated in space, spread throughout the cell; they may respond in a wave as calcium spreads across the cell or their response is simultaneous and coordinated—much as ours is when, after waiting so quietly in the dark room on the birthday, the door is opened and we suddenly and simultaneously, each in our own voice, shout, "Surprise!"

Another example of the power of combining domains is seen in the process that triggers cell division. As you can imagine, cell division must be carefully controlled through inputs from many sensors to ensure that it takes place when, and only when, it is needed. Too much division can grow a tumor. Too little division can leave a tissue damaged, as if our skin were not fully replaced after an injury. A protein that is able to integrate information from different sources can be built up from domains that respond to distinct signals. Part of a signaling pathway that leads to cell division is initiated by a signaling domain that remains inactive until it is turned on by another domain of the same protein, an activator domain. The activator domain may turn on the signaling domain by, for example, changing its shape, which it can do by attaching a few atoms, such as a phosphate group, to the signaling domain. But the activator domain can turn on the signaling domain only if the activator domain is itself turned on. The activator domain is turned on by a signaling system upstream from it, perhaps by an enzyme that puts a phosphate on it too. Therefore, the activator domain will activate the downstream signaling domain, which can lead to cell division, only if the upstream system that signals the activator domain is turned on.

But there is another level of regulation. Even when it is turned on, the activator domain may be unable to activate the signaling domain because it may be physically blocked by another part of the protein. This blocking domain will not release its block until and unless it too is activated by a separate upstream signaling system. Thus the signaling domain can trigger the downstream pathway that may lead to cell division if, and only if, the signaling systems that regulate the activating domain and the blocking domain are both active.

Because of the way in which its three domains interact, this protein carries out the molecular equivalent of reasoning. The combination of three protein modules becomes a logic gate: "If this (what signals the activator domain) and this (what signals the blocking domain), then do this (what the signaling domain triggers)." Only if the signals to both the activator domain and the blocking domain are present will the protein's signaling domain send its cell division signal forward, where it is likely to be integrated with other signals in the network of regulation that controls cell division.

By combining domains or motifs into multidomain proteins, a genome can create and explore such logic gates, integrating signals from different signaling pathways and "learning," through selection, what types of connections are most likely to be useful. Once a logic gate protein is in place, copying and varying the gene that encodes that protein can lead not only to more copies of one type of gene, but also to new signaling systems. In other words, whenever there are two domains in a protein, or indeed two proteins, that work together to do a job, we have more in hand than just these two proteins and this one specific task.

Once two proteins that can communicate with each other are encoded in the genome, their interaction (the possibility of a signal) also is encoded, indirectly, in the genome. When the proteins are copied and varied, the concept of a signal will be copied too. As copies of the two interacting proteins vary and evolve and make new connections, the signal that they encode can become attached to different triggers and to different messages. When the genes encoding two proteins that interact have been copied and varied many times, two large families of proteins that interact with each other will emerge.

The serine protease clotting cascade is one example of a large signaling system that has been built up from duplication, variation, and adding modules to genes. Two other very important signaling systems involve enzymes called kinases and phosphatases. A kinase can change the activity of certain other proteins (which may themselves be kinases or phosphatases) by adding a phosphate group. A phosphatase can reverse the effect of a kinase by taking the phosphate back off. Whether, and to what extent, such proteins are active will depend upon the relative activity of the pathways that turn on the kinases and the phosphatases that act on that protein. Important regulatory networks affecting whether our cells will divide or die, our immune system will function, and myriads of other day-to-day vital signaling systems in the cell are controlled by the balanced, and timed, action of kinases and phosphatases turning on and off proteins in our cells, and by the action of proteins that cut or chew up other proteins.[8]

For the cells of our body to work together as a system, it is not enough for each cell to monitor its environment in isolation. Cells have to be good communicators; they have to send signals to other cells about what they sense.

One very large gene family helps our cells work together; without it, our many kinds of cells wouldn't be coordinated. This gene family can respond to messenger molecules that may travel through our blood. Out of the corner of your eye, you spot a large form leaping toward you. "LOOK OUT! An SUV OUT OF CONTROL!" The messenger molecule adrenaline released from your nerves rushes through your body, signaling the cells lining your blood vessels to constrict, and preparing your muscle cells to mobilize energy.

Adrenaline changes the behavior of your blood vessels and muscle cells without actually getting inside them. It only has to knock on their doors. Specific proteins on the surface of all those cells that recognize adrenaline, such as muscle and blood vessels and fat storage cells, transmit the signal that there is more adrenaline than usual in the blood to the inside of the cells. The proteins that first receive the adrenaline signal are called *receptors*.

Adrenaline receptor proteins are rooted in the membrane that is the interface between the outside world and the world inside each cell; the receptor protein sticks its molecular equivalent of head and arms out to catch passing adrenaline molecules and keeps its foot on the molecular gears inside the cell. Inside the cell, it transmits the signal that adrenaline has come.

It sends this message through its effect on another protein, called a G protein. Therefore, the receptor protein that receives a signal and transmits it to a G protein is called a *G-protein-coupled* receptor. When adrenaline binds to the receptor, parts of the G protein shove another protein that broadcasts the signal through the cell.

You might expect that evolution would grab this signaling system and use it again and again, and you would be right; indeed, it is not unique to adrenaline. Serotonin has its own set of G-protein-coupled receptors that are on the lookout for it; so does dopamine, and so do hundreds of other signaling molecules that are coursing through our blood right at this moment. We have about 1000 different G-protein-coupled receptors. Each time a receptor or a G protein or the broadcaster protein is duplicated and varied, the emergent concept of the signaling system is itself duplicated and varied. The families of genes that code for these signaling and receptor proteins work together to allow us to transmit a multitude of signals from the fluid outside each of our cells to the inside of those cells.

We are not the only ones who fight or fly, smell food, experience pain and pleasure, and regulate our blood pressure through molecular signaling. For example, there is *Caenorhabditis elegans*, the tiny roundworm, less than 1 millimeter (1/20th of an inch) long. It must sense, that is, smell, the mixture of molecules in its soil environment, find nourishment, avoid harm. Perhaps its largest gene family is devoted to keeping its cells aware of its surroundings. One out of every 20 proteins in *C. elegans* appears to be a G-protein-coupled receptor.[9]

Much as turning on the light at the surprise birthday party has effects throughout the roomful of people, a signaling pathway may turn on many genes at once in a complex cascade. Turning on a gene means triggering the copying of the information in the gene into messenger RNA, the first step in making a protein. A string of letters in the DNA that form a module that promotes the copying of the DNA is called a *promoter*; other types of modules that enhance the copying of the DNA are called *enhancers*. A promoter might contain a string of letters that attach to the machine that copies instructions from DNA into RNA. For example, it could hold onto the machine by linking to a finger protein that recognizes this specific string of letters in the DNA. Wherever this DNA module is within the DNA, neighboring DNA may be copied or a neighboring gene turned on. Modules can adjust the level of gene activity intrinsically or can adjust the level that will be achieved in response to a given signal.

Each time a gene is turned on, it can have effects throughout the cell, as if different colored filters were put over the lights for the surprise party, with each color signaling different people throughout the room to dance and signaling others to change the lights to yet another color. The protein product of a gene that is turned on may in turn bind to other regulatory modules elsewhere in the DNA, and turn on (or off, dial up or down) other genes, in a multistep signaling system.

Whether or not a gene sends a message to the protein-making machinery can depend upon the conditions in which the cell is growing. The letters in the DNA next to the gene[10] might attach to the messenger-making machine only under special circumstances—say, when the cell is running out of glucose. The information in the neighboring gene would be used only if there is too little glucose in the cell. All genes with these letters next to them are turned on when the cell needs glucose. It is very useful to have this signaling string of letters next to genes for enzymes that can help the cell get energy by making glucose from other sugars—an activity that is sorely needed if the glucose disappears. It would be a waste of energy to make these other enzymes when the cell is swimming in glucose.

You can make many different things by combining screws, axles, and wheels. You can make many different life forms by combining nerves, muscles, and bones. You can build many different kinds of antibodies by combining variable pathogen-binding domains and conserved effector domains. You can make many different biochemical signaling pathways by combinations too.

Such combinations may lead to the evolution of a protein that responds to a signal, and to a relay system of other proteins that communicates that signal to another protein that turns a gene on or off. To turn a gene's activity on or off, a sequence of DNA must evolve, next to the gene, that will interact with the proteins that will regulate it. Such a sequence may happen to evolve there through random mutation, but that is not the only way. It can be pasted in there too. Often, sites in the DNA that regulate whether a gene is turned on or off are duplicates of strings of letters that are found elsewhere in the genome next to other genes. Copying regulatory regions and moving them around[11] links the behavior of genes that are far away from each other in the genome.

Additional promoter elements that turn on neighboring genes in different kinds of cells or different circumstances can be added in a stepwise, modular fashion during evolution, [12] without interfering with the activity of promoters that already are next to the gene. Promoters can be linked up like a long German word, or even interdigitated aisntehxiasmple, as a genome tries out new networks of gene regulation. This whole signaling system—from the signal, to the protein that responds to the signal, through the relay system and the protein that turns on the gene, the regulatory module on the gene, and the function of the protein encoded by the gene inside the cell—becomes a higher-level signaling module, which can, with time, be duplicated and varied too.

All of the cells in our body have the same genome.[13] It is conditional regulation—which ensures that some genes will be off and others on—that makes our heart cells and our brain cells and our pancreas cells so different. The most dramatic example of the power of turning genes on and off may be the moth and the caterpillar. As Barbara McClintock has pointed out, the moth and the caterpillar are two different organisms encoded by the same genome.[14]

To get an organism from a fertilized egg into the form of a caterpillar, person, or tree, groups of genes turn on and off in a complex dance. Regulatory sequences in DNA play a central role in the evolution and sculpting of body form through a family of *Hox* genes, which turn other genes on and off by recognizing specific sequences near the genes and binding to them. There are Hox genes in both plants and animals. The number of its Hox genes and the regulatory modules that turn each Hox gene on determine the shape of the developing organism. How many Hox genes you have is important; it determines whether you are a tetrapod (something with four limbs, like crocodiles and us) or a fish. As clusters of Hox genes were copied and varied through the course of evolution, more creativity in body form emerged. But the order in which Hox genes are turned on, from future head to future foot, which specifies the body axis, is preserved (except, of course, in laboratories, where people rearrange things).[15]

A Hox gene can be turned on in various places within the genome of the early embryo, turning other genes on. Variations in how long a Hox gene is on let the embryo reach out in new directions, creating new body shapes. Changes in the patches of DNA near each Hox gene determine where, when, and for how long the gene is turned on in the developing organism. Changes in these regulatory regions are an important route to evolution of new body forms;[16] they allow the genome to use changes in the sequence of regulatory patches near genes to explore physical space and architecture. In tomatoes, if a specific Hox gene is turned on in the cells that start the growth of a leaf, the leaves will be broken into leaflets, rather than growing to be one large leaf.[17]

How do the genes in a cell know where the cell is within a developing embryo? They orient themselves by being sensitive to certain proteins around them;[18] the level of a Hox protein tells a cell how far it is from the cells that are making that Hox protein much as the noise of a crowd fades as you walk away.

Hox proteins can work in species that look very different from one another. Walter Gehring and colleagues in Basel inserted a gene for a similar kind of protein, the mouse Pax-6 gene, which controls eye formation, into a fruit fly genome in such a way that it would be turned on in an unusual place, on the fly's antenna. This mouse gene caused an eye to form on the fruit fly's antenna; some antenna cells thought they were in the eye region. But even though the eye program was turned on by the mouse gene, the eye did not look like a mouse eye; it was a fruit fly eye. The master gene simply had switched on the fruit fly's eye program by binding to the little patch of letters next to the relevant genes.[19]

There is another family of genes that encode proteins that turn other genes on and off and is very important in the formation of the body. All the members of this family contain a string of amino acids called a *MADS* box; such strings are found in animals, seed plants, and yeast.[20] MADS box proteins are essential for some signaling pathways and for complex body structures of multicellular organisms, including muscles in animals and structures that seed-bearing plants use in reproduction. So, our muscles have a hidden kinship to flowers. One single-celled organism took a genetic step to become the ancestors of plants. Another stepped to a different path to become our ancestors. The MADS genes already were there.

Regulatory modules dispersed throughout the genome allow coordinated behavior involving many genes with many roles to play. Their importance is very clear when we look at the mustard weed. We might ignore this small plant if we passed by it in a field, but we shouldn't. It was the first plant genome to be sequenced, and it is teaching us a lot. Like most plants, the mustard weed may look as if it is just standing there, but in fact it has a busy schedule every day.[21] First, just before dawn, the mustard weed gets ready for the sunlight by turning on a particular group of 23 genes. These genes encode enzymes that are needed to make pigments that absorb visible and ultraviolet light. Genes that encode the proteins that digest sugars or transport them to storage sites become most active toward the end of the day. Then, near dusk, to get ready for the evening, genes that make enzymes that modify plant lipids are turned on, to increase the little mustard weed's resistance to the chill of the coming night. During the night, when the plants cannot make sugars from sunlight, they draw on the starch they have stored. As you might expect, genes that encode the enzymes needed to use this stored starch are turned on during the night.

Next to each set of genes for the plant's daily tasks, there is a module of DNA that allows the gene to respond to signals from the plant system that notes the sunrise and keep the plant clocks running. For example, there is an evening module made up of the nine letters AAAATATCT. If you wanted to find genes in the mustard weed's genome that were turned on at the end of the day, you would look for this evening module in the DNA next to the gene, just as the plant's RNA-making machinery does.

Out of the simple mustard weed's total of about 8000 genes, 450 respond to its clock. We too are affected by a clock; our sleep/wake cycles prepare us for the inevitable cycle of sunlight as this planet on which we were formed turns on its axis each day. For us, too, these cycles are affected by small strings of letters next to our genes.[22]

Through multiple combinations of modules in proteins and modules next to genes, genomes make connections; they gain new skills, and begin to "reason." Regulation—to what extent a gene is on or off, whether a protein is made at all—and how active the protein is once made can become more and more sophisticated as the regulatory regions next to the genes become more complex and the ability to sense and respond to multiple regulators is added to the protein itself.

New levels of interaction and regulation rarely arise through letter-by-letter random mutation of random DNA sequences. Whole clusters of Hox genes are duplicated. Gene regions encoding protein domains, and the regulatory region next to genes, move around the genome and land next to something new. Since the industrial revolution, we have made our interchangeable parts in factories, using precision tools. The parts of our genome find creative new roles without the help of our engineers, factories, and distribution centers. New combinations of molecular skills emerge, selection measures their usefulness and adjusts interactions and responses, and generations of new lives are created, seeking a place in the world.

15

Jumping Genes

We are here for this . . . to make mistakes and to correct ourselves . . . nature is . . . not impermeable to the intelligence; we must . . . look for the opening or make it.

—Primo Levi[1]

Barbara McClintock spent a lot of time looking at chromosomes. She worked with simple tools—a cornfield and a microscope[2]—yet a scientific admirer, Jim Shapiro, has suggested that McClintock "may well be seen as *the* key figure in 20th century biology."[3]

In the first half of the twentieth century, looking through her microscope, McClintock noticed that in one unusual line of corn plants, from generation to generation, one of the chromosomes had a tendency to break—not all of the chromosomes, just one of them, chromosome 9. Two parts of chromosome 9 would just dissociate from each other. Not only was it always chromosome 9 that kept breaking in this line of plants, but the place where it broke was always the same. In other words, this strange tendency for two parts of chromosome 9 to dissociate at this particular spot was inherited. Biologists give names to inherited characteristics, and Barbara McClintock did the same thing for this unstable place in the chromosome; she gave it the name "Dissociation" (Ds). On the other hand, chromosome 9 did not always break. McClintock figured out that something else had to be present in the same genome to activate the chromosome-breaking behavior of Dissociation. She called this factor "Activator" (Ac).

By 1948, just four years after the Avery lab published its discovery that the genetic material is DNA, and four years before the publication of the structure of DNA, McClintock not only had described Dissociation and Activator, but also had observed that in another line of corn, chromosome 9 broke in a completely different place. Dissociation could "change its position in the chromosome"; in other words, Dissociation could move around the genome, or "transpose." A gene could jump. This observation was greeted by much of the scientific community with what most generously might be called denial. McClintock found that Activator could move around the genome too.

In addition, she found that Activator could do more than activate Dissociation's chromosome 9-breaking effect. Activator also could destabilize some previously stable mutations. In other words, a gene might have been damaged by a mutation and, as one would expect, remain damaged from generation to generation. But if a plant with this mutation was bred with a plant that contained Activator, the mutated gene might suddenly start working again. Activator seemed to undo the mutation.

McClintock had bred lines of corn with mutations that changed the color of the plant. It turned out that some of these mutations were due to Dissociation's landing in a gene that was needed if the plant was to synthesize its pigment; without its pigment, the plant was pale. Since Dissociation could not jump without Activator, it would stay put in the pigment genes, and the plant's progeny would be pale too. The color would suddenly reappear many generations later if the plant was bred with a genome that had Activator in it, and Dissociation jumped back out of the pigment genes. When Dissociation jumped during the life of a corn plant, the plant would have freckles on its kernels.

When Activator itself jumped into a gene and mutated it, these mutations were inherently unstable because Activator could jump back out without help; it was a "complete" transposable element. In contrast, Dissociation could not jump by itself. This is why it needed Activator. What Dissociation was missing, and Activator could make, was an enzyme that cuts the jumping gene out of the DNA and pastes it in somewhere else. (But no one knew this until over 30 years later;[4] since jumping genes are called transposons, this enzyme was called a transposase.)

Later, McClintock found other transposable elements, many of which would not budge even in the presence of Activator. These other transposons have their own version of Activator. In other words, there are many families of transposable elements, or jumping genes, each of which has its own incomplete elements, like Dissociation, that depend upon other active elements, like Activator, to provide the needed transposase. Each transposase looks for a different DNA sequence and cuts and moves only genes that have that specific sequence on their edges. Many transposons have been found in many species, including us; some have been given names like hopscotch, hobo or mariner, tourist, or sleeping beauty.

Barbara McClintock's insights were so perceptive that for decades only a few people realized the importance of what she was saying. She figured out that genes in one place in the genome could affect the behavior of genes at other places in the genome. She explained that gene behavior, even jumping, could respond to the environment and could change under stress. Bit by bit, other people, in other systems, rediscovered these effects. But that took years. During all my years in graduate school (and I received my Ph.D. in molecular biology in 1973 from the school that had been rated tops in my field), Barbara McClintock never was mentioned, not even once, in any of my classes. She was awarded the Nobel prize for her work in 1983, 35 years after she first explained the breaks in corn chromosome 9.

It turns out that there are many ways in which genes can move around the genome. Jumping genes like Activator and Dissociator can travel by *cut and paste*: A piece of DNA is cut out—for example by a transposase, which recognizes special sequences at its borders—and pasted in elsewhere. Transfer of information by cut and paste can be a little like mailing a letter. The DNA where the information lands does not necessarily have to touch the DNA that had been close to the jumping DNA before the jump. Information also can move around the genome by *copy and paste*: The genes stay put, but the information in their DNA is copied into RNA, then copied back into DNA at another place in the genome. Copy and paste is like mailing a copy of a letter; the original piece of DNA retains the information and can send out other copies too.

Aside from using a molecular post office, information can be transferred between two DNA molecules in a sort of molecular hug, called *recombination*. In order for the two DNA double helices that are about to exchange information to hug, they need to have a way to hold on to each other. They use their pairing rules: An A on one double helix finds a T on the other. For this to be a tight hug, there needs to be a long string of letters than can be matched up. The longer the match, the tighter the hug, and the more likely it is that the DNA strands will hold together long enough to recombine.[5]

Why would genomes tolerate genes moving all over the place, for many millions of years? Surely some very strict protection mechanisms would be in place to immobilize these agents that threaten to jump in and break up active genes—(in fact, break up chromosomes), just as we have developed a sophisticated immune response to get rid of pathogens. Yet these jumping genes seem to have made themselves very much at home.

Suppose you were given a 10-foot-high bag filled with parts from a machine and challenged to figure out how the machine worked. Where would you begin? Suppose you found that one type of part filled about half of the bag. As you reached in, you would very occasionally find another type of part, mixed through the 10-foot-high bag. By themselves, these other parts would have filled only about 2½ inches of the bag, so when they were scattered throughout the bag, it was hard to find them. Those little bits hidden in the bag are the parts of our genome that actually code for our proteins. They probably would not be the first things to capture out interest were we to look at a genome for the first time, with open eyes. Most of our genome is made up of something else, and about half of it appears to be derived from transposable elements. Maybe instead of asking why the genome puts up with them, we should ask what they are doing there.

Natural selection wouldn't have to get rid of jumping genes if it could capture their skills and put them to work—if it could tame them. Indeed, it is possible to regulate the time and the place that they jump. Transposons can fall under biochemical regulation just like other parts of the genome.

Even when McClintock's plants had Activator in their genome, chromosome 9 didn't always break. Activator didn't always jump, and it didn't always make Dissociator jump either. We now understand that very well. A gene can be present in a genome but be inactive until it is turned on. Like any other gene, Activator's transposase could be off. It could be turned on, for example, by stress, such as DNA damage, perhaps responding to the corn equivalent of the SOS response. In fact, ultraviolet light can get jumping genes hopping around the corn genome.[6] We now know that in organisms from bacteria to corn, stress can cause DNA that has jumped into a spot in a genome to jump out.

A half-century ago Barbara McClintock perceived that one gene can affect the activity of another. She also perceived that a genome could sense stress, and that when it did so, its genes could jump. As she put it, when the genome senses stress for which it is unprepared, it "reorganizes itself."[7]

Much work has been done since then, and molecular biologists have been getting data that have led us back to Barbara McClintock's explanations many times, but we have not yet fully caught up with this last bit— that when a genome "senses stress for which it is unprepared," genes jump, and the genome "reorganizes itself." Just don't everybody jump at once! As nearly a half of our genome consists of pieces of DNA that have moved in the past and/or can jump, the potential for reorganization when transposons are released is significant. We now know that there are global mechanisms that can turn the tendency to jump on and off, but we don't fully understand their im-plications. In this book I have mostly been focused on variation within a species, but how do other species arise? How do chromosomes get rearranged to create a new species? It must happen here too, as the germ-line genome is preparing to move forward. The importance of jumping genes in the biology of multicellular organisms—and perhaps in the emergence of new species—remains in the realm of discussion and speculation.[8]

Transposons are found among the many repetitive sequences in the genome that have been called "junk" DNA. They are by no stretch of the im-agination useless junk, however. With their ability to move whole pieces of DNA around, transposable elements clearly have played an important role in evolution. They can spread pathogenicity and antibiotic resistance among bacteria. We too benefit from jumping genes; in fact, we would not be here without them.

The invasion of an ancient animal germ-line genome by a transposon appears to have created the vertebrate immune system. The enzymes that move the antibody V genes do their cutting and pasting very much like the way transposases operate, so it seems that our immune system itself is a gift from jumping genes. Living in a sea of microbes as we do, without an immune system, we simply would die. Without this creative leap of a trans-poson into our ancestor's genome, the whole vertebrate lineage would lack this protective immune system. It would have had to wait on the edge of evolution until another mechanism of immunity emerged.[9]

A transposon may have brought the information that encodes protein pieces—called *helix-turn-helix domains*—into an ancestral animal genome. These protein pieces control whether genes are on or off. In fact, one sur-vey suggests that around 50 human genes appear to be directly derived from transposons.[10]

It is not just the jumping of genes themselves that is shaping our genome. Their movement creates places in the genome where there are stretches of DNA that are similar enough to pair and exchange informa-tion. Genes with similar sequences, such as those in gene families, can recom-bine. Repetitive sequences that are present throughout the genome enable the exchange of information between unrelated genes by recombination. Jumping genes that can't jump any more still can hug.

We can envision starting with gene pieces, each of them a module, dis-persed throughout the genome, each bordered by repetitive DNA on its edges that acts as the molecular equivalent of Velcro. Then we can envision pulling up these pieces of Velcro and exchanging their connections, changing which pieces of DNA are next to each other. A piece of DNA with Velcro on each side can get moved around the genome and thus becomes a mobile information module.

Because these mobile modules can have a wide range of different roles, moving them around facilitates the exploration of new combinations of their functions. Thus, a genome can go beyond simple variation around a theme; it can combine short themes into a longer melody—the calcium sensor attached to the enzyme, for example. Repetitive DNA—molecular Velcro—has far more destructive and creative power than do point mutations; jumps and Velcro provide a vehicle for bringing two different parts of the genome together. Once two functional pieces of DNA move together, they may come to work together in a creative way, with real synergy.

This vision of a "modularized" genome, described by Nina Fedoroff[11] and Jim Shapiro,[12] gives us a glimpse into how a genome can be built up to be responsive to the outside world. This vision represents a strong disagreement with the idea that the repetitive mobile DNA in the genome is useless, parasitic junk. Instead, repetitive DNA can serve as guideposts for recombination.

Landing randomly can cause problems. If you jump over the fence when your neighbor is having an elegant garden party, you may land on the buffet table, breaking the punch bowl. Or, you can learn to land between people talking on the lawn; no real harm is done, and perhaps an interesting conversation begins. If genes were to keep jumping into protein-coding DNA and knocking out important functions, natural selection would tend to eliminate them through the death of the organisms they enter; killing these organisms eliminates the chance that the gene that just jumped will be carried forward in time.

There clearly are favored landing spots in the genome, and other places where gene jumps tend to be excluded.[13] Jumping genes and molecular Velcro are definitely not dispersed randomly through the genome. There are places in the genome that seem to be filled with repetitive DNA. They look like landing pads, where gene after gene has jumped in, seemingly on top of one another. In our X chromosomes, there is a region of 200,000 letters where nearly 100 percent of the genome is made up of strings of letters that look like jumping genes.[14] Other places seem very quiet. One quiet stretch of genome is the Hox region, which makes sense. Hox may be duplicated as a full block, but it would lose its neatly aligned position information— from head to foot—if it got broken up inside. Each of our four Hox clusters has regions of around 100,000 letters that have less than 2 percent of these repetitive sequences. This is true not only for us, but also for several other mammals that have been examined. Even regions that do not encode proteins are highly conserved in the Hox region, a sign that they exclude jumping genes.

Thus natural selection can drive transposons and repetitive elements into parts of the genome where they can be more creative and do less damage. Many of them are in between genes, in the regulatory region, and in the parts of genes that get transcribed into RNA but are not translated into proteins. Repetitive DNA can attract gene "silencing" effects that turn off whole blocks of a chromosome, not just the gene that they have jumped in next to,[15] and can attract mechanisms that increase both their own mutation rate and the mutation rate of genes that look like them or that are near them.

When they parachute into the genomic landscape, many jumping genes avoid smashing through roofs—they may have been tamed well enough by natural selection to avoid landing, for example, within a codon. But are there biochemical mechanisms that can begin a conversation between the probability of gene jumping and the activity of other genes in the cell, or with the activity of the gene at the landing spot? There are. For example, the jumps of a particular transposon in yeast are regulated in two ways. First, the transposon is turned on to jump only during mating, which means that it will create diverse members of the next generation. Second it is specifically copied into the regulatory area next to the genes.[16]

One jumping gene in fruit flies favors jumps into the left end of genes, in the control regions that turn genes on and off. Rather than favoring a specific sequence of letters within the DNA, it appears to favor a certain DNA structure and pattern of chemical groups sticking out of the DNA.[17] Others may be attracted to certain spots by interacting with proteins that bind there. The extent to which jumping genes become attracted to certain patterns throughout the genome, and thus the extent to which different regions of the genome attract and avoid transposons, can become a selectable trait.

A jumping gene may tend to jump into the regulatory region of genes that are turned on at the same time because opening these regions up and turning them on makes them more accessible; if these genes are on at the same time, they may be functionally connected, even though they are dispersed throughout the genome.[18] If a jumping gene leaves the same bit of regulatory DNA next to many different genes in several spots in the genome, those genes may come to be turned on and off in a coordinated way.

Many jumping genes clearly have been tamed, and indeed contribute to evolution. A genome that cuts and pastes modules has hit on a more efficient strategy for creating and trying out new genes than a genome that can make only random DNA changes in random places. But this doesn't guarantee that the changes themselves will provide a selective advantage; it does not guarantee fitter progeny. It doesn't even protect the genome against serious mistakes. It only opens a path through the landscape of an incomprehensibly larger number of theoretically possible genome changes. An increased probability of recombination at repeat sequences does no more than provide a more focused strategy for genetic exploration than wandering the vast landscape of random base change. A sign may keep you away from the loose stones at the edge of the cliff, but you still might step on a snake.

As pieces of the genome are rearranged, some connections are in fact miswired. Progeny with certain rearrangements and connections die. But some will survive. A genome that tends to make harmful connections will, over the course of generations, have fewer surviving progeny. A genome that tends to avoid harmful connections will do better; its progeny will also tend to avoid harmful connections, inheriting hard-earned mechanisms that avoid deadly mistakes and increasing their numbers relative to the progeny of a genome that keeps stumbling. A genome that tends to make creative connections might have even more progeny over the centuries. The survivors, in the process of survival, have learned which types of new connections can be useful.

Genes are jumping and recombining in us, too. In the ancestors of about two out of every three of us, a gene has jumped into a spot on our chromosome 1. In the other one out of three of us, the gene has not jumped there. It is not there in chimps and gorillas either,[19] and we all seem to be fine. On the other hand, footprints of moving modules have been found in people, including in children who differ from their parents in a way that hurts them. Velcro-like sequences of repetitive DNA can be found in abrupt changes in the DNA sequences, as if something was pasted in there or removed. For example, in the DNA of many women with breast cancer, a big piece of the BRCA1 gene is missing; left behind is the footprint of a mobile module that has jumped away.[20] This loss of a chunk of BRCA1 increases a woman's risk of breast cancer. In some Japanese with the heart problem X-linked dilated cardiomyopathy, it was clear that a mobile module had jumped into and disrupted an important heart muscle gene.[21] Two thousand letters had jumped into the large dystrophin gene of a person with muscular dystrophy.[22] Different jumps into the hemoglobin A gene can cause hemophilia.[23]

For evolution, we focus on things that jump when they are being passed from parent to child. However, just as corn kernels can have freckles, genes can jump during our lifetimes, too, and a tendency for them to do that may be inherited and selected for as well. For example, in a colon cell, the transposon L1 sometimes jumps into and damages a gene that is needed to separate chromosomes properly at cell division. This makes the genome unstable, because its chromosomes are not evenly divided between the daughter cells, and can lead to colon cancer.[24] Other jumps may be more benign, and simply leave us as a mosaic of cells with slightly different genomes.

A genome that has explored something less optimal than is common in the population is said to have a *genetic disease*. Genetic diseases are exploratory stumbles by genomes that tolerate variation. We do not notice the successes, for we assume that our brilliant, beautiful, healthy children got the genes exactly right from us. But when we are able to read our family tree in genomes, some creative activity is certain to appear. Is this creativity worth the risk of breast cancer, of X-linked dilated cardiomyopathy, of other genetic stumbles caused by jumping genes? To accept this, we want to hear clear stories of important, creative, positive jumps in our genome. Obviously creative things happened in the past. But now that we can read—and begin to manipulate—the genome, we are faced with a difficult question: Do we want to stop all these changes? Aren't we OK now?

When we listen to the story of evolution, we are rooting for our tiny ancestor, the little mammal that scampers away as the foot of a dinosaur steps down from above. We are rooting for our apposable thumb to appear, and for our cortex to get big, and for language to come. But now, do we want this evolution stuff to stop and leave us alone? Like immigrants to a new landscape who came to make a better life for their children, our primate ancestors' genomes made the molecular choice to keep changing, to allow diversity; thus their distant descendants would have opportunities that they themselves might not have had as the world changed around them. These primate ancestors may be gone now, but we are here. Do we want to take a bet on the future? Which knows better, our brain, which is just learning about genomes, or our genomes themselves—which, by the way, enable the connecting together of our brains?

16

Be Prepared
for the Unexpected

*HORATIO: O day and night, but this is wonderous
strange!*
HAMLET: And therefore as a stranger give it welcome.
There are more things in heaven and earth, Horatio,
Than are dreamt of in your philosophy.

—William Shakespeare, Hamlet, Act I, Scene 5

This chapter is here for scientific humility. A few decades ago, we thought we had it all figured out. The information in DNA is copied into a similar but less stable molecule, RNA. This RNA serves as a messenger, carrying the instructions from DNA into the cell's protein-making machinery. The proteins are made and go on to do things like carry oxygen to our tissues, fight infections, operate our muscles, and so on. The important actors were DNA and proteins. Yes, the protein-making factories contained a lot of what we assumed was structural RNA, and the decoder that translated the information into proteins involved RNA, but basically we thought of RNA as a simple messenger; it carried instructions from DNA to the factory, and that was all.

The first hint that RNA might be much more than an unquestioning messenger was spotted by Howard Temin[1] in the 1960s. Temin was studying a virus that causes cancer in chickens. Actually, it already was known that some viruses, such as polio and flu, use RNA rather than DNA for their genomes. But we thought the information just was stored in their RNA, and then translated into protein. So they didn't have DNA; these viruses essentially skip a step, and some "RNA viruses" do.

However when Temin added a molecule, actinomycin D (Act D), that blocks an infected cell's ability to copy information from DNA into RNA, this chicken RNA virus couldn't spread. Something that blocks the copying of information from DNA to RNA shouldn't have had any effect on this RNA virus, because an RNA virus can copy its information directly from RNA into protein.

Temin creatively speculated that maybe this chicken RNA virus goes through a "provirus" stage in which its information is stored in DNA inside the infected cell. If so, this would explain why Act D got in its way; Act D would block the virus' ability to get the information back out of the provirus, from DNA into RNA. But for information to be stored in a DNA provirus, the information in the virus' RNA would have to be copied from RNA into DNA. Many people told Temin that there must be something wrong with his observations.

However, Temin found that the chicken cancer virus has an enzyme that actually does copy information from RNA into DNA,[2] and this DNA actually is inserted into the DNA of the cell that the virus infects. The virus does store its information in DNA as the provirus that Temin had predicted. The virus carries its information from cell to cell via RNA, but when it gets into a cell, it makes a DNA copy of that information and inserts it into the cell's DNA. According to the view that information moves from DNA to RNA to proteins, copying (or transcribing) information from RNA into DNA was backward, so the enzyme was named *reverse transcriptase*.

The discovery of reverse transcriptase shook people up a bit and made them think. So, it was not so simple, just proteins and DNA with RNA as a messenger. By the early 1980s, other researchers had discovered that RNA even can act as an enzyme,[3] a role that had previously been assumed to belong exclusively to proteins. RNA gained new respect. Many people began to speculate that the first life forms on Earth used RNA to carry their information and catalyze their reactions, with DNA and proteins added later as specialists.

Temin's discovery of reverse transcriptase turned out to be important for much more than just explaining why the chicken cancer virus was blocked by Act D, or even for increasing our range of questions about how the first life on Earth might have evolved. Reverse transcriptase became one of the central research tools in molecular genetics laboratories. It enabled people to take all of the RNA messages in any given cell and turn that information back into DNA. With the help of other enzymes, such as one from bacteria that live over steam vents in Yellowstone Park, it became straightforward to make many copies of this DNA in the laboratory, and this enabled us to get enough material to study the information content of all the messages in a cell, and thus of all the genes that are turned on in a given cell, to catalogue which genes are turned on in which tissues of the body, to compare a breast cancer cell with a normal breast cell.

And, the discovery of reverse transcriptase came just in time for the tragedy that struck a decade later, because HIV uses reverse transcriptase to slip the information from its RNA genome into our DNA genome. Because of this, HIV is called a "retrovirus." Knowing about reverse transcriptase helped us in our efforts to figure out how HIV works and led to the first treatment for HIV, AZT, which blocks this enzyme.

Some viruses use the cell that they infect as a temporary factory, taking over the machinery and killing the cell, then bursting out to infect other cells. Instead, HIV creates a long-term relationship with the infected cell, sending out progeny by budding off the cell surface, leaving the cell intact as an HIV factory. HIV inserts itself into our DNA, using its reverse transcriptase; then it is copied, faithfully and carefully, by our DNA copying machinery. Our own genome copying machine is much more careful than HIV's. While we do have genetic variation, our optimal mutation rate is orders of magnitude below that of HIV. Each of us, after all, can't afford to lose tens of thousands of children. In contrast, HIV may generate 10 billion new particles each day in one person.[4]

By settling in as DNA, HIV establishes a genetic "base camp" in each cell that it infects, a secure source of more HIV. From this base camp, it sends out progeny like experiments, wrapped in protein. The progeny set up shop in neighboring cells, and there, in the neighboring cell, HIV's creative, deadly genius emerges. Before slipping into the new cell's DNA for faithful replication, HIV makes less accurate, unrepaired, copies of itself. The somewhat sloppy copy is inserted into the cell's DNA, and a new genetic base camp is established. Thus the HIV in each infected cell can be slightly different from its parent back at the base camp. HIV plays theme and variations on its whole genome. If the progeny of this slightly different HIV are viable, they too will explore variations around their new genetic theme. Each crop of progeny is like a new set of experiments, varied around a stable, successful source, as HIV explores new ways to spread and learns how to break in through the coreceptor of yet another type of cell.

With its suddenly central position, RNA gained new respect and certainly got our attention. It keeps grabbing our attention. While retroviruses led us to reverse transcriptase, it turns out that viruses are not the only things that use reverse transcriptase. Many jumping genes, including some in our own genome, use their own reverse transcriptase to move around. The messenger RNA's (mRNA) copy of the information in certain stretches of DNA can be copied back into DNA and inserted into the genome somewhere else. Because the RNA moves (transposes) the information to a new place, and is copied backward (RNA copied into DNA), these are called *retrotransposons*. Things are not so quiet in our genome. Based on watching human cells in the laboratory, there seem to be about 50 L1 transposons actively jumping around our genome;[5] laboratory mice may have more than 3000. L1s have been jumping around genomes for a long time. All mammals have them; in fact, jumping genes that look a lot like L1 are found in frogs, bony fish, corn, weeds, and a slime mold. They probably popped up around 600 million years ago. We can watch engineered L1s jump around in human cells in the lab and have seen them grab patches of 30 to nearly 1000 letters from their right side. When the L1 lands in another place in the genome, it pastes the extra letters in beside it, perhaps adding them to a gene. Among the things that L1s can move around the genome are exons and promoters, linking new protein domains and new regulatory regions; this may be one widely used route to the evolution of new genes.[6] In fact, reverse transcription appears to have played an important role in the evolution of our genome.

Some of the information that is moved around the genome by reverse transcription seems to be in a kind of storage. There are none of the right signals nearby to attract the machinery that would be needed to get the information out of those pieces of DNA into proteins. However, bits and pieces of those genes can be patched into other, similar genes, generating little patches of diversity.

When genetic information is passed through RNA (whether RNA is a viral genome or a retrotransposon), its mutation rate is likely to increase because, in contrast to mutations caused by DNA polymerase, mutations caused by RNA polymerase are not corrected by proofreading activity, nor are they corrected by repair of errors that are left over after copying and proofreading is finished. Just as with DNA, there can be hot spots of genetic change in RNA retrotransposons as a result of nonrandom patterns of decreased fidelity, switching between templates, or even untemplated extensions.[7] Thus, if gene duplication occurs through an RNA intermediate, the probability of a particular mutation in the duplicate is likely to differ from the probability of that same mutation in genomic DNA.

We speak of them as RNA, but in fact, just like HIV, retrotransposons spend most of their time as DNA, sitting in our genome. About 10 percent of our genome is made up of 1 million members of the Alu family of these, which are copied back into DNA and inserted into our genome. Their presence can favor recombination and exchange of information between different places in the genome, and also can make inheritance very complicated because repetitive sequences can cause blocks of genes around them to be turned off in a way that is partially inherited.[8]

RNA that is copied into DNA may contain introns that will be spliced out, but the intron may contain another gene, backward, on the other strand of DNA. The intron also might contain an exon for this very gene that will be spliced out in one tissue, but included in the protein in another tissue; one estimate is that well over one-third of our genes do this alternative splicing of introns. Little pieces of RNA that come from somewhere else play a central role in the machinery that selects where to cut out the introns and when to cut out which intron.

At M.I.T., Alan Herbert and Alex Rich point out that if simply turning on a gene is not enough to define what protein will be made, the genome is, in a sense, "soft-wired";[9] other information that is dispersed throughout the genome and is under separate regulation can have a hand in deciding how the RNA is spliced, and thus what the protein will look like. Even more than that, they note that some quirky things can turn up.

RNA can be edited. In other words, an RNA molecule can be changed not just by removing introns, but also by changing the actual sequence of the letters that were copied from the DNA. Thus the sequence of the RNA message becomes different from the sequence of the gene that encodes it. For example, this type of editing happens to the messenger RNA of glutamate receptor, a protein that is involved in signaling in our brain. The message is edited just after the DNA is copied into RNA and before the intron RNA is removed to create the messenger. The intron loops back onto the message, a lot like the hairpin loops Lynn Ripley saw in DNA that were described in Chapter 4, but this loop is in RNA rather than DNA.

Once the mRNA loops, an enzyme cuts a little piece off of a very specific A in the message, changing it to the letter I; this changes the codon CAG to CIG. I looks less like A than like G to the protein factories, so CIG is read by the protein factory as if it were CGG. Thus instead of the amino acid Q, which would have been put into the protein if the CAG had not been edited, the amino acid R will be added to the growing protein chain. This happens in our brains; it is happening right now. This is not a minor

change. This change from Q to R actually adds a positive charge to the protein and changes its signaling speed.

Fish DNA already encodes an R at that spot in the gene for the protein.
Why can't our genome too just get the codon for R into the DNA instead
of going through the complication of editing? Perhaps it's because this complication allows for some creativity. Sometimes there is more editing, sometimes there is less. We can increase or decrease the speed of signaling by
increasing or decreasing the editing. One gene can encode different proteins.
Different introns can be cut out or left in, yes. But editing means that it isn't
only the choice of which introns to cut out that can vary a protein; the
sequence of an exon can be changed by an editor in a way that can be regulated by circumstances. The protein channel can signal more quickly, or be
dialed down by more and more editing so that it signals more slowly.

Herbert and Rich suggest that the advantage of editing is that it allows
changes to be tried out in different tissues to different extents, and even to
be adjusted up and down under different circumstances. If the changed
sequence works better all of the time, there is always the possibility that
reverse transcription of the edited message will insert the altered sequence
into the DNA. Editing may sound like a minor thing—dotting i's and crossing t's—but missing an editing enzyme can be lethal.[10]

So, our messenger RNA can get edited a bit. But before we get too
proud of this genetic skill, there is a real genetic gymnast that we should
talk about. In the case of our brain glutamate receptor, one letter gets
changed for another. In the case of certain genes in the parasites called
trypanosomes, multiple blocks of letters are inserted and deleted. All of
the letters inserted are Us. (When DNA is copied into RNA in us, too,
the RNA uses the similar U instead of T. Like T, U pairs with A; that is,
wherever there is an A in the DNA, the RNA copy is made with a U
instead of a the T that would be in a DNA copy.) In the trypanosomes,
many, many extra Us are inserted. These Us turn up in the RNA that is
about to be copied into proteins at places where there is no letter in the
DNA; that is, they turn up in between the letters that were copied in a
string from the DNA.

For example, the DNA sequence CCCCTCCCCTCTCCAAAAAAA-
CTC is copied as GGGGAGGGGAGAGGUUUUUUUGAG. This is what
we consider normal: A is copied to U, T to A, C to G, and G to C. But then
something extraordinary happens. Small "guide" RNAs partner with this
RNA copy of the genome, leading a protein enzyme to cut the RNA copy
and another enzyme to start adding Us to the cut end. If it adds too many Us,
they hang over the end of the guide RNA, and the extras will be trimmed

off by another enzyme. Yet another enzyme stitches the other edge of the original cut RNA to the new Us that were added on the other side of the cut. Editing is not limited to adding Us. Some of the Us in the original RNA get taken out too.

So, the message GGGGAGGGGAGAGGuuuuuuuGAG gets turned into GuGuuGuuGuuAuuuuuuuGuuuGuGuuGuAGAuGGGuuuuuuuAuG.[11] (The Us that are added and removed by editing are indicated here in lower case, but they really are normal Us. Actually, the original and edited RNA sequences are much longer; I just included a small piece here, for illustration.) If we did not have the DNA and the original RNA to look at, we would have assumed, of course, that the Us were encoded in the DNA by As, although we might wonder about there being so many of them.

This newly built sequence actually encodes a protein. The amino acids encoded by the edited stretch of letters shown above are VLLLFFCLCCR-WVFLC; in contrast, if no editing had taken place, the DNA would have encoded the amino acids GEGSGFFE. (A bit confusingly, there is an amino acid, glycine, that is called G just as the DNA building block guanine is called G. They are not related to each other, other than that, as it turns out, GGG encodes glycine; they were named separately, decades before this relationship was discovered.) The FF amino acid pair is encoded entirely by inserted Us (one of the codons for F is UUU[12]). We would have no clue about this pair of amino acids FF if we looked at the original piece of DNA; all of the other codons have one or even two of their letters contributed by the inserted Us.

So, the information encoding the protein that actually is made is not explicit in the DNA. It is cryptic. If you knew the table of codons and saw the DNA sequence, you would not be able to figure out the protein this sequence encodes at all unless you knew a lot more about the guide RNA than we know now. In fact, you would be misled. These are called *crypto-genes*. Horatio, if you come to ask me about this, I will reply as did Hamlet. For the latest on this, follow the research of Larry Simpson, a professor at UCLA. In addition to the work with guide RNAs that I have described above, Simpson and his colleagues have compared the sequences of genes from different trypanosomes and found that the edited message sometimes gets reverse transcribed and inserted into the genome; in that case, the gene sequence in the DNA will come to match the protein that actually is made.

RNA seems to work as a guide in many other situations, too. It guides the removal of introns, positioning the machinery at the intron/exon boundary, even making the splice to cut out the intron. A small RNA serves as an adapter, recognizing the codon on the messenger RNA and positioning the

correct incoming amino acid in the right site to be connected to the growing protein chain. This adapter may slip if the codons are in a run of
repeated letters, especially if there is a hairpin structure nearby in the RNA,
rather like slippery DNA. Rather than mess up copying, for some RNA,
including HIV, this slip will shiftt her eading frame to give us a new protein
that is encoded in a different frame in the same message, using different
codons.[13] In other words, if the message is read UUU UUA GGG (which
encodes FLG), when the reading slips backward, one of the Us is read twice,
so the message is read UUU UUU AGG (which encodes FFR).

A look at the draft of the genome[14] shows thousands of parts of it that
do not encode proteins look as if they could be copied into RNA—they are
copied from DNA to RNA, and that's that. RNA is busy in the cell, taking
on many roles other than simply acting as a messenger to the protein factory. These jobs include active roles inside the protein factory: matching up
the correct amino acid with its codon, working with proteins to become the
factory structure itself, helping to get newly made proteins across certain
cell membranes, and perhaps the central step in making proteins using the
genome's information, actually forming the bond between two amino acids.
In addition to its work getting proteins made, RNA is also busy back in the
nucleus, in some ways that we know and in some ways that we do not yet
know; it is the needle-threader that helps one strand of the antiparallel
DNA double helix to be copied backward, and it works with proteins and
unusual DNA structures to finish the DNA at the ends of the chromosomes, like crocheting to finish the edge of a knit scarf.

And what about all of the RNA in the introns that does not get translated into proteins? Is it all just thrown away? People used to assume that
it was, but this doesn't make sense. All that extra RNA contains some
potentially useful information: each time the DNA encoding a specific
protein is copied, the intron RNA is, of course, copied too. When that RNA
is cut out of the messenger, it could travel to other parts of the cell and
around the genome, carrying the message that the gene it encoded has been
copied. Each time the gene is copied, another bit of the chopped-up intron
RNA could travel, and this could serve as a counter. Has this potential for
usefulness been captured by evolution? I don't know yet, but I expect that
it has. What we do know is that, indeed, not all of the intron RNA is simply chewed up and thrown away.

There is, of course, the intron RNA that folds over and is used for editing the message of the brain glutamate receptor. And there is another kind
of RNA, called snoRNA,[15] which directs the activity of specific proteins—
as if the snoRNA were the dog on the scent and the protein were the per-

son following behind to do something when the dog gets him or her to the right spot. If you look around the genome for DNA that encodes snoRNA, one of the places where you will find it is in introns.

One group of proteins that snoRNA directs attaches methyl groups not to DNA, but to RNA, not to the letter, but to the sugar that links the letters to on another. One recently discovered snoRNA, found only in the brain, guides a protein to attach a methyl group onto an A in one of the brain receptors for the neurotransmitter serotonin.[16] This particular A often gets edited to an I, but the researchers who discovered this methyl group suspect that it may make the A less likely to be edited; in other words, this snoRNA might be involved in regulating the activity of the serotonin receptor. SnoRNAs are relatively recent discoveries. Researchers are still sorting out all that they may be up to.

Sometimes RNA, including some snoRNAs, is involved in imprinting. We have 23 pairs of chromosomes; one of each pair comes from mom and the other from dad. Strangely, some DNA is copied into RNA only from one parent's chromosome; the fate of a patch of the genome is imprinted by the parent of origin. Thus, a specific RNA might be copied from DNA on the chromosome that you got from your father, but not from the equivalent chromosome that you got from your mother. If that parent-specific copying is messed up, you might inherit a severe disease, even though the very DNA that you need is there on the other chromosome, perhaps a chromosome that your mom got from her father. A lack of copying of snoRNAs that are usually copied from dad's chromosome 15 is on the list of suspect causes of a disease that strikes about 1 in 15,000 births, causing failure to thrive, weak muscles, and other very serious problems for the infant. Imprinting is an interesting story that still is being deciphered.[17]

I will close this RNA chapter with more recent unexpected news: RNA interference. The first strange observation was in petunias. Researchers inserted a gene for a pigment-making protein to make the color more intense, and instead the color disappeared in blotches, although it reappeared in later generations. Then RNA interference was found in worms: Pieces of RNA that were *fed* to the worm could turn off genes that have sequences that are similar to the RNA. Then RNA interference was found to be common. When there are two strands of RNA that can pair with each other using the pairing rules, as if they were trying to be double-stranded DNA, all kinds of strange things can happen in a genome. When these are small pieces of RNA, they can get chopped up by an enzyme called *dicer* into bits of about 22 letters each. These bits then attach to messenger RNAs that have the complementary sequences and serve as guides to direct (possibly reversible) inactivation of these messages before they can get to a protein factory.[18]

For researchers, this discovery is a tremendous gift, for by putting the right bits of two-stranded RNA in a cell, we can selectively inactivate the RNA copied from a particular gene and find out what happens—what function is lost, what the gene is needed for. However, it also means there are forms of regulation within the cell that we are just beginning to peek at. Sometimes they seem to block the jumping around of retrotransposons. Another observation is that if these chopped up bits of RNA get near the chromosomes, they sometimes affect which genes are turned on and which turned off in ways that are inherited between generations. We can begin to wonder what happens if these bits of RNA, which can travel from tissue to tissue and affect the whole genome, get into our germ-line cells, which will become eggs or sperm and which contain the DNA that we will package for the next generation.

This chapter has focused on the surprising behavior of RNA, while the focus of the discussion of evolution traditionally has been on changes in our DNA. But RNA's surprises, which continue to dance on the stage before us, remind us that the enzymes that interact with some -NA, and the some *same* -NA itself, do not stick with our script of simple linear tracking of information, with the occasional mutagenic stumble. If RNA can do some things that we did not expect, perhaps DNA can too, either through interactions with RNA, through the RNA it encodes, or on its own. We should contemplate this question with some humility as we consider our own genome, and evolution.

17

Mixing Up Genes
for the Children

"We shall not cease from exploration
And the end of all our exploring
Will be to arrive where we started
And know the place for the first time."

—Thomas Stearns Eliot

If I were put in conscious charge of my genome, I would be very careful
with it. I wouldn't want to drop it, scratch it, or mess it up. I want to stay
me. I would take especially great care with if I were assigned stewardship
of the human germ-line genome, the genome that is set aside to be copied
and passed through egg and sperm—from parent to progeny to progeny forever. The future of the species depends on its integrity. Yet when a genome
is passed between generations, it gets shuffled up and recombined. Mistakes
are not so rare; there are major errors in about one in five of all human con-
ceptions. A person may get two of mother's chromosomes 1 and neither of
father's chromosomes 1.[1] (Chromosomes are numbered in size order, with
number 1 being the biggest.) We notice these missteps when they create
serious challenges (including miscarriages[2]). For example, if a cell gets three
copies of one of the smallest chromosomes, chromosome 21, the child will
have Down's syndrome.

To understand evolution in animals, in yeast, and in trees, we have to look
closely at this moment, when the sperm and egg genomes are being prepared

for the next generation, and think carefully about the interaction between specific DNA sequences and the enzymes that recognize and act on them. It may seem strange at this point of the book, after we've reviewed complex genetic mechanisms, to come to a description of meiosis, the special cell division that takes place in our germ line, which we all learned about in school. However, the research described in this book, with its focus on the generation of diversity and on evolution, brings a new perspective to meiosis.

A standard-issue genome for a human being is 46 chromosomes in 23 pairs, with one chromosome in each pair coming from mom and one from dad. Because we have two copies of each of our 23 chromosomes (that is, if we are women, with two copies of the X chromosome; guys of course have just one X and a Y), we are *diploid*. The genome in an egg or a sperm has room for only one set of 23 chromosomes; it is *haploid*. We can give each child only part of the DNA that we carry forward from our parents. The rest, of course, must be left aside to make room for the DNA carried by the person who joins with us to create a child.

Most of the cells in our body divide by mitosis, which produces two daughter cells with a full complement of 46 chromosomes. But as our germ-line genome prepares for the moment of mating, in the form of a haploid egg or a sperm, it first divides by mitosis, then undergoes meiosis; and then the sperm divide by mitosis again. In sporting events, to keep track of the players on a crowded field, we give them T-shirts with numbers. One way that is used to keep track of the players at cell division is to label each chromosome in a numbered pair M or D, for mom or dad. Thus each of us has two chromosomes 1—one 1M chromosome and one 1D. We have one 2M and one 2D, . . . one 10M and one 10D, . . . one 22M and one 22D, and one XM and one XD (for females) or YD (for males), for a total of 46 players. When a chromosome is duplicated, it is a DNA double helix at its core that is copied. If, after duplication, we were to give each of the resulting matched pairs T-shirts, there would be two players wearing the 1M shirt, two wearing the 2M, and so on. These pairs are called sisters (though they are more like twins). Each member of this matched pair has one new strand and one strand of the original DNA double helix that was duplicated; its sister has the other original strand.

Here is where the T-shirts really come in handy. When the cell divides after duplicating all of its DNA, the resulting 92 chromosomes must sort into the correct two sets of 46. During mitosis, the sisters leave each other and move to opposite sides of the cell. After mitosis, each daughter cell will have only one player with a 1M T-shirt, not two, and only one with a 1D T-shirt, not two, and so on, for a matched diploid set of 46.

In meiosis, after the cell copies its DNA once, it separates its chromosomes and divides not once but twice. At the start of meiosis, 46 chromosomes in 23 pairs are cramped within a single cell. If stretched out end to end, they would be about 5 feet long, over 30,000 times longer than the diameter of the cell. This cell is destined to generate an egg or sperm cells, each with a single set of 23 chromosomes, yet rather than simply divide the 46 chromosomes between two cells, meiosis begins by duplicating all 46 chromosomes.

Then, after duplication, at the first division in meiosis, something unusual happens. Rather than separating as they do in mitosis, the sisters stay together. So, when the cell splits, each cell gets an unusual set of chromosomes: one cell gets both 1M sisters, and the other cell gets both 1D sisters. This means that the cell that got the 1M pair is missing the information that left when 1D, which had come from dad, went off into the other cell. If the cell with the 1M pair got the 12D pair, it also lost mom's information, which is unique to 12M.

If dad packed your lunch, he might have chosen the peanut butter or the egg salad sandwich for you, but not both. Did he put in the chocolate milk or the juice; the brownie or the apple? Assuming that dad's choices were independent of one another, these three pairs of choices gave dad eight possible lunch options, $2 \times 2 \times 2$. Did you get the peanut butter sandwich, the chocolate milk, and the apple? Did your big sister get the egg salad, the juice, and a brownie? Did your lucky little brother get the peanut butter sandwich and the chocolate milk and a brownie?

Long before lunch, the first important package each of your parents gave to you was a set of chromosomes.[3] When packaging chromosomes for the egg that became you, a choice was made 23 times, once for each of mom's 23 pairs of chromosomes: the chromosome handed down from grandmother or the one from grandfather? The total number of different combinations of mom's 23 chromosome pairs that she can pack in an egg for you or your siblings is $2 \times 2 \times 2 \times 2 \times 2 \times 2 \times 2 \times 2 \times 2 \times 2 \times 2 \times 2$ $\times 2 \times 2 \times 2 \times 2 \times 2 \times 2 \times 2 \times 2 \times 2 \times 2 \times 2$ (2 times 2, 23 times; in other words, 2^{23})—over 8 million. For example, perhaps you got 1M, 2M, 3D, 4M, 5M, 6D, 7D, 8D, 9M, 10M, 11D, 12M, 13D, 14M, 15M, 16D, 17D, 18D, 19M, 20M, 21M, 22D, and XM.

So, if your parents could keep making babies forever, how many different brothers and sisters could you have just from chromosome assortment alone—no mutations? Since each of your parents can give you or your siblings one of 8 million chromosome combinations, the odds that little you were handed a specific combination of chromosomes, and therefore a specific combination of genes, were 1 in 8 million times 8 million or 64 trillion—while there are 6 billion people alive today, and all of the people who have ever been born on Earth is estimated to be 100 trillion.[4] So, except for identical twins, each of us receives a package of DNA that has never been made before and probably will never be made again.

This mixing of chromosomes may give our species a lot of potential diversity, but there is a serious constraint. Simply mixing chromosomes cannot send into the future a particularly good combination of genes that might come into a genome on different chromosomes. Suppose your mother's version of a gene on the top of chromosome 4 and your father's version of a gene on the bottom of chromosome 4 work particularly well together. You, of course, are lucky to have them both, one on your 4D and one on your 4M, and you gain whatever extra fitness this combination of genes might bring. But, when it came time for you to pass your genes on to your children, after the chromosomes you got from mom and dad separated, some children would get 4M, and some would get 4D; none would get both. Your lucky combination of genes would leave each other, like ships passing in the night. So, if you were packaging genes for the kids, you might want to do some cutting and pasting. And you can, for just at the point where the DNA is being transferred into cells that will become the egg or sperm that will seed our children, just when we envision the crown jewels—the genome, the book of life—being carefully handed down, protected in glass, to the next generation, on a tray lined with soft velvet, just now, at this very moment, rather than being protected from all harm and damage, our DNA is cut into pieces.

DNA is cut in meiosis when a molecular scissor protein called Spo11 is turned on. Just as special proteins are turned on in a heart cell or a neuron, special proteins are turned on in germ-line cells that handle the genetic footwork of meiosis and mitosis.[5] During meiosis, after each M and D chromosome is copied and there are 92 chromosomes packed inside the cell, the mom and dad chromosomes exchange information through a programmed sequence of steps. This sequence begins when Spo11 cuts through both strands of the DNA double helix of a chromosome (see Figure 17-1). Where Spo11 cuts, letters are chewed off the DNA in opposite directions on each of the two strands. This leaves a patch on each side of the cut where there is only a single strand of unpaired helix.

The new single-stranded edge of the broken DNA can reach out and explore. It will pause at something familiar—a sequence that is similar, but not necessarily identical, to its own. To find a new partner, this single strand of DNA can "invade" an intact double helix and pair off with one of the

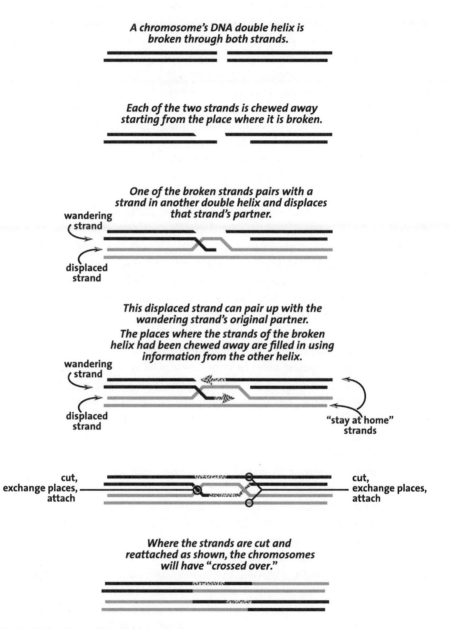

A chromosome's DNA double helix is broken through both strands.

Each of the two strands is chewed away starting from the place where it is broken.

One of the broken strands pairs with a strand in another double helix and displaces that strand's partner.

wandering strand

displaced strand

This displaced strand can pair up with the wandering strand's original partner.

The places where the strands of the broken helix had been chewed away are filled in using information from the other helix.

wandering strand

displaced strand

"stay at home" strands

cut, exchange places, attach

cut, exchange places, attach

Where the strands are cut and reattached as shown, the chromosomes will have "crossed over."

Figure 17-1   Recombination in meiosis.

strands, pushing the second strand of that helix aside. In turn, this displaced strand can move over to partner with the wandering strand's former partner. This displaced strand will provide new information, filling in the places where the DNA had been chewed away and restoring a double helix.

When DNA in a chromosome is damaged, it usually turns for help to its sister, the chromosome that has the other half of its parent DNA molecule. Thus one of the 4M sisters could restore its lost information by turning to the other. But in meiosis, something extraordinary happens. The chromosome that is cut by Spo11 does not turn to its sister. Instead, mom's chromosome turns to dad's for information, and dad's turns to mom's.[6] 4M turns to 4D. At any given region of DNA, mom and dad's chromosomes are very similar, but probably not identical. Thus, when the wandering strand invades the other helix, it creates a biparental DNA double helix. Copying, cutting, and pasting of the strands of the two interwoven helices restores a pair of separate, intact, but now recombinant molecules in which information from mom and dad is connected on the same chromosome. At least once for each mom/dad pair,[7] after Spo11 has started the chromosome wandering and recombining, the stay-at-home strands get cut, and the portions from the cut to the end of the chromosome move with their former partner over to the other chromosome. If the DNA strands of the chromosomes from the cut to the end exchange places, they have *crossed over*. In other words, it is as if you noticed that the house next door, and all the houses from your neighbor to the corner, have exchanged places with the houses that used to be on the other side of the street.

In meiosis, before 4D and 4M go their separate directions into future generations, they kiss and exchange notes. Cutting and pasting chromosomes creates a memory, carried forth in the human genome, that your father had this father and that mother. A memento of your paternal grandparents' marriage became inscribed in the collective human genome when your father formed the sperm that entered your mother's egg around your age plus nine months ago.

Back to you, squished inside the cell, with a scissors, tape, and a flashlight. How could the wandering single-stranded patch of DNA from 4M have found the corresponding patch of DNA on 4D in the tangled mess of 92 chromosomes? If a piece of mom's chromosome 4 is wandering, it is most likely to find the corresponding spot on dad's chromosome 4 close by, because during meiosis the two parents' chromosomes cuddle up next to each other.[8] But another spot on dad's chromosome could be similar enough—with enough As in the right places to match its Ts, Gs in the right paces to match its Cs, and so on—to attract the wanderer. This similarity between neighboring patches of DNA is certain to be there, for example, if members of a gene family sit next to each other along a chromosome. In that case, the wandering DNA from mom's chromosome could reach over, slip into some other gene on dad's chromosome that is nearby, and pick up a patch of information from it. Or, wandering DNA that sits in a neighborhood with other gene family members could even loop over and find a similar sequence in a neighboring gene on its own chromosome, and capture information from it. One double helix can get an extra gene in this way, and one can lose one. For descendants of the child that gets the duplication, it will become even more likely for additional duplications to take place, as DNA can wander into the new copy too.

This type of gene loss and duplication is not rare at all. Something like this happened on an ancestor of our chromosome 11 to create a string of five hemoglobin genes. Gene families are more restless than single genes. When the mouse genes that match the human genes on chromosome 19 were compared, single genes looked like homebodies compared to the moving around and changing numbers of the genes in gene families, especially gene families that keep getting copied in tandem.[9]

There is a place on the X chromosome where genes encoding proteins that sense red and green light sit beside each other. Guys get only one X chromosome, so they can't compensate for any fooling around with these genes. Since the red- and green-sensing proteins are about 98 percent identical, a wandering piece of DNA here can slip next door. One cell can get an extra copy of the green gene, while another loses what may be its only copy. Some guy may just have become red/green color blind.

It is easy to see how wandering DNA from the green and red genes find each other, for the two genes are so very close and so very similar. But even genes that are very different can interact in this gain/loss way if they are in the neighborhood of repetitive DNA. As half of our genome is made up of repetitive sequences, wandering strands of repetitive DNA will have a lot of partners to choose from—another indication that "junk" DNA definitely is not just taking up space. Any one instance of interaction between these repetitive sequences may be rare, but in the aggregate there are so many similar sequences that pairings between them are not that rare over time.[10]

Though this is much less likely, a wandering DNA sequence may find a similar sequence on a chromosome with a different number and penetrate the helix there, moving information between, say, chromosome 5 and chromosome 19. Moving large blocks of DNA around like this may cause severe problems, but sometimes it turns out OK. The children with reshuffled blocks of chromosomes live, but may be heading off in a different direction, perhaps toward another species. The two sides of our chromosome 16 got together before there were baboons. Our chromosome 7 got organized after chimps and people headed together down a genetic path that diverged from that of other apes,[11] then somewhere along the way a bit of chromosome 5 got inverted, among other things, as chimps and people parted. And rearrangements still are happening. A copy of 15,000 letters of chromosome 6 was put onto chromosome 16 in some people; other people have only the chromosome 6 copy of those letters, just like the apes.[12]

It is one thing to envision how mom's and dad's chromosomes, once they're lined up, might exchange information. It is quite another to visualize how, in the mass of threads of DNA on 92 chromosomes packed and twisted throughout the cell, a patch of DNA could find a similar sequence somewhere else in the genome. In the laboratory, when researchers moved a mouse gene to a different chromosome, its partner found it. The researchers found that about 1 in 200 mouse sperm exchanged a patch of DNA between the two copies of a gene that they had placed on different chromosomes.[13] Apparently, the DNA in our cells can probe just about[14] our whole genome to find and interact with sequences that are complementary to itself.[15]

The chance that any two chromosomes will exchange a piece of DNA is affected by how close together they are in the nucleus.[16] DNA is found in different "territories" within different cells in our body; the parts of the chromosomes that are near each other in thyroid cells may not be near each other in breast cells.[17] Different chromosomes have their own territories, which are separated by channels.[18] Genes that are active are turned toward the channels, probably so that the RNA copied from them can move out to be processed (to have introns removed) along "tracks" that get to the cytoplasm. We do not yet know what underlies this organization.

When we consider how DNA sequences can find each other in a crowded, tight space, let's reflect on the skill of the ciliate, a little free-living cell with tiny hairs around it. The ciliate has only one cell with two separate nuclei, one containing its germ line and the other containing its operating genome (used to make RNA messages that direct the synthesis of its proteins). The ciliate's germ-line genome has two full sets of chromosomes, one set from each of its parents. When this ciliate prepares to mate, its germ-line genome undergoes meiosis, and so becomes haploid. When ciliates mate, they give each other one haploid nucleus; the haploid nucleus that the ciliate receives as a gift and its remaining haploid nucleus fuse to form the ciliate's new diploid genome. After sex, the ciliate's new diploid nucleus divides once by mitosis.

So far, there's nothing unusual in this. What comes next, however, is a head turner. David Prescott, of the University of Colorado, explains that as one of the ciliate's two new nuclei begins to change into a new operating nucleus, its chromosomes fragment into thousands of pieces. From these scattered fragments of its genome, the ciliate rapidly reassembles a part of its DNA. Somehow, after tossing aside about 90 percent of its DNA, chopping its chromosomes into about 24,000 small pieces, and making 1000 copies of each gene, it ends up OK. Ciliate genome tossing has been going on for many millions of years. Clearly, DNA sequences can rearrange in ways that are massive, nonrandom, and controlled.

We might envision a biochemical machine moving down the ciliate's DNA double helix and somehow selecting pieces about 14 to 500 letters long, each surrounded by a repeat of 2 to 7 letters, to cut out; around each piece that is cut out, the ends of the DNA that will be kept are stitched back together. But it is not that simple, for in the germ-line nucleus, the pieces of DNA are in the wrong order—or, at least, are in a different order from the way they will be in the operating nucleus.

So to make an operating genome, pieces have to be cut out of the germ-line genome, then the remaining pieces have to be unscrambled and put back together in the right order.

The only way we can tell which pieces of the germ-line nucleus will be eliminated in creating the operating nucleus, and which order of the pieces is "correct," is to look at an operating nucleus. Perhaps the ciliate does this too.[19] It may well be that before it is replaced, the DNA from the old operating nucleus, which was running the cell before mating, helps to guide the cut sites and the order of the genes. But if the old operating nucleus does guide the cutting and pasting to form the new one, this would mean that the germ-line genome must find the necessary information from among the 24 million pieces of DNA in the operating nucleus, where its letters are separated and stitched in a different order. It must be able to do this even though the sequences in the new genome that was formed after mating are not identical to it—which is, of course, the whole point of sex.

How does the little ciliate keep track of where everything goes when it shatters its genome? After throwing a ball over his shoulder into the basket, the young Bill Bradley explained, "You develop a sense of where you are."[20] The ciliate's breath-taking genome tossing suggests that letters in DNA can have a sense of where they are in the complicated landscape of a genome.

When we are talking about living things, underneath a "sense of where you are," there must be biochemistry. There must be molecules that can keep everything straight. It seems very likely to me that as we figure out how the ciliate manages its genome, we will be led to ask questions that as yet we have not imagined about our own germ-line genome. Clearly, the cell nucleus is not just a bag full of disorganized squirmy chromosomes.

Generally, we think of DNA as being rather nearsighted and helpless. Yes, we know that it is full of information, like a book on a shelf. But, on a day-to-day basis, we assume that the main job of any letter is to be there, holding hands with its partner across the newly forming double helix when it is being copied, As paired with Ts and Gs paired with Cs. If there is a problem—say an A is incorrectly paired with a C—then a protein (one of the hard workers that really runs things) must notice the misshapen bump in the helix and fix it. Like a revered but not-very-competent monarch, DNA depends upon its valets and handlers to get through the day intact.

Before the Avery team showed that DNA is the genetic material, researchers dismissed it as a simple molecule and assumed that genetic information was carried by the proteins, which are more complex and interesting. So too do we discount the ability of DNA to find its way around the nucleus. When DNA is damaged, if it is lucky, it may find, very nearby, a similar sequence that it can use for repair, with the help of proteins. But except possibly when it is paired up at cell division, we don't think that a little piece of DNA sequence notices from day to day that there is other DNA in the cell.

We even limit, in our imagination, the role of proteins. Proteins can bind to DNA and to each other, thus controlling which genes are turned on and off. They can spot and fix mismatches, and cut into DNA. Might proteins emerge during evolution that are turned on in the germ line, that are able to recognize specific types of DNA sequences, sequences that carry information affecting how likely it is that a spot of DNA will be cut and which genes will recombine? And, of course, there's RNA. It can guide proteins to DNA sequences and move around. What else might it be up to? Might DNA be reaching out and feeling its way around?[21] How does organization emerge? As our chromosomes recombine to generate diversity, is the genetic change that results completely unstructured, completely random?

18

Sculpting the Genome

A want of the habit of observing and an inveterate habit of taking averages are each of them often equally misleading.

—Florence Nightingale[1]

When we speak of evolution, it often seems like something that happened over such a long time and so long ago. Yet, of course, evolution can happen here, and quickly. As described in Chapter 7, bacteria evolved to become antibiotic-resistant within an infant who was only a few months old. OK, so that happens with bacteria, but for humans, especially, as we peer through glass in our museums at the bones of other primates and contemplate the millions of years that separate us, evolution seems very distant indeed. We don't expect to suddenly see a newly evolved primate species. And yet, as our experience with malaria and HIV show us, selection is something that can, even today, sweep through a human community like a wall of water in a tidal wave. Even within a generation, an epidemic can leave behind a human genome with a different mix of genes. While disease is the clearest and most dramatic example of selection at work, it is not the only such example. In an isolated community that was forced to high ground by war or an earthquake, the mix of genes carried by people like me, those who are extremely sensitive to altitude, would not fare well. Selection acts on variations. If selection sometimes happens quickly, we can't relax and imagine that we always have generation after generation of time to adjust as each new challenge gradually turns up the pressure. If, over and over again, quick sidesteps may be needed, then to fully understand what happens in evolution, we have to begin to focus on the other part of the process, variation. Have repeated episodes of selection begun to structure the mechanisms of genome variation? How do variations arise in our genome—is it only by completely random mutation?

Now, not just for bacteria, but for those of us who are yeast and rice and flies and people—now that our genome has been sequenced and a wide array of computational and laboratory tools have become available, we can begin to ask whether genome variation really is only random. We can do this by sampling information from a range of the species that go through meiosis, examining the types of differences we find between genomes. We can compare genomes from different individuals. We also can follow the progress of one individual's genome as it travels through cells in the germ line.

One landmark we can examine is the location of double-strand cuts in meiosis. Because each of these opens the door to genetic variation between generations, the chance that a stretch of DNA will vary between generations can depend upon how likely it is that a cut will be made in the neighboring DNA, and how far the DNA is from a spot that is likely to be cut.[2] If you had the scissors and paste ready, where would you cut, and where would you paste?

In asking whether double-strand cuts occur randomly throughout our chromosomes, let's reflect again on the two meanings of random. Is genetic change random with respect to sequence? If it is not, then we can ask whether it is random with respect to the type of information encoded in the DNA. The answer to the first question—whether cuts in the germ-line genome are random with respect to sequence—is that they are not. Chromosomes are not cut randomly.

Along each double helix there are hot spots, places that are likely to be cut and therefore to change. There also are cold spots. We can see that, in some organisms, a specific sequence of letters tends to be the site of the chromosome cuts during meiosis. Other times, all that is clear is that the cuts tend to occur in certain regions of DNA and not in others. In some species, we can see that hot spots happen where the DNA attracts specific proteins,[3] which in turn can create landing pads for enzymes that cause double-strand cuts in DNA. Is there a completely equal chance of crossing over at every letter in the genome.

In some organisms that live as single cells (say a fungus such as yeast or bread mold), it is easy to get a close-up look at hot spots because it is actually possible to catch the four cells that are the product of the two divisions of each single meiosis and to look at their DNA. In one study, the average frequency of gene conversion (when a patch from one gene is put into another) during meiosis at any one spot in the brewer's/baker's yeast genome was found to be about 1 in 40. This was the average, but from spot to spot the probability varied from less than 1 in 100 to more than 1 in every 2 cells.[4] In one kind of yeast, about half of the exchanges between the two parents' chromosomes happen at the sequence ATGACGT.[5] However, you would have to explore the neighborhood around each cut to spot this hot spot, because the double strand cuts are not within ATGACGT itself, but rather about 50 to 200 letters away.

During meiosis in people, a stretch of 26 letters, spread throughout our genome within the repetitive sequence Alu, can attract cuts that set the DNA to wandering. This stretch of letters was the site of DNA cuts in two out of a group of five people who were missing large blocks of their hemoglobin genes.[6] Because these letters include 5 of the sequence of 8 letters that promotes the exchange of genetic information in *Escherichia coli*,[7] CCAGC, cuts at these letters in our DNA may turn out to be descended from a very ancient mechanism that can focus recombination. Not only can Alu attract cuts, but once the DNA is cut, when Alu is part of the edge of the DNA that starts wandering, it can contribute to duplications and deletions of blocks of genome by being similar enough to one of the estimated millions of other Alus across our genome to exchange DNA near the Alu.[8]

Double-strand cuts often are between genes, near the promoters that determine whether the gene is on. To pack 46 pieces of DNA, with a range of sizes, totaling approximately 5 feet in length, into a cell with a diameter much smaller than the width of a hair from your head, the DNA must be intricately wrapped around itself, wrapped around proteins, and folded and folded and folded and folded again in each chromosome of each of our cells. Several groups of researchers have suggested that double-strand cuts often happen between genes because DNA is "unwrapped" near promoters and so may be more accessible[9] to, for example, Spo11.

In addition to Alu, other DNA sequences, repeats, and structures attract cuts. One example is a piece of the DNA helix where letters can loop out in a hairpin comprised of one strand partnered with itself, A with T, G with C, as seen in Lynn Ripley's palindrome.[10] Long strings of ATs on human chromosomes 11 and 22, which can form loops, can cause rearrangements of DNA between these two chromosomes.[11] Long, slippery CAG repeats can form hairpin structures, when they momentarily become single-stranded during copying, and be cut by Spo11.[12] In DNA from people in 150 different families with Huntington's disease, stretches of CAG repeats

37 to 86 repeats long changed in length 80 percent of the time they passed through the genetic footwork of the germ line.[13]

There are differences in what happens to the same sequence of DNA in different cells because different cells contain different proteins, enzymes that can cut the DNA, such as Spo11, components of the mismatch repair system, different RNAs, and other molecules that can affect the DNA. DNA encoding an antibody attracts a region-specific[14] cut in the context of certain cells of our immune system. This cut happens in the switch region, the first step in moving the pathogen-binding module next to a new effector module. The cut has been called region-specific because, although it is not always between the same two letters in the DNA, it always is within the switch region. It has taken a while to work out the mechanism of this region-specific cut. This cut seemed to require copying of the switch region DNA into RNA, but it does not require copying of this RNA into protein. For a while it wasn't clear whether the RNA copy really was needed, or if the DNA just had to be accessible, as it is when it is about to be copied. We now know that as part of the class switch mechanism, an RNA copy is made of a G-rich region of DNA.

DNA cutting that takes place in meiosis also may be region specific. Some experiments indicate that an RNA copy has to be made, but some people wonder whether the DNA just has to be accessible, as it is when it is about to be copied. So, it is reasonable to ask whether RNA might be involved in attracting cuts to certain sequences in germ-line cells.[15]

Because what happens to a sequence depends upon both the sequence itself and on other molecules that are present in the cell, the likelihood that a particular place will be cut between generations becomes susceptible to regulation by whatever controls the action of these other molecules. A colorful palette of biochemical tools may affect where in our genome DNA is cut during meiosis and mitosis in the germ line. Some form(s) of RNA is (are) likely to have surprises for us here.

In addition to asking what proteins (and RNA) are present in large amounts during meiosis and mitosis in the germ line, what types of DNA sequences they may tend to act on, and where they have access to the DNA, we should look at the specific timing of their activity within the hours when the genome is being manipulated. Copying our genome is a big job, and it is done in stages. The DNA in some sections of the nucleus routinely is copied before the DNA in others. For example, housekeeping genes, which are needed in essentially all of our cells, appear to be copied in one wave.[16] Because different parts of our germ-line genome are copied separately during mitosis and meiosis, it is possible for different sections of the genome to experience different types of mutation, due to local differences in what other molecules are present. It may be that there are places and mechanisms that have emerged in the genome that are like laboratories, where new DNA sequences tend to be generated. The genome may also have evolved other regions, perhaps those where housekeeping genes live, that are more stable.

At different times, and in different places in the nucleus, a gene may experience different pols (polymerases) and different pools, and thus different extents and types of genetic variation. First, the different pools. While polymerases are copying the genome in the germ line, the probability that one letter will take the place of another—in other words, the chance that a specific type of mutation may occur—will be different depending upon the relative amounts of A, T, G, and/or C in the pool of letters that float in and out of the helix as the polymerase approaches. We saw this with the ras gene in tumors that was described in Chapter 11. If the pool of one of the letters, say G, becomes depleted as the DNA is being copied,[17] there will be a tiny (but over generations perhaps significant) shift toward, for example, As and Ts in the genes that are copied later. In fact, some (but not all) regions of the genome that are copied later do seem to be richer in As and Ts. This may contribute to what has been called the different "flavors"[18] of our genome—some stretches are more full of As and Ts than of Gs and Cs, whereas others are more G- and C-rich.[19] Because there are differences in the physical properties of GC-rich and AT-rich DNA, once these different-flavored sections of the genome form, they are likely to continue to experience a distinct spectrum of mutations.

In addition to differences in the pools, difference in the pools that have access to DNA sequences will have an effect on genetic change. If, for example, machinery that copies part of the genome during the later wave has a slight tendency to favor inserting A or T over inserting G or C, this also could explain a shift to more AT in the section of the genome that is copied later, although there is no evidence for this. What we do know is that when the amount of the SOS polymerase dinB was increased in E. coli, mutation increased tenfold, but mutations did not all increase to the same extent. Most mutations made by dinB were shifts in strings of identical letters, the slippery DNA. This laboratory study of the effect of increased dinB may be relevant to our germ line, for when samples of adult human and mouse tissue were examined, our dinB SOS polymerase was found in the highest amounts in testes.[20] In fact, there are high amounts of several unusual polymerases, which tend to make distinct types of errors, in testes[21]—where we would expect to find them if they have an effect on genetic change between generations. Polymerases with unusual activities clearly are present in germ-line cells, but we don't know whether they are attracted to specific classes of DNA sequences. They might be attracted to specific sequences either by distinct molecules that are active around cuts in DNA or because distinct sequences are available to be copied at the particular time the polymerase is expressed during each mitosis or meiosis in the germ line.

While there is a lot that we do not know yet, it is clear that genetic change in our genome can be affected by which proteins are present, which sequences are accessible, and the pools of different letters in which they are immersed. Therefore, the genome becomes susceptible to organization, such as by the timing of copying, into regions that experience different classes of genetic variation.

Spo11, which cuts DNA, repair proteins, and unusual polymerases are not the only proteins turned on in the germ line that encourage genome variation. A conservative genome would try to keep transposons as quiet as possible as it is being handed down between generations. Yet some transposons are, quite specifically, turned on in the germ line of fruit flies.[22] Well, OK, you say, they're fruit flies, so let their little eyes turn from red to white.

But genes clearly are jumping in our germ line too. The jumping gene L1 carried 526 new letters into a dystrophin gene, disrupting its function; the young man who was born with that gene had muscular dystrophy. About one in five times that a jumping gene takes off, it grabs a piece of DNA from its right and inserts it where it lands. This can make us a little nervous as we envision a transposon ricocheting around our genome out of our control, fooling around with our DNA before we've given it to our children. The rest of our cells seem to have come up with ways to keep many transposons in check, yet they get away with jumping around in—of all places—the germ line. To jump into the future, however, transposons must learn to avoid breaking the punch bowl in the germ line too often.

One estimate is that there is at least one jump in every 50 to 100 human germ cells. Another estimate is that one in eight children is born with a genome in which an L1 transposon has moved.[23] Some changes weaken the child for life in our world; we see what looks like a dramatic mistake and call it a genetic disease. Indeed, some of these changes are so bad that a sperm with such a mutation will not even make it to an egg, as we experience selection during our little haploid stage of life.[24] Out of 600 apparently harmful mutations in people that are known so far, 33 were jumps.[25] We know about these jumps because they broke the punch bowl or otherwise made a splash.[25] We are less likely to notice other jumps, although we sometimes see their footprints in the genome if we look closely. Places where L1 retrotransposons landed and inserted pieces of genes are flanked by small duplications of between 7 and 20 letters; these rearrangements represent about 0.5 to 1 percent of the human genome. As of now, DNA gymnastics that introduce diversity in children that are free of special challenges still pass mostly unnoticed. But we will see the jumps if it becomes routine for everyone to look at their genome, and that of their children, much as people have come to bring home a print of the sonogram taken before their child is born.

Right now, as we have begun to compare the genomes of different people, it is becoming clear that some patches definitely are much more diverse than others.[26] The probability of genetic change *is* different for different DNA sequences. But what about the other definition of random? Has a selective advantage gone to the genomes in which intrinsic differences in the probability of, for example, DNA cutting tend to facilitate creating new combinations of functions, rather than those in which it tends to destroy active genes? Is genetic change in our germ line random with respect to the type of information that is encoded in the DNA?

Now that we have whole genomes, we can begin to look into this. For example, when the whole yeast genome was examined, one group of researchers reported that there did seem to be some functional difference between hot spots and other regions of the genome. They reported that genes that encode proteins that build amino acids appear to be closer to the hot spots of double-strand cuts than genes that transport other molecules around the yeast cell.[27] We might, for example, scan our genome the way Moxon scanned *Haemophilus influenzae* for four-letter repeats, to ask whether places that we know tend to slip, like TTTTTTT and CAGCAGCAGCAGCAGCAG, have tended to pop up in strategic places within our genome too.[28]

Although by now this is not a surprise, it is very clear from looking at our genome that there is a great deal of gene duplication and reverse transcription of RNA copies involved in building gene families in our genome. The first hint that new proteins can evolve by duplication of genes, rather than by random mutation of DNA, came in 1964, long before we were able to look at our genes, when two proteins with related functions were found to have very similar amino acid sequences.[29] An innovation that led to the emergence, expansion, and diversification of gene families such as those involved in signaling between cells may well have been part of the evolution of new families, indeed new phyla, of organisms.[30] If, as we see more dramatically with our antibodies, successful gene families do encode a framework that affects the probability of distinct types of variation, this would be likely to favor gene duplication and include relative hot spots of DNA cuts, recombination, and/or attraction of creative polymerases, although we may find rougher edges than in our immune system.

Now that we can peek at the genome, the source of new gene creation will sometimes be clear. For example, many "zinc finger" genes (a family that regulates whether other genes are turned on or off) are located on our chromosome 19.[31] The genes on chromosome 19 appear to have evolved by repeated duplication of a specific gene, followed by specialization to do slightly different jobs. It is likely that the place in the genome where the original gene sits has a strong tendency to be duplicated, relative to most other sites in the genome. "Strong" doesn't mean that this will happen at the border of every generation. One explanation for so many recent duplications of a gene would be that every place in the genome is equally likely to duplicate, but that only duplications of this particular gene in this particular place were selected for every million years or so because of a selective advantage from each one of these duplications. However, an increase in the intrinsic tendency to duplicate in the region encoding zinc fingers seems much more likely, especially given some unusual features of the genes' DNA neighborhood, described by a team that sequenced it as "a complex genomic architecture . . . [with] three [identified] hierarchical levels of organization."[32] We are taking the first steps to understand what determines the probability that specific patches of DNA sequences in our genome will duplicate. Selection will favor genome sequences that tend to recombine at spots and in ways that, over and over again, provide a potential advantage.

When new copies change more quickly than the original gene, perhaps the duplicating process itself adds variation to the new version of the gene. Alternatively, the genomic context where those copies land may generate an increased tendency for the copies to vary in the germ line at specific places along their length, while the original gene, exposed to less variation, remains a stable source of new gene family members with a tendency to vary in the germ line at specific places along their length.

Within the gene families of our vertebrate immune system, biochemical machinery has evolved that is able to focus genetic exploration at appropriate sites in our genome when forming antibodies during each of our lives, and also between generations. In fact, so far, the genes in the germ line that may be most variable from person to person are the several histocompatibility genes on our chromosome 6, one of which comes in more than

240 varieties. They are called histocompatibility genes because they determine whether tissue (*histo-*) that is transplanted between people is compatible or will be rejected, but these genes evolved before transplant surgeons. One of their roles is to protect us from viruses.

From generation to generation, we change our cells' coats, protecting ourselves against pathogens through the great variability in our histocompatibility genes. Many variations among histocompatibility genes arise when a patch from one gene is pasted into the corresponding place on another gene (gene conversion). In mice, there is so much variation that if you pick any two histocompatibility genes, you will find that they have exchanged patches in somewhere between 1 in 10,000 and 1 in 2 million sperm. This exchange is not distributed evenly even within the histocompatibility genes. In the male germ line, some information exchange by gene conversion seems to happen in cell divisions before meiosis, at sequences that are made up mostly of Gs and Cs.[33] In human sperm, the borders of the patches that get moved around between some of the histocompatibility genes do in fact turn out to be hot spots of crossover in meiosis.[34] This is a good place for us to learn the genomic rules that focus germ-line exchanges at the edges of the blocks that we see when we compare histocompatibility genes among many different people.

The histocompatibility region of our genome clearly represents a region where hot spots of variation are aligned with function, in this case the need for an intrinsically high rate of variation in that region to protect against pathogens. If hot spots correlate with biological function here, then they also could evolve at biologically promising spots in other gene families. But we will need to look more closely for such hot spots because variation at specific sequences within these other gene families, while higher than average for the genome, may be much rarer than in the histocompatibility hot spots and so have not yet captured our attention.

The genome cannot know that a specific new version of a gene family protein will be useful. It cannot know that a new virus X will evolve the ability to bind to surface protein Y. But it can know, from several billions of years of experience, that it is useful to evolve new gene family members, with variation focused at specific spots, and to vary certain surface proteins. In varying surface proteins, our genome changes the locks and hides doors, such as the HIV coreceptor CCR5, that specific lines of pathogens may have traditionally used to enter, for pathogens have been passing around keys to certain kinds of locks.

Survival itself selects effective strategies for survival, from among different tendencies. It is as if you and a large group of friends have been lost.

You really don't have a goal, other than to survive. You found yourselves in a vast landscape, and after you ate the food in your immediate vicinity, you started wandering. Some of you were drawn to live among the swamps, which are moist, where you could include the abundant plants in your diet and sip the water, impervious to all but the most severe drought. Once quicksand claimed some of the group, most of those who remained tended to stay on higher ground and survive by hitting on the observation that you can catch the occasional rainwater in hats. And there was the tragic experience of a few of your friends who have disappeared (which we will not go into here)—those friends who felt comfortable entering the caves, which turned out to be filled with venomous snakes.

Everyone has been free to wander in his or her own direction. You decide to spread out, but to whistle for one another at dusk so that you can get together to share information about good survival strategies. This system of wandering and exchanging information works well, in general. Some of you have come to call the exchange of information at dusk "recombination"; others refer to it as "mating."

Gradually, you learned to adapt to the habitat. Some people spread far out over the landscape, randomly searching for places where water might have pooled. Others tended to come often at dusk, focusing their exchanges of information in a way that improved their skills at building, out of available material, enormous but lightweight hats for gathering rainwater. You do notice that some people don't come to share information when you whistle at dusk. Perhaps they have moved too far away. However, you also note that after a dry spell many of the people who searched randomly for water rather than regularly exchanging information about hats are gone, and that all of the people who had a tendency to walk through the swamps seem to have disappeared too.

Once the group noted the absence of the swamp people, none of the remaining group went anywhere near a swamp—or, of course, a cave. One of the swamp people did in fact survive, and that person turned up one summer evening to exchange the information that swamps are fine in the daylight, with one adaptation: To be sure to escape from the quicksand, he carried a long, sturdy pole wherever he went. This did not reassure the hill people, although a few times, when food and water was getting scarce on the hill, one of the hill people did try to wander across a swamp at noon carrying two long poles, and found it actually a rather good strategy during dry spells. She also found that when favored foods ran out, she could use the sturdy poles to kill—for a carefully dissected protein dinner—the occasional snake, readily available at the caves.

While the group of friends has retained some diversity and may have just recently begun to explore an adaptation to swamp life, there has been a clear selection in favor of those who tended to stay on high ground and who tend to focus their information exchange on the hat family.

The genomic landscape is huge. Random wandering through the landscape of possible mutations is not the most efficient strategy for long-term survival. In our own case, random mutation would mean that any one of the more than 3 billion spots in our genome had the same probability of each kind of change. Eventually, as genomes evolve and are built up over countless generations—indeed, passing through distinct species—variation should become better than random. There has been enough time. Better than random does not mean that there are better than even odds that any specific change will provide a survival advantage. It does not mean that all mutations are precisely targeted. It does means that caution and welcome signs can emerge across a genomic landscape.

If this all sounds too fantastic, our immune system, with its startling peaks of variation, is there to point out that, yes, these things are possible—and to shine a light that suggests what to look for. Its mechanisms that focus genetic change at useful spots, move exons around, and create targeted variation may be a paradigm for what happens, albeit more slowly, in genome evolution. We too have to change and explore in order to survive, and our genome knows this. It learned this because, starting in the form of a single cell, it is descended from a long line of explorers who survived.

19

Decoding DNA

*We have to learn to read DNA more as poetry than as
expository prose. Each line of the text can convey multiple meanings, and they are all biologically important.*

—James Shapiro[1]

I remember the summer day in 1996 when, sitting in a beach cottage,
I read the first report of what was then an unprecedented accomplish-
ment: A long sequence of the human genome had been revealed—685,000
letters, in order.[2] It seemed to me that this was a glimpse, through a barrier, into a hidden dimension that underlay the visible world in which we
participate. Although I was reading a technical article in a scientific journal,
I thought of Martin Luther King, Jr., his resonant voice proclaiming: "I have
been to the Mountaintop, and I have seen the Promised Land."

Now our entire genome is coming into view; there is a great deal in the
landscape that we expected to find there, but there also is much that we
still do not perceive. Along the familiar double helix, with its strings of
base pairs and genes coding for proteins, there is a great deal of room in the
genome for new kinds of information. About 19 of every 20 letters in our
genome do not appear to encode the amino acids that comprise our proteins, and, because the genetic code is degenerate, there is room for still
more information under the letters that do encode our proteins.[3] Some of
this additional information encodes such things as whether a protein will
be made in a heart cell or a liver cell. But there is much more that is await-
ing discovery.

As our own genome opens before us, there is so much that we want
to ask of it. What should we explore first? Researchers program computers

to go through our 3 billion As, Ts, Gs, and Cs to find the scattered fragments of DNA sequences that might be genes, using rules such as these: Genes are sequences that are not too short and that are surrounded by recognition sites for the machinery that starts and stops transcribing the information into RNA. This software is by no means perfect, for finding scattered genes is not a straightforward task, but an automated search certainly is better than staring at a string of more than 3 billion letters the size of those in this book, spread out across the field at Yankee Stadium.

We build lists of all of the genes that look as if they might encode receptors or serine proteases, or that must be members of many other gene families that we know and we make lists of mystery genes, which don't look like anything we have seen before. We make lists of genes that appear to be copied into RNA but that are not copied into proteins. We can make lists of control regions, which interact in hierarchies of regulation[4] to determine whether a gene will be on or off. As we increase the sophistication of our computers and develop laboratory methods that will let us check the status of every protein present in a cell at once, we can begin to fill in the huge blanks in our knowledge of what groups of genes might be turned on and off at each step in the immune system, or in brain cells that are learning.

Now we can ask, in a more global, strategic way than had been possible before, How is it is written, in code, to get us to a four-limbed, one-headed creature from a single fertilized egg? What do you do first? How do you know what to do next, and how do you know when is next? How are we organized to respond effectively to predictable challenges, such as to an infection? What if this challenge is a new virus? A bacterium? A fungus? A parasite? Or is it a splinter? How do mere molecules figure this out? For each challenge, we can ask what goes wrong when the response is inadequate or is overblown. If we can read the strategic information in our genome, we will better understand what "alive" means.

And we can begin to focus on what affects the rate, type, and location of genetic change from place to place in the genome, from generation to generation. We can make lists of genes that encode the enzymes that copy DNA and those that cut damaged letters out of DNA. We can identify proteins that look like those that participate in fixing mismatches, and enzymes that make double-strand breaks. We can ask what affects the activity of each of these, and what controls their access to different spots on our DNA. We eventually will come to see what encodes the balance between the forces that maintain genetic stability and—the fundamental requirement for evolution—the mechanisms that generate diversity between generations.[5]

As genomes evolve and build up over evolutionary time, classes of sites that tend to experience similar types of genetic variability can emerge. One example of a class of sites with an increased probability of genetic variability would be those sequences that tend to serve as molecular Velcro within the context of that genome, facilitating the copying and rearranging of the sequences it surrounds. Another class of sites might experience the equivalent of the hypermutation that is experienced by the pathogen-binding regions of our antibodies after they are moved into a particular genomic context. So far, we have seen focused variation in our immune system: in histocompatibility genes across generations and in antibody and T-cell receptor genes during our lifetime. But other gene families have their own needs for focused variation. To generate new family members, they too must change some amino acids while keeping others constant to conserve the common function of the gene family.

Indeed, in gene families, the rate of variation between what should be synonymous codons does vary along the genes.[6] Once established within a gene, information that modulates variation will be copied when the gene is copied and thus will become a conserved property of a gene family, much as is seen in the gene families of our immune system.

To the extent that these variations in the probability of variation are aligned with the functional and structural requirements of active members of the gene family, the evolution of additional members of the gene family will be more efficient. This efficiency emerges from selection that has taken place at the gene family level, through the evolution of mechanisms that modulate the rate of variation at specific classes of positions, rather than through the random generation of variation in new family members followed by selection letter by letter across the DNA. The new genes' effects experience selection, of course, but the event that created them and their subsequent mutations would not be completely random.

For each genome, certain genetic changes are orders of magnitude more likely to occur than others simply because of the physical properties of different sequences of DNA. If each of these genetic changes were an independent event, then once the change happened, the genome that "let" it happen would be changed at that one place, and there would be no effect on the probability of mutation elsewhere in the genome—and while the probability of slips back and forth at that one position would experience selection, mutation elsewhere would remain random with respect to its effects on the survival of the organism's progeny. But mutations in a genome are connected by the fact that each one takes place in the context of the biochemical recognition between proteins, RNA, and stretches of

DNA that is characteristic of that genome. Other sites in the DNA that are similar to the place that mutated remain in the genome unchanged after the mutation, as does the enzyme that may have slipped at a run of Ts or did not catch the insertion of the wrong letter in a certain place, or that cut and moved a piece of DNA, resulting in the mutation. These related sites will all continue to experience—with consequences for survival—the increased or decreased tendency toward genetic change that is characteristic of that type of sequence of DNA in that genome.

The gene encoding proteins that take part in copying DNA, including the DNA polymerases themselves, can mutate, affecting the future probability of distinct types of mutations at myriad places throughout the genome. When these mutations start happening, their effect on the viability of generations of progeny will determine whether organisms that inherit this new polymerase—along with its unique classes of more and less probable mutations—will survive. Or a protein that affects where the genome tends to be cut during meiosis may mutate, with consequences throughout the genome, both at sites where cuts tended to happen before the mutation and at sites where cuts tend to happen after the mutation. If a gene jumps into a genome, the types of sites where it tends to land will affect the likelihood that the organisms with this gene will survive, carrying it into the future.

As described throughout this book, for some high-frequency forms of variation, such as pathogen surface-antigen variation, four-letter repeats in bacteria, and somatic variation in the vertebrate immune system, we are well aware that focused variation exists. We are likely to discover other examples if we take the time to look for them.[7]

But finding information that can focus mutation will be a challenge. It is a challenge to find all the genes in our genome. It is even more difficult to write software that can recognize information that we suspect is there, when we are uncertain how this information might be encoded. And then there is overlapping information we might not even notice if we tripped across it, information that we have not yet imagined exists.

The Lyme spirochete tells us that evolutionary information may be encoded not just in the sequences themselves but also in the relationships between sequences. To find mechanisms that may be recognized by the machinery that cuts and pastes DNA and that generate variability among gene family members, we might want to look for patterns of very high conservation of DNA sequence that surround regions of very high sequence variability. Once we know what to look for, a Lyme-like repeated sequence is easy to spot, but information may be encoded in the genome in ways that are harder to decode. For example, region-specific information may be harder to spot.

Much of the difficulty in getting all of the information from our genome is that we are focusing on DNA sequences as we write them, in strings of letters, yet molecules recognize something other than the sequence itself. Specific sites on the DNA tend to form structures that differ from the textbook DNA double helix. DNA that can form shorter, fatter structures often occurs at the edges of places where genes are duplicated and patches of DNA sequences are exchanged.[8] However, with a few exceptions—such as this short fat structure, palindromes that can form hairpin loops, and the stacks of G tetrads—we are not yet able to predict tendencies to form unusual DNA structures by examining DNA sequence alone.

Someday we will be able to make predictions. We will go across the whole genome, calculating the subtle changes in DNA context—the breathing, tilt, and propeller-like twist of the steps on the helix; the unique physical and chemical properties presented by different strings of letters[9]—and assess how these subtle differences in structure may affect the rate, nature, and location of genetic change and to what extent these differing rates, nature, and location of genetic change have emerged in locations that might provide a selective advantage. But as we set off to ask global evolution questions about the structure of our own genome, we face this hurdle: Right now, we cannot in general read point-to-point variations in the fidelity with which DNA is copied just by looking at the DNA sequence. To assess the probability of genetic variation along a genome—from sites that may attract breaks and recombination during meiosis, to landing sites for jumping genes, to regions copied by polymerases of varying specificities— it will not be enough to stare at letters, or even at relationships between letters, such as repeats and hairpin loops. We must learn another language if we are to be able to perceive meaning in DNA in the language that proteins understand.

Much as bats can see with sonar and dogs can use their exquisitely sensitive sense of smell to pick up sensations to which we humans are (except in our laboratories) effectively blind, the enzymes that copy, repair, and move DNA sequences live in a sense world that is different from ours. Completely different combinations of letters can build patterns in space that proteins recognize as similar. The properties that proteins and other molecules sense along a strand of DNA do depend upon that strand's sequence of letters, but similar messages can be encoded by completely different letters, much as something that is attracted to round shapes would find the words COO, ORB, and GROSS more attractive than the words KILN, MAT, and WALL.

As we begin to examine the genome for classes of sites with different probabilities of mutation, it remains controversial to suggest that the probability of mutation may not be completely random with respect to effects on the potential usefulness of the mutation.[10] Yet focused, regulated variation clearly is biochemically possible. Indeed, starting perhaps with the slippery sequences in bacterial genomes, focused genetic variation existed long, long before we did. It is unlikely that our ancient ancestors' genomes left this skill behind. If it helps to use light and darkness to guide behavior, information that encodes eyes can evolve. If it helps to focus mutation, information that affects the probability of different types of mutation at different sites in the genome can evolve too. A genome encodes many strategies; how to get from a single cell to us is a dramatic example. Is evolution another?

Current evolutionary theory states that variation results from genetic changes that remain forever random, and that selection operates upon the results of this random genetic variation. It is time to incorporate the observations described in this book into evolutionary theory. Mechanisms, such as polymerase fidelity, DNA cutting at meiosis, mismatch repair, and recombination, that determine the genome's unique probability of distinct types of genetic change at different types of sequences feel the effects of mutations on survival because of selection among generations of progeny descended from the genome—a key piece that has been missing from evolutionary theory. The result of such selection is that genomes that tend to generate the most adaptive types of variation will tend to have more surviving progeny for generation after generation. Thus, the abundance of organisms with a tendency to more strategic genetic variations should increase in the population, making the further evolution of new capabilities more efficient. Because genomes do not inhabit a completely random world, generations that survive selection should evolve into genomes that are increasingly favored by repeated cycles of selection.

By looking in a global way for information that affects the likelihood of mutation, we can begin to ask how a genome evolves a worldview of which classes of changes have a better chance of yielding a new function and are less likely to destroy something essential, such as cutting and pasting between modules rather than cutting up the module itself. DNA learns about the world as it moves from generation to generation. Selection is a form of education. Through natural selection, starting from intrinsic sequence-dependent differences in the physical properties of DNA, information that adjusts the probability of mutation can emerge in a genome. This does not imply that there are no longer any random mutations or that all mutations are helpful. Rather, it suggests that while a genome may not have a trail to follow or a goal in the huge landscape of possible genetic changes, it is likely to have a topographic map.

As we contemplate the long road from the first life to the present, the fact that mechanisms can emerge that tend to organize genome diversity makes the journey more conceivable. The ability to handle predictable, repeated challenges is in fact the major challenge of evolution. Perhaps the most important factor in genome evolution will prove to be that the generators and stabilizers of variation themselves feel the pressure of natural selection.

Since I use the word *strategy* in talking about genomes, I have been asked whether I am calling DNA "intelligent." How should I answer that question? Can we actually use words like *intelligence* to refer to DNA, to *molecules*?[11] In table salt, sodium gives up an electron to chlorine. We could say that sodium "likes" chlorine, but if we use words that imply intelligence for such a thing, they become drained of meaning. When do we cross the border as we journey from the simple chemistry of a salt crystal to the DNA that encodes the development of our brain, and finally to the intelligence of our operating brain itself?

Is it the interaction of our brain with our environment, as we develop, that makes us become intelligent? But our genome set up the brain to experiment with the world effectively, to learn so well. Where do we get the toddler's overwhelming instinct to ask why, to insist that others "let me" do it, to see what will happen after a hard tug on the tablecloth? If the human brain is intelligent, can we avoid considering that the human genome is intelligent in some sense, since it carries the information that in the proper context develops into a functioning human brain?

I am not trying to enter into a debate about the meaning of intelligence, or to ignore the importance of the environment in which our genome finds itself, starting with a fertilized egg. Rather, I mention intelligence here to encourage us to pause to reflect on the apparent wisdom of our shared human genome, which connects us across time through generations of partnerships. This reflection has important implications for genetic medicine. We can harvest and dissolve salt crystals, but should we look at our own genome in the same way, as a set of building blocks to play with?

If we see a "broken" regulator that turns genes on, perhaps we should consider the possibility that this "malfunction" may protect some people from a renegade gene somewhere else in the genome by keeping it safely off. The same gene that may be helpful in one person's genome, with its unique mix of genes, may actually be harmful in someone else's genome, because of interactions between the activities of different genes. When we see "mistakes," should we blithely start "fixing" them when we do not understand so much of the information that our genome contains? Until we understand the genome's multiple, networked interactions, can we, with confidence, remove something from the human germ line and assume that we know what we did?

Whether in our own immune system, in our developing, learning brain, or in our nine-month journey from a single cell to a new beloved individual, the apparent wisdom that we have glimpsed in genomes should in fact humble us in the face of what we do not yet understand. With even more trepidation than that expressed by Lewis Thomas,[12] who had no doubt that he would rather take command of a 747 airliner on which he was a passenger than be put in charge of his own liver, we should approach our germ-line genome with humility—indeed, with awe.

Suppose HIV's timing had been a little different, so that it did not catch our global attention until some years into the twenty-first century, after whole genome surveys and "fixing damaged genes" might have become feasible, or even routine. Might we have been tempted, in the interim, to fix those broken CCR5 receptors, perhaps because fixing them would protect some people from a virus we had encountered in the interim? Had we purged the broken CCR5 from our collective genome, even more people could have died from AIDS when HIV burst on the scene.[13] Our genome would not have had a chance to teach us the potential advantages of inactivating genes such as those that encode CCR5. Does a "broken" gene protect some people who survive exposure to the Ebola virus? "Fixing" human diversity destroys information that we may need as microbes continue to probe our bodies and challenge our chronically underfunded international public health infrastructure.[14]

As we look at the germ-line genome, we should begin our study not as teachers, engineers, and doctors, but rather as students. Then, as we look closely, will we come to see intelligence in genomes? Perhaps we will. After all, how did we get to be so smart?

Epilogue

What Became of the First Genome?

None of them died, they only changed, were always reborn, continually had a new face . . . and all these forms and faces rested, flowed, reproduced, swam past and merged into each other, and over them all there was continually something thin . . . this smile of unity over the flowing forms.

—Siddhartha Hermann Hesse, trans. Hilda Rosner

The hair mother brushed from your head when you were four turned to dust then. Taken up by the birds of the air, some still blooms, even now, within flowers in the gardens of the place where you were raised.

You are no longer that small child, but still you are connected to that child. Through our breath and from our food, molecules come into us and stay for a while. They are broken up into their atoms, which we use to construct the molecules of our lives. They pass through us—perhaps through our heart, or our biceps—and then out. Atoms that connect in our bones, or in the backbone of our DNA, may stay longer. Atoms in a molecule that signals part of a thought between our nerves may be gone in less time.[1] But as atoms come and go, we remain here, ourselves.

This will last for some time—a rich time, full of all the joys and sorrows of a life. As we move through the world, organizing atoms into us, something in turn has organized us. A unique variation of the human genome, a gift from our parents, was the seed of our entry into this world. The genome we carry came to us as a cousin of all of the genomes on Earth, borne by generations of connections reaching back across time. Information in today's genomes will move on to new progeny and new experiments, generation after generation into the future.

Much as atoms flow through us in a lifetime, genes flow through us between generations. When our genome is moving through us to be reassorted in pieces and shared in the future with the genomes of many others whom we may never meet, do we feel no kinship with these others? I envision a large, inverted family reunion picnic gathering together all of the people now alive who will become my relatives in the future. Two hundred years from now, their descendants might marry into "my" family by marrying a descendant of my nephews or nieces. If these descendants' daughter were to come back to us from the future and read the newspapers, she might be alarmed at how we are treating each other. She might warn us that we are about to injure one of her great-great-grandfathers. Instead, she might say, we should invite him to the picnic.

As I visited the Gettysburg battlefield—so peaceful now, covered with green grass—I thought of absent friends, the empty spaces in our world, and the courageous fallen, whose never-born great-grandchildren are missing from our world today. What would those soldiers have said to us as they died on that field in Pennsylvania? Perhaps some would have been as eloquent as Dawid Graber, a 19-year-old lost in the Warsaw Ghetto, who left us a buried note: "We would be the fathers, the teachers, and educators of the future. We would be the grandfather of the bards who tell to the grandsons, to the young, the story of victories and defeats of staying alive and of perishing. How they would cock their ears."[2] And how we would listen to the struggles and triumphs of those who came before.

Now when I hear the words "shadow of death," I forever will recall a large shadow that passed over me quickly, moving north to south, on a sky-blue September morning. Concentrating on my work, I did not focus on the large airliner that flew too low, 400 feet above me. Less than a minute later, it crashed into the north tower of the World Trade Center. From those burning hours of terror emerged beautiful gifts too, bought at an immeasurable price in lives, sorrow, and pain. We were awed by the courage of those who rushed toward the flames, the determination in their hearts to rescue endangered lives. We watched the diverse faces of people with roots throughout the world fleeing from the collapsing towers, and heard their varied accents as they described the horror that had engulfed them.

Crying in the candlelight of the next days, we could see emerging from the terror a more hopeful vision of life, a vision that counters those who would divide human from human into antagonistic groups. We knew that these people who were leaning on one another as the tragedy was unfolding live in peace and enjoy one another's company, music, food, laughter, and the smiles of their children, together in New York City. These diverse people will be the seeds of generations of children that will be linked to so many others in other places around the Earth.

From the crossroads of immigration in New York, I envision the scattered houses where my grandparents and great-grandparents were born, those ancestors who first traveled here, from San Angelo all'Esca, Kiev, Warsaw, and Liverpool. After a few generations, my individual ancestors and their surroundings fade from view, but I can imagine, given the high cheekbones on my mother's side, that some were born much farther to the east.

If I stop to calculate, assuming four generations each century, it appears that, at the time the colonies declared independence here in 1776, there were, scattered throughout Europe and I have no idea where else, over 500 individual people (more if we count multiple generations alive at the same time) who knew few of the others, but all of whom became my ancestors. I step back to their place and look forward in time. How inconceivable it would have been for them that nine generations in the future a descendant of theirs would live in New York City, in a building that is considered unremarkable though it rises over 400 feet above the ground—someone who is routinely carried up and down the center of that building using a source of power that would be mysterious to them. This humbles me as I look toward the future from here.

Was one of these 500 ancestors your ancestor too? Who and where was the last ancestor that you and I share? Simply by calculating two parents for each individual, and two parents for each of them, four generations each century, you or I would have a million ancestors walking the Earth as recently as 1492. Continuing this calculation, in the year 0, the number of each of our ancestors was ten thousand billion times greater than the number of people who ever were born. This calculation is completely wrong because it counts the same ancestors over and over again; it does not capture the fact that the people we meet, whether we marry them or simply pass them on the street, are our distant cousins; our ancestors met and married distant cousins too.

The information carried in each piece of our DNA survives through a chain of individuals. Links in the chain that brought your grandfather's genes to him, yours to you, and mine to me eventually reach back to those who would count as their descendants every person on the planet. Then, from these extraordinary ancestors, there are other links, extending even further back. Much further back, there emerge some very unusual, and un-expected, distant cousins.

When we think of life on Earth, we think of the larger forms of life that we see around us: people—many of them, all around, most of the time—dogs, cats, perhaps the occasional gorilla (at least in a zoo), cows, birds, bugs, and maybe a raccoon, deer, or bear—oh, yes, and trees, flowers, celery, and house plants. These forms seem to dominate the living landscape, but if we did an actual head count, all of us big things, from people to trees, would be stuck together in a tiny corner of an inventory that would be dominated by the microbes.

In our little corner of the inventory sit all of life that can come from a fertilized egg that divides, becoming muscles, nerves, branches, leaves, and more eggs or sperm for the future. And in our little corner with us we would find a very tiny worm that we have given a fancy name, *Caenorhabditis elegans*. Although we may feel a greater kinship to a tall, imposing tree, if truth be told, this little worm, which lives in soil and rotting vegetation, eating meals of bacteria, is a much closer relative of ours than the tree. This tiny worm made history for it was the first animal genome for which we had the complete DNA sequence, and it teaches us much about ourselves. From its tiny fertilized egg grows a new adult worm, with 302 neurons, making worm decisions, sensing and responding to the world around it, to tastes, smells, temperature changes, and touch. Some of our decisions are the same as those made by the worm: Move toward food when hungry, and avoid very hot things.

Most of the genes that create us arose and survived in the ancestors of these tiny worms, and of fruit flies, tigers, bats, and seals. Many of the genes that we carry within us arose in the ancestors of the redwoods, and of the grass that sweeps across savannas and that we plant and then cut back on our lawns. Ancestors of the protozoa that cause malaria are links in *our* chain. Further back in our DNA's chain are ancestors of the fungus that makes penicillin, the bacteria that grow in the gut of a termite, the bacteria that you burn when you cook chicken thoroughly, and the bacteria that grow in hot springs. Their ancient ancestors were our ancient ancestors too.

Like us, countless other creatures must make four limbs and a head from a single fertilized egg. Flowers share with us genes that cause our cells to grow into the space around us, creating forms. Yeast, no less than we, must get through the gene mixing of meiosis. Useful genes survive and then participate in many life forms. The currents of ions that conduct our heartbeats, our muscle movements, and our thoughts rely on protein molecules similar to those used by the worm. These proteins share ancestry with proteins in the little ciliate *Paramecium* as well, enabling it to swim. All appear to be descended from the same gene, the one that cracked the problem of en-coding a protein that could allow charged molecules to move through oily membranes.[3]

The BRCA2 gene first caught our attention when we learned that in its damaged form, it increases the risk of breast cancer. When it is working properly, BRCA2 helps our cells use recombination repair to respond to DNA damage. But BRCA2 did not arise suddenly when people, or even breasts, first arose. All life on Earth faces genome damage. On the mustard weed's chromosome 4, there is a gene that encodes a protein in which nearly 40 percent of its amino acid sequence is the same as that of our BRCA2.[4] This is a close resemblance, considering that, since there are 20 amino acids to choose from, there is only a 5 percent chance of two proteins being the same at any individual amino acid. A protein like mustard weed BRCA2, which has 126 amino acids, would have $(1/20)^{126}$ chance of matching our BRCA2 sequence. The last common great-great-great-etc.-grandparent of the mustard weed and of us—a single cell with a nucleus, whom we certainly would not recognize, or even notice, if we passed it on the street—lived about 1.5 billion years ago.

The plants and even the tiniest bacteria—and even the tinier-still viruses—are all profoundly connected to us at the heart of life, for like us they all have genomes of DNA or RNA. The fact that we all use proteins and carbohydrates means that we share even more, for we all must copy our chemically similar genomes and build up our chemically similar molecules using highly similar molecular infrastructures, and must power ourselves with the same sources of energy. In this there is a line of kinship connecting all life on Earth, a kinship that separates us from the gray stones we walk upon and the blue sky whose molecules we breathe.

In a family, one son and his children and their children may carry on the family business while one daughter and her children and their children go into medicine. So, too, some lines of life on Earth, descended from a common parent, continued to thrive as single cells, while others began to explore variations that were multicellular. From their first days on Earth, and continuing from generation to generation, life and genomes have been explorers.

Some evolutionary theorists calculate that, since we share half of our genes with our brothers and sisters and an eighth of them with our first cousins, it is in our interest to be altruistic. We would sacrifice our lives, these theorists suggest, to save two siblings or eight cousins in order to pre-serve the information in our genome. Of course, when we rush to an endangered family member's side, it is out of love, not calculation. Aside from discounting love and family partnership, these calculations make a fundamental error in that they focus on the differences between each individual and all the rest of life, when we are in fact so similar.

A look at the genomes themselves makes it quite clear that the information in the genes of any two people on Earth, even if they are "perfect strangers," is in fact 99.97 percent shared.[5] If we were to seek to save half of the information in our genome, how far away among the species would we have to wander? Right now, the widely quoted estimate is that we share 98 percent of the sequence of our genome with our closest relative, the chimp.[6] While I expect that differences in repeated sequence and genome structure will lower this number, genome structure also connects us with many other species. Although the last ancestor that we shared with mice is estimated to have lived about 100 million years ago, most of our chromosome 20 has similar genes to those on mouse chromosome 2, lined up in a similar order. A stretch of over 90 million letters on human chromosome 4 is descended from the same ancestral patch of DNA as the letters on mouse chromosome 5. Our chromosomes have large blocks of segments in common with fish, and even with invertebrates such as the fly and the worm.

We are connected to other beings by heritage, but also by specialization and cooperation. We have learned to share, as if one family member grew the tomatoes and another made the tomato sauce. We have come to rely on plants (and the bacteria in our guts) to make the vitamins that we need to keep our metabolism running, but that our genome has forgotten how to make for itself. Because we kept eating plants, we lost the family recipe for vitamins. We cannot live without the products of the plants, just as the pathogens that live inside our cells, like *Mycobacterium leprae*, which feed on many of our metabolic juices, could never live without us animals. As we eat the energy that plants have stored from the sun, either by eating the plants themselves or by eating other animals that have eaten the plants, we transform this from stored to fast energy, using much of the same chemistry and enzymes similar to those of all life on Earth.

Successful genomes—those that have been handed down from generation to generation and have reached us across billions of years—have learned quite a bit about how to survive in changing circumstances. Starting with the tiny ones, genomes have been built up. Once a concept is in place, such as how to move ions across a cell membrane, variation creates selectivity for different ions, and regulation connects the actions of those individual molecules into an emerging whole life. A genome is copied, varied, and shared among its multiple descendants, learning by selection what thrives and what doesn't survive—a form of education about the world that becomes incorporated into our DNA. We are like our parents, but not exactly; both the resemblance and the exploration keep our chain of life reaching to the future. Many organisms don't get it exactly right and many die,[7] but rather than representing an unavoidable destructive force, the risk taking inherent in mutation generates the variation on which selection acts. Through it all, life continues to build on possibilities. There are many viable forms of genomes that have not yet been conceived. Changes in a genome serve as questions about the world, and represent ripples of hope that no matter what we encounter, there will be genomes on this Earth that will be survivors. Will the survivors always include human genomes?

The image of our isolated home, the Earth, an inviting blue world wreathed in white clouds circling in the deep blackness of space, should stop us in our tracks. It should spur us on to protect our planet, with its thin rim of air and its diverse gifts of life, but somehow we get distracted, day to day. So, too, should we take a step back and absorb the knowledge we carry within us, encoded in an ancient helical ribbon. Soon, when the view of our genome no longer is limited to a few thousand scientists in laboratories busily sorting it all out, when we all can look at it and understand it and talk about it, we will see our deep kinship to one another and our connection to all life on Earth. We were created together, and in the long run our fates are intertwined.

Glossary

AMINO ACID   Molecules that contain, in addition to other atoms that define the particular amino acid, two groups of atoms called amino and acid groups, respectively. Amino acids play a variety of important roles in biology. Twenty specific amino acids, ranging in size from 10 to 27 atoms, are the "building blocks" of our proteins. In forming proteins, the acid group of one amino acid is connected to the amino group of the next amino acid in the chain.

BASE PAIR   Letters A and T or G and C paired with each other in a double helix. In this book, I have generally used the term *letter pair* instead of *base pair*.

CHROMOSOME   A single DNA molecule at its core. Chromosomes carry genetic information from generation to generation. Chromosomes are numbered in order from the largest (1) to the smallest. Most humans have 46 chromosomes in 23 pairs; they receive one chromosome in each pair from their father and one from their mother.

CODON   Three letters that specify which amino acid to add to a growing protein chain (listed in Figure 3-1).

DEGENERATE CODE   A code that has more than one way of encoding the same thing. For example, the same amino acid can be encoded by more than one codon.

DNA   A widely used abbreviation for the technical term *deoxyribonucleic acid*. DNA is a double helix. Each of the strands of the helix is a linear string of letters, A, T, G, and C, which represent the chemical building blocks of DNA. The letters are linked together through the sugar deoxyribose and phosphate groups, which are made up of atoms of oxygen and phosphorus. The different information that is carried by different DNA molecules is encoded in the order of the letters.

DOUBLE-STRAND BREAK   A cut that extends across both strands of a DNA double helix.

ENZYME   Usually a protein, but sometimes RNA, that serves as a catalyst. Such catalysts are essential to life; they enable chemical changes to happen much more rapidly than they would without such a catalyst present.

EXON   The sequence that remains in RNA after the introns are removed.

GENE   A stretch of letters in a genome that encodes a specific function, such as a stretch of DNA that encodes the information needed to make a protein.

GENE CONVERSION   Changing the information in a patch of one DNA molecule to match the information in a patch from another DNA molecule.

GENE EXPRESSION   Transcribing the information from a gene into RNA.

GENE FAMILY   Genes with similar, but not identical, sequences that are related in that they are descended from extra copies of the same gene.

GENETIC CODE   The code by which the amino acids that make up our proteins are encoded in our DNA, as given in Figure 3-1. (This is its most widely used meaning; technically, this term also can and has been used to include other information encoded in DNA.)

GENOME   All of the information carried between generations by DNA (or, in the case of a few viruses, RNA).

HAIRPIN   A structure that arises when one strand of DNA loops back and partners with itself, generally obeying the pairing rules (A with T and G with C), as described in Chapter 4.

HOT SPOTS AND COLD SPOTS   Intrinsic variations in the probability of mutation at different points along the DNA.

HOUSEKEEPING GENES   Genes that encode the proteins that are involved in the routine, everyday chores of life shared by most cells, such as turning sugar into energy, copying and repairing DNA, and constructing protein-making machinery.

HUMAN GENOME   Three billion letters that carry, through their order, the information transmitted between generations.

HYPERMUTATION   Mutation that is much more rapid than at other locations in the same genome.

INTRONS   Letters that are transcribed from DNA into RNA, but then cut out of the RNA before, for example, the RNA goes to the protein factories.

LAGGING STRAND   The strand of DNA that is copied in a discontinuous way as described in Chapter 4; this method of copying is required because the two strands of DNA are antiparallel, yet both must be copied from left to right.

LEADING STRAND   The strand of DNA that is copied straight through.

LETTERS   The term used in this book for chemicals that are linked together to build DNA: A, T, G, and C, which encode, through their order, the information that is contained in a molecule of DNA. These letters represent four different but related chemicals, adenine, guanine, thymine, and cytosine. A and G are similar to each other, and bigger than T and C. RNA uses U (uracil) in place of T.

MEIOSIS   A form of cell division that takes place in the germ line; DNA is copied once, but the cell divides twice, taking a diploid cell to a haploid cell, which then will combine with another haploid cell (e.g., sperm and egg) to form a new diploid cell that is thus a member of the next generation.

MEMBRANE   A lipid-containing barrier; for example, the barrier between the outside world and the inside of each cell.

MESSENGER RNA   A polymer that carries the instructions from DNA to the protein-making machinery.

MISMATCH   A place in the DNA double helix that does not obey the **pairing rules**.

MITOSIS   A form of cell division that produces two daughter cells, each with the same number of chromosomes as the cell that divided (46 for a typical human cell).

MODULE   The term used in this book to mean any functional unit in the genome; a module may encode a region of DNA that is involved in turning a neighboring gene on or off, or it might encode part of a protein with a specific structure and function.

MUTAGEN   Something that causes a mutation.

MUTATION   A change in one or more letters in the genome.

NATURAL SELECTION   The term that Darwin used when he proposed that those most fit for life in a given environment would be more likely to survive and breed.

NUCLEOTIDE   A letter attached to a linker, the building blocks of DNA and RNA.

PAIRING RULES   In a DNA double helix, an A on one strand is paired with a T on the other strand, and a G on one strand is paired with a C on the other.

PLASMIDS   Extra pieces of DNA in bacteria in addition to chromosomes.

POLYMERASES   Enzymes that build strands of genetic material. An enzyme that copies DNA into DNA is a DNA polymerase; an enzyme that copies DNA into RNA is an RNA polymerase.

PROOFREADING   One of the DNA copying machinery's tasks; it double-checks that it has inserted the correct letter in the growing DNA chain. It assumes that the information in the template strand is correct.

PROTEIN   A molecule made up of one or more strings of amino acids; the amino acids in each string are connected in the order that they are encoded in a genome using the genetic code. Proteins have a wide range of jobs in our bodies; for example, distinct proteins carry oxygen to our tissues, fight infections, make up our muscles, and serve as enzymes, including those that copy DNA.

READING FRAME   Since information in DNA is a string of letters, and since amino acids are encoded by groups of three letters, it is necessary to know where to begin reading the information encoded in the DNA so as to block it out into the correct groups of three letters.

RECEPTOR   A protein that specifically binds to another molecule and signals the cell of the other molecule's presence.

RECOMBINATION   Transfer of information between two DNA molecules.

RNA   A substance that is similar to DNA, but that uses a different sugar as a linker between its letters and uses the letter U (uracil) instead of T. Typically, RNA is single-stranded, but it folds up using the pairing rules as well as through more complex structures, often involving modifications of its letters. The genome of some viruses, such as polio and flu, is made of RNA rather than DNA, and can be double stranded; RNA plays a wide range of roles in all organisms, including acting as the messenger that carries the protein-coding information transcribed from DNA, taking part in the operation of the protein factory, and helping in DNA synthesis; some of its many roles are described in Chapter 16.

SEQUENCE OF A GENOME   All of the letters in a genome, in order. Once this is determined, it remains necessary to decode the information encoded by these letters. Protein coding information, for example, is decoded using the genetic code illustrated in Figure 3-1.

SERINE PROTEASES   A family of protein-cutting enzymes that share the concept of using the amino acid serine (S) as a molecular sword to cut through other proteins.

SLIPPERY DNA   Sequences such as TTTT or CAATCAATCAATCAAT where the template and the new DNA strands may become misaligned, for example, during copying, leading to the addition or deletion of a repeat unit.

SUBSTRATE   For each enzyme, a specific molecule that the enzyme can change into another molecule. An enzyme can have more than one substrate.

SYNONYMOUS CODONS   Different groups of three letters that encode the same amino acid; it is possible to have synonymous codons because the genetic code is degenerate.

TEMPLATE STRAND   When the two strands of DNA in a double helix separate to be copied, each of these strands becomes a template strand and is used by the DNA copying machinery to determine the order in which letters are connected in the strand that will become its partner in a new double helix.

TRANSPOSE   To move DNA to a new location.

TRANSPOSON   A "jumping gene"; a piece of DNA that can move from one place in a genome to another, and also sometimes can move between genomes. To move, a transposon depends upon an enzyme called a transposase. Some transposons can move in the form of RNA; if so, they are copied back into DNA that is inserted into a new spot in the genome.

TRIPLET CODE   Amino acids are encoded by letters taken three at a time as illustrated in Figure 3.1. For example GAC instructs the protein-assembling machinery to add the amino acid D. As each of the three letters in a codon can be any one of DNA's four letters, there are $4 \times 4 \times 4 = 64$ possible codons.

TUNING KNOBS   A term proposed for DNA sequences such as TTTTTT that tend to lengthen and shorten more easily than the rest of the DNA in that genome.

TURNING ON A GENE   Activating the machinery that copies the information in a gene into RNA; for regions of DNA that encode proteins, copying the information in the gene into RNA is the first step in making a protein.

Notes

Preface

1. Alfred Russel Wallace, *The Malay Archipelago* (1869; reprint, Oxford: Oxford University Press, 1991), p. 419.
2. F. Sanger, A. R. Coulson, T. Friedmann, et al., "The Nucleotide Sequence of Bacteriophage phiX174," *Journal of Molecular Biology*, 125, no. 2 (1978): 225–246.
3. Lynn Helena Caporale, "Is There a Higher Level Genetic Code That Directs Evolution," *Molecular and Cellular Biochemistry*, 64 (1984): 5–13.
4. Harley McAdams and Adam Arkin, "Simulation of Prokaryotic Genetic Circuits," *Annual Reviews of Biophysics and Biomolecular Structure*, 27 (1998): 199–224.

Prologue   Chance Favors the Prepared Genome

1. http://www.netspace.org/MendelWeb/.
2. Miroslav Radman, "Mutation: Enzymes of Evolutionary Change," *Nature*, 401 (1999): 866–869.
3. Werner Arber, "Involvement of Gene Products in Bacterial Evolution," in Lynn Helena Caporale, ed., *Molecular Strategies in Biological Evolution, Annals of the New York Academy of Sciences*, 870 (1999): 36–44. In several places in these notes I have referred to this Annals volume, rather than to other sources in which the author discussed the referenced subject. I have chosen the Annals volume because its goal was to put the talks in context, with an introduction to the papers in each session; it also includes summaries of the discussions.
4. Lynn Helena Caporale, "Is There a Higher Level Genetic Code That Directs Evolution," *Molecular and Cellular Biochemistry*, 64 (1984): 5–13.
5. Charles Darwin, *On the Origin of Species*, available on line at http://www.talk origins.org/faqs/origin.html.

Chapter 1   Diversity or Death

1. Y. Feng, C. C. Broder, P. E. Kennedy, and E. A. Berger, "HIV-1 Entry Cofactor: Functional cDNA Cloning of a Seven-Transmembrane, G Protein-Coupled Receptor, *Science*, 272 (1996): 872–877.
2. Kunal Saha, Jianchao Zhang, Anil Gupta, et al., "Isolation of Primary HIV-1 That Target CD8+ T Lymphocytes Using CD8 as a Receptor," *Nature Medicine*, 7 (2001): 65–72.

3. Alshad S. Lalani, Jennifer Masters, Wei Zeng, et al., "Use of Chemokine Receptors by Poxviruses," *Science*, 286 (1999): 1968–1971.
4. Allan Rosenfield, *Dean's View*, Mailman School of Public Health, fall 2000, New York: Columbia University.
5. http://mosquito.who.int/amd/abuja2002_facts.htm.
6. http://www.who.int/bulletin/pdf/2001/issue8/vol79.no.8.704–712.pdf.
7. A little bird, its skin raw in spots where its feathers were rubbed off as it pushed over rocks to look for seeds, during drought that decimated the finch population, was observed by Peter and Rosemary Grant and their co-workers and described in Jonathan Weiner's book *The Beak of the Finch*, Vintage Books, 1995. David Modiano, Gaia Luoni, et al., "Haemoglobin C Protects against Clinical *Plasmodium falciparum* Malaria," *Nature* 414 (2001): 305–308.
8. Alfred Russel Wallace, *My Life, My Life: A Record of Events and Opinions*, 2 vols. (New York: Dodd, Mead, 1905).

Chapter 2   The Magic Staircase

1. From a March 1953 draft of a paper by Franklin and Gosling, prepared before learning of the Crick-Watson structure as described in a biography written by a friend of Franklin's, Anne Sayre, *Rosalind Franklin and DNA* (New York: W H Norton & Co., 1975). See also Aaron Klug, "Rosalind Franklin and the Discovery of the Structure of DNA," *Nature*, 219 (1968): 808–810. Rosalind Franklin's ground-breaking research is mentioned briefly in Chapter 7; for those interested in reading more about Franklin, I recommend Sharon Bertsch McGrayne's *Nobel Prize Women in Science* (Carol Publishing Group, 1998).
2. See Chapter 3, especially Figure 3.1, for a fuller explanation.
3. M. S. Boosalis, J. Petruska, and M. F. Goodman, "DNA Polymerase Insertion Fidelity," *Journal of Biological Chemistry*, 262 (1987):14689–14696.
4. R. M. Schaaper and R. L. Dunn, "Spontaneous Mutation in the *Escherichia coli* lacI gene," Genetics, 129 (19991): 317–326.
5. As Roel Schaaper describes it (personal communication), to prevent Cs from replacing Ts, mismatch repair is most likely removing Gs that were added across from Ts. (It is much more unusual to find a C added across from an A.) To prevent Ts from replacing Cs, mismatch repair is mostly removing not only Ts added across from Gs but also As added across from Cs.
6. J. Jiricny, "Mediating Mismatch Repair," *Nature Genetics*, 24 (2000): 6–8.
7. Toshiro Matsuda, Katarzyna Bebenek, Chikahide Masutani, et al., "Proof-reading of DNA Polymerase η-Dependent Replication Errors," *Journal of Biological Chemistry*, 26 (2001): 2317–2320.

Chapter 3   Predators Battle Prey in the Genome

1. *Buddhism without Religion* (Riverhead Books, 1997).
2. http://grimwade.biochem.unimelb.edu.au/cone/deathby.html.
3. Baldomero M. Olivera, "E. E. Just Lecture, 1996: Conus Venom Peptides, Receptor and Ion Channel Targets, and Drug Design: 50 Million Years of Neuropharmacology," *Molecular Biology of the Cell*, 8 (1997): 2101–2109.

4. Baldomero M. Olivera, C. Walker, G. E. Cartier, et al., "Speciation of Cone Snails and Interspecific Hyperdivergence of Their Venom Peptides: Potential Evolutionary Significance of Introns," in Lynn Helena Caporale, ed., *Molecular Strategies in Biological Evolution, Annals of the New York Academy of Sciences Annals of the N Y Academy of Science*, 870 (1999): 223–237. It is very interesting, and it may be a hint as to the mechanism that in the midst of all of this variation, codons for the structurally important amino acid cysteine (also known as "C") are reported not to change, even between synonyms. See Silvestro G. Conticello, Yitzak Pilpel, Gustavo Glusman, and Mike Fainzilber, "Position-Specific Codon Conservation in Hypervariable Gene Families," *Trends in Genetics*, 16 (2000): 57–59.
5. J.-R. Zhang, J. M. Hardham, A. G. Barbour, and S. J. Norris, "Antigenic Variation in Lyme Disease *Borreliae* by Promiscuous Recombination of VMP-Like Sequence Cassettes," *Cell*, 89 (1997): 275–285.

Chapter 4   Mutation Is Not Monotonous

1. Lynn Ripley, "Predictability of Mutant Sequences," in Lynn Helena Caporale, ed., *Molecular Strategies in Biological Evolution, Annals of the New York Academy of Sciences Annals of the N Y Academy of Science*, 870 (1999): 159–172.
2. M. A. El Hassan and C. R. Calladine, "Two Distinct Modes of Protein-Induced Bending in DNA," *Journal of Molecular Biology*, 18 (1998): 331–343.
3. Ripley, loc. cit.
4. Reiji Okazaki, Tuneko Okazaki, Kiwako Sakabe, et al., "In Vivo Mechanism of DNA Chain Growth," *Cold Spring Harbor Symposium on Quantitative Biology*, 33 (1968): 129–143. A recent review is Ulrich Hübscher and Yeon-Soo Seo, "Replication of the Lagging Strand: A Concert of at Least 23 Polypeptides," *Molecules and Cells*, 12 (2001): 149–157.
5. R. R. Sinden, V. I. Hashem, and W. A. Rosche. "DNA-Directed Mutations: Leading and Lagging Strand Specificity," in Caporale, ed., *Molecular Strategies*, op. cit., pp. 173–189.
6. For example, see D. J. Futuyma, *Evolutionary Biology* (Sunderland, Mass.: Sinauer Associates, 1986), p.12.
7. Charles Darwin, *On the Origin of Species*, available online at http://www.talk origins.org/faqs/origin.html.

Chapter 5   What the Antibody Genes Tell Us

1. Ernst Mayr, *What Evolution Is* (New York Basic Books, 2001).
2. The original demonstration that DNA actually changes during development of the immune system was reported in this classic reference: N. Hozumi and S. Tonegawa, "Evidence for Somatic Rearrangement of Immunoglobulin Genes Coding for Variable and Constant Regions," *Proceedings of the National Academy of Sciences of the USA*, 73 (1976): 3628–3632. More information about much of the unreferenced material regarding gene rearrangements in the

immune system can be found in most introductory biochemistry and immunology textbooks.

3. This legend is supported by my father, who listened to the game on the radio.

4. J. Yelamos, N. Klix, B. Goyenechea, et al., "Targeting of Non-Ig Sequences in Place of the V Segment by Somatic Hypermutation," *Nature*, 376 (1995): 225–229.

5. There is a high rate of errors at specific codons (often at purine-rich codons, e.g., RGYW motifs) in the right sequence context. The initial statistical analysis that specific sequences hypermutate is reported in I. B. Rogozin and N. A. Kolchanov, "Somatic Hypermutagenesis in Immunoglobulin Genes: II. Influence of Neighbouring Base Sequences on Mutagenesis," *Biochimica et Biophysica Acta*, 1171 (1992): 11–18.

For an introduction to the issues of sequence context and focused hypermutation, see C. Rada and C. Milstein, "Sequence Context: The Intrinsic Hypermutability of Antibody Heavy and Light Chain Genes Decays Exponentially," *EMBO Journal*, 20, no.16 (2001): 4570–4576. This report contains references to the classic (1966) proposal of targeted mutation by Sydney Brenner and César Milstein. See also Beatriz Goyenechea and César Milstein, "Modifying the Sequence of an Immunoglobulin V-Gene Alters the Resulting Pattern of Hypermutation," *Proceedings of the National Academy of Sciences of the USA*, 93 (1996): 13979–13984, a discussion of what focuses mutation on a certain sequence, including a report that changes between "synonymous" codons change the sites of mutation.

6. Recent initial support for the hypothesis that mutations may be targeted by an enzyme that cuts a piece off some Cs in DNA can be found in S. K. Petersen-Mahrt, R. S. Harris, and M. S. Neuberger, "AID Mutates *E. coli*, Suggesting a DNA Deaminating Mechanism for Antibody Diversification," *Nature*, 418 (2002): 99–103.

7. Julian Sale, D. Calandrini, M. Takata, et al., "Ablation of XRCC2/3 Transforms Immunoglobulin V Gene Conversion into Somatic Hypermutation," *Nature*, 412 (2001): 921–926.

8. P. J. Gearhart and R. D. Wood, "Emerging Links between Hypermutation of Antibody Genes and DNA Polymerases," *Nature Review of Immunology*, 1 (2001): 187–192.

9. Tasuko Jonjo, Kazuo Kinoshita, and Masamichi Muramatsu, "Molecular Mechanism of Class Switch Recombination: Linkage with Somatic Hypermutation," *Annual Review of Immunology*, 20 (2002): 165–196.

10. Hui Sun, Akiko Yabuki, and Nancy Maizels, "A Human Nuclease Specific for G4 DNA," *Proceedings of the National Academy of Sciences of the USA*, 98 (2001): 12444–12449.

Chapter 6   Slippery DNA and Tuning Knobs

1. Barbara E. Wright, "Minireview: A Biochemical Mechanism for Nonrandom Mutations and Evolution," *Journal of Bacteriology*, 182 (2000): 2993–3001. Barbara Wright's experiments explore the controversial concept that when

bacteria are stressed by lack of nutrients, mutations become more likely in those genes that are turned on by that stress and copied into RNA, in effect "focusing" mutation on genes that may be useful in overcoming the stress. In certain yeast, starvation leads to the genetic variation inherent in mating, and, in addition, the sites of variation may be affected by nutritional status (see Chapters 17 and 18 for a discussion of meiosis; also see Mohamad F. F. Abdullah and Rhona H. Borts, "Meiotic Recombination Frequencies Are Affected by Nutritional States in *Saccharomyces cerevisiae*," *Proceedings of the National Academy of Sciences of the USA*, 98 (2001): 14524–14529.

2. R. Kelly, M. Gibbs, A. Collick, and A. J. Jeffreys, "Spontaneous Mutation at the Hypervariable Mouse Minisatellite Locus Ms6-hm: Flanking DNA Sequence and Analysis of Germline and Early Somatic Mutation Events," *Proceedings of the Royal Society of London, Series B: Biological Sciences*, 245, no. 1314 (1991): 235–245.

3. Juan José Miret, Luis Pessoa-Brandão, and Robert S. Lahue, "Orientation-Dependent and Sequence-Specific Expansions of CTG/CAG Trinucleotide Repeats in *Saccharomyces cerevisiae*," *Proceedings of the National Academy of Sciences of the USA*, 95 (1998): 12438–12443.

4. T. Simonsson, "G-Quadruplex Structures: Variations on a Theme," *Biological Chemistry*, 382, no. 4 (2001): 621–628.

5. http://www.woodyguthrie.org/biography.htm.

6. The Huntington's Disease Collaborative Research Group, "A Novel Gene Containing a Trinucleotide Repeat That Is Expanded and Unstable on Huntington's Disease Chromosomes," *Cell*, 72 (1993): 971–983.

7. http://www.hdsa.org/.

8. E. P. Leeflang, S. Tavare, P. Marjoram, et al., "Analysis of Germline Mutation Spectra at the Huntington's Disease Locus Supports a Mitotic Mutation Mechanism," *Human Molecular Genetics*, 8, no. 2 (1999): 173–183. There is a report, based on work in mice, that further expansion of CAG takes place in those brain cells that are most affected by this disease: Laura Kennedy and Peggy F. Shelbourne, "Dramatic Mutation Instability in HD Mouse Striatum: Does Polyglutamine Load Contribute to Cell-Specific Vulnerability in Huntington's Disease?" *Human Molecular Genetics*, 9 (2000): 2539–2544.

9. C. J. Cummings and H. Y. Zoghbi, "Trinucleotide Repeats: Mechanisms and Pathophysiology," *Annual Review of Genomics and Human Genetics*, 1(2000): 281–328.

10. C. L. Liquori, K. Ricker, M. L. Moseley, et al., "Myotonic Dystrophy Type 2 Caused by a CCTG Expansion in Intron 1 of ZNF9," *Science*, 293 (2001): 864–867.

11. Christopher D. Bayliss, Dawn Field, and E. Richard Moxon, "The Simple Sequence Contingency Loci of *Haemophilus influenzae* and *Neisseria meningitidis*," *Journal of Clinical Investigation*, 107, no. 6 (2001): 657–666.

12. Alex van Belkum, Stewart Scherer, Loek van Alphen, and Henri Verbrugh, "Short-Sequence DNA Repeats in Prokaryotic Genomes," *Microbiology and Molecular Biology Reviews*, 62 (1998): 275–293.

13. Yulin Cheng, Sara M. Dylla, and Charles L. Turnbough, Jr., "A Long T · A Tract in the upp Initially Transcribed Region Is Required for Regulation of upp Expression by UTP-Dependent Reiterative Transcription in *Escherichia coli*," *Journal of Bacteriology*, 183 (2001): 221–228.

14. S. Hammerschmidt, A. Muller, H. Sillmann, et al., "Capsule Phase Variation in *Neisseria meningitidis* Serogroup B by Slipped-Strand Mispairing in the Polysialyltransferase Gene (siaD): Correlation with Bacterial Invasion and the Outbreak of Meningococcal Disease," *Molecular Microbiology*, 20 (1996): 1211–1220.

15. Belkum et al., loc. cit.

16. Bayliss et al., loc. cit.

17. H. P. Gerber, K. Seipel, O. Georgiev, et al., "Transcriptional Activation Modulated by Homopolymeric Glutamine and Proline Stretches," *Science*, 263 (1994): 808–811.

18. Lesley A. Sawyer, J. Michael Hennessy, Alexandre A. Peixoto, et al., "Natural Variation in a *Drosophila* Clock Gene and Temperature Compensation," *Science*, 278 (1997): 2117–2120.

19. Edward Trifonov, "Elucidating Sequence Codes: Three Codes for Evolution," in Lynn Helena Caporale, ed., *Molecular Strategies in Biological Evolution, Annals of the New York Academy of Sciences*, 870: 330–338.

20. Y. Kashi, D. King, and M. Soller, "Simple Sequence Repeats as a Source of Quantitative Genetic Variation," *Trends in Genetics*, 13, no. 2 (1997): 74–78.

21. Charles Darwin, *On the Origin of Species*, available online at http://www.talk origins.org/faqs/origin.html.

22. A. J. Jeffreys, V. Wilson, and S. L. Thein, "Individual-Specific 'Fingerprints' of Human DNA," *Nature*, 316 (1985): 76–79.

23. George W. Cox, Lynn S. Taylor, Jonathan D. Willis, et al., "Molecular Cloning and Characterization of a Novel Mouse Macrophage Gene That Encodes a Nuclear Protein Comprising Polyglutamine Repeats and Interspersing Histidines," *Journal of Biology and Chemistry*, 271 (1996): 25515–25523.

24. This is a brief reference to an important field of discussion in evolution involving functional modules that interact with one another. The author of a soon to be published book on this subject kindly sent me a few chapters: Mary Jane West-Eberhard, *Developmental Plasticity and Evolution* (Oxford University Press, 2002). Also see the notes to Chapter 14.

25. S. T. Pullarket et al., "Thymidylate Synthase Gene Polymorphism Determines Response and Toxicity of 5-FU Chemotherapy," *The Pharmacogenomcs Journal*, 1 (2001): 165–170. There is more discussion of the relevance of slips to cancer prognosis in Chapter 11.

Chapter 7   Everyone Has Something to Teach Us

1. Werner Arber, "Science for the Twenty-First Century, World Conference on Science, UNESCO, 2000, pp. 24–25. Werner Arber received the Nobel prize in 1978 for his work on understanding what determines whether and where bacteria will chop up the DNA that enters them. As discussed in the introduction, this chapter, and Chapter 19, he has written about "evolutionary genes," genes that generate diversity. Professor Arber's efforts currently are focused on work with international scientific organizations, with the goal, described in the cited reference, of improving the well-being of people and their environments around the world.

2. For all of the *E. coli* calculations, I am indebted to the enthusiasm and creativity of Stephen Farrier.

3. Maclyn McCarty, *The Transforming Principle: Discovering that Genes Are Made of DNA* (New York: W.W. Norton & Co., 1985).

4. Oswald T. Avery, Colin M. MacLeod, Maclyn McCarty, "Studies on the Chemical Nature of the Substance Inducing Transformation of Pneumococcal Types," *Journal of Experimental Medicine,* 79 (1944): 137–158.

5. The observation that A = T and G = C was named *Chargaff's rules* after the discoverer of these fixed ratios. Erwin Chargaff," Chemical Specificity of Nucleic Acids and Mechanism for Their Enzymatic Degradation, *Experientia,* 6 (1950): 201–209.

6. Quoted by René J. Dubois in *The Professor, The Institute, and DNA* (New York: The Rockefeller University Press, 1976).

7. Watson describes this theft in his book *The Double Helix.* Aaron Klug, who was awarded the Nobel prize in 1982 for his ability to determine the structure of complexes between large molecules such as DNA and protein, analyzed Rosalind Franklin's notebooks to assess how close Franklin had been to solving the structure of DNA without the need for Watson and Crick. Klug is quoted as saying, "It is rather heartbreaking to look at these notebooks and to see how close she had come. . . ." (Sharon Bertsch-McGrayne, *Nobel Prize Women in Science,* Carol Publishing Group, p. 323). Francis Crick became friends with Franklin in the years after the discovery and before her death at age 37; he is quoted (Ann Sayre, *Rosalind Franklin and DNA,* New York: WH Norton & Co., 1975, p. 166) as saying that Franklin would have arrived at the correct structure in "perhaps three weeks. Three months is likelier."

8. C. L. C. Wielders, M. R. Vriens, S. Brisse, et al., "Evidence for In-Vivo Transfer of mecA DNA between *Staphylococci, Lancet,* 357, no. 9269 (2001): 1674–1675.

9. M. M. Hobbs, A. Seiler, M. Achtman, and J. G. Cannon, "Microevolution within a Clonal Population of Pathogenic Bacteria: Recombination, Gene Duplication and Horizontal Genetic Exchange in the opa Gene Family of *Neisseria meningitidis," Molecular Microbiology,* 12, no. 2 (1994): 171–180.

10. Nicole Perna et al., "Genome Sequence of Enterohaemorrhagic *Escherichia coli* O157:H7," *Nature,* 409 (2001): 529–533.

11. J. Allan Downie and J. Peter W. Young, "The ABC of Symbiosis," *Nature* 412 (2001): 597–598. Howard Ochman and Nancy A. Moran—"Genes Lost and Genes Found: Evolution of Bacterial Pathogenesis and Symbiosis," *Science,* 292(2001): 1096–1098 emphasize the point that ancestors to pathogens already were adapted to live inside us peacefully before acquiring "pathogenicity islands" from other bacteria.

12. Dean A. Rowe-Magnus, Anne-Marie Guerout, Pascaline Ploncard, et al., "The Evolutionary History of Chromosomal Super-Integrons Provides an Ancestry for Multiresistant Integrons," *Proceedings of the National Academy of Sciences of the USA,* 98(2001): 652–657.

13. E. L. Tatum and Joshua Lederberg, "Gene Recombination in the Bacterium *Escherichia Coli," Journal of Bacteriology,* 53 (1947): 673–684.

14. H. O. Smith, J. F. Tomb, B. A. Dougherty, R. D. Fleischmann, and J. C. Venter, "Frequency and Distribution of DNA Uptake Signal Sequences in the *Haemophilus*

influenzae Rd Genome," *Science*, 269(1995): 538–540. The full DNA password is 29 letter pairs with the important core being the 9 letter pairs. The identity of the other 20 letters is more flexible; some can be any base, others A or T, and still others A or G. Sometimes, the password sequence can form a hairpin with an inverted repeat of itself that is nearby.

15. Werner Arber, "Involvement of Gene Products in Bacterial Evolution," in Lynn Helena Caporale, ed., *Molecular Strategies in Biological Evolution, Annals of the New York Academy of Sciences Annals of the NY Academy of Science*, 870 (1999): 36–44.

16. L. Quillet, S. Barray, B. Labedan, et al., "The Gene Encoding the Beta-1,4-Endoglucanase (CelA) from *Myxococcus xanthus*: Evidence for Independent Acquisition by Horizontal Transfer of Binding and Catalytic Domains from Actinomycetes," *Gene*, 158, no. 1 (1995): 23–29.

17. Elie Wollman and François Jacob, "Sur les processus de conjugaison et de recombinaison chez *Escherichia coli*," *Annales de l'Institute Pasteur*, 93(1957): 323–339.

18. Norton Zinder and Joshua Lederberg, "Genetic Exchange in *Salmonella*," *Journal of Bacteriology*, 64 (1952): 679–699.

19. A. J. Simpson et al., "The Genome Sequence of the Plant Pathogen *Xylella fastidiosa*: The *Xylella fastidiosa*," Consortium of the Organization for Nucleotide Sequencing and Analysis, *Nature*, 406 (2000):151–157.

20. John F. Heidelberg et al., "DNA Sequence of Both Chromosomes of the Cholera Pathogen *Vibrio cholerae*," *Nature*, 406 (2000): 477–483.

21. N. Figueroa Bossi, S. Uzzau, D. Maloriol, and L. Bossi, "Variable Assortment of Prophages Provides a Transferable Repertoire of Pathogenic Determinants in *Salmonella*," *Molecular Microbiology*, 39(2001): 260–272.

22. N. Figueroa-Bossi and L. Bossi, "Inducible Prophages Contribute to *Salmonella* Virulence in Mice," *Molecular Microbiology*, 33, no. 1 (1999): 167–176.

23. Andrés Vazquez-Torres, Yisheng Xu, Jessica Jones-Carson, et al., "*Salmonella* Pathogenicity Island 2-Dependent Evasion of the Phagocyte NADPH Oxidase," *Science*, 287 (2000): 1655–1658.

24. N. E. Kohl, E. A. Emini, W. A. Schleif, et al., "Active Human Immunodeficiency Virus Protease Is Required for Viral Infectivity," *Proceedings of the National Academy of Sciences of the USA*, 85 (1988): 4686–4690.

25. J. A. Shapiro, "Genome System Architecture and Natural Genetic Engineering in Evolution," in Lynn Helena Caporale, ed., *Molecular Strategies in Biological Evolution, Annals of the New York Academy of Sciences*, 870 (1999): 23–35. Lynn Helena Caporale, "Lessons from the Most Innovative Genetic Engineer," *Nature Biotechnology*, 16 (1998): 908–909.

26. Werner Arber was one who asked, as can be seen in his Nobel lecture of December 8, 1978 (available on line at http://www.nobel.se/medicine/laureates/1978/arber-lecture.html). In addition, this lecture provides an excellent intellectual history of the discovery of the existence of a chemical "stamp" that bacteria can put on viral DNA that affects whether the viral DNA can survive inside, and thus infect, bacteria of the same species.

27. Lynn Margulis and Dorion Sagan, *Microcosmos: Four Billion Years of Microbial Evolution* (New York: Simon & Schuster, 1991).

28. http://www.annefrank.com/site/af_student/study_AFHH.htm.
29. E. Andersson, Alireza Zomorodipour, Jan O. Andersson, et al., "The Genome Sequence of *Rickettsia prowazekii* and the Origin of Mitochondria SIV G," *Nature*, 396 (1998): 133–140.

Chapter 8   The Genome Sends an SOS

1. E. M. Witkin, "Ultraviolet Mutagenesis and the SOS Response in *Escherichia coli*: A Personal Perspective," *Environmental and Molecular Mutagenesis* 14, suppl. 16 (1989): 30–34 and personal communication.
2. Quoted in E. C. Friedberg, *Correcting the Blueprint of Life, an Historical Account of the Discovery of DNA Repair Mechanisms* (Cold Spring Harbor, N.Y.: Cold Spring Harbor Laboratory Press, 1997), pp. 12–13.
3. Ibid., p. 177.
4. W. M. Rehrauer, P. E. Lavery, E. L. Palmer, et al., "Interaction of *Escherichia coli* RecA Protein with LexA Repressor. I. LexA Repressor Cleavage Is Competitive with Binding of a Secondary DNA Molecule," Science, 271(1996): 23865–23873.
5. Y. Luo, R. A. Pfuetzner, S. Mosimann, et al., "Crystal Structure of LexA: A Conformational Switch for Regulation of Self-Cleavage," *Cell*, 106 (2001): 585–594.
6. Magdalena Maliszewska-Tkaczyk, Piotr Jonczyk, Malgorzata Bialoskorska, et al., "SOS Mutator Activity: Unequal Mutagenesis on Leading and Lagging Strands," *Proceedings of the National Academy of Sciences of the USA*, 97, no. 23 (2000): 12678–12683.
7. E. C. Friedberg, R. Wagner, and M. Radman, "Specialized DNA Polymerases and the Genesis of Mutations," *Science*, 296 (2002): 1627–1630; F. Hanaoka, "DNA Replication," *Nature*, 409 (2001): 33–34.
8. J. R. Nelson, C. W. Lawrence, and D. C. Hinkle, "Deoxycytidyl Transferase Activity of Yeast REV1 Protein," *Nature*, 382, no. 6593 (1996): 729–731.
9. R. D. Wood, M. Mitchell, J. Sgouros, and T. Lindahl, "Human DNA Repair Genes," *Science*, 291 (2001): 1284–1289; P. M. Burgers, et al., "Eukaryotic DNA Polymerases: Proposal for a Revised Nomenclature," *Journal of Biological Chemistry*, 276 (2001): 43487–43490.
10. Y. Zhang, F. Yuan, H. Xin, et al., "Human DNA Polymerase Kappa Synthesizes DNA with Extraordinarily Low Fidelity," *Nucleic Acids Research*, 28(2000): 4147–4156.
11. T. Matsuda, K. Bebenek, C. Masutani, et al., "Low Fidelity DNA Synthesis by Human DNA Polymerases-eta," *Nature*, 404 (2000): 1011–1013.
12. R. D. Wood, "DNA Repair: Variants on a Theme," *Nature*, 399 (1999): 639–640.
13. R. E. Johnson, M. Todd Washington, S. Prakash, and L. Prakash, "Bridging the Gap: A Family of Novel DNA Polymerases that Replicate Faulty DNA," *Proceedings of the National Academy of Sciences of the USA*, 96 (1999): 12224–12226.
14. B. Alberts, D. Bray, J. Lewis, et al., *Molecular Biology of the Cell* (New York: Garland Publishing, 1983).
15. J. Nakamura, V. E. Walker, P. B. Upton, et al., "Highly Sensitive Apurinic/ Apyrimidinic Site Assay Can Detect Spontaneous and Chemically Induced Depurination under Physiological Conditions," *Cancer Research*, 58, no. 2 (1998): 222–225.

16. P. J. Pukkila, J. Peterson, G. Herman, et al., "Effects of High Levels of DNA Adenine Methylation on Methyl-directed Mismatch Repair in *Escherichia coli,*" *Genetics,* 104, no. 4 (1983): 571–582.

17. C. Bucci, A. Lavitola, P. Salvatore, et al., "Hypermutation in Pathogenic Bacteria: Frequent Phase Variation in Meningococci Is a Phenotypic Trait of a Specialized Mutator Biotype," *Molecular Cell,* 4 (1999): 435–445.

18. H. Hendrickson, E. S. Slechta, U. Bergthorsson, et al., "Amplification-Mutagenesis: Evidence That "Directed" Adaptive Mutation and General Hypermutability Result from Growth with a Selected Gene Amplification," *Proceedings of the National Academy of Sciences of the USA,* 99: 2164–2169.

19. I. Matic, M. Radman, F. Taddei, et al., "Highly Variable Mutation Rates in Commensal and Pathogenic *Escherichia coli,*" *Science,* 277 (1997): 1833–1834; A. Giraud, I. Matic, O. Tenaillon, et al., "Costs and Benefits of High Mutation Rates: Adaptive Evolution of Bacteria in the Mouse Gut," *Science,* 291 (2001): 2606–2608.

20. M. Radman, "Mutation: Enzymes of Evolutionary Change," *Nature,* 401 (1999): 866–869.

21. A. Giraud, M. Radman, I. Matic, and F. Taddei, "The Rise and Fall of Mutator Bacteria," *Current Opinion in Microbiology,* 4 (2001): 582–585.

22. J. E. LeClerc, B. Li, W. L. Payne, and T. A. Cebula, "High Mutation Frequencies among *Escherichia coli* and *Salmonella* Pathogens," *Science,* 274 (1996): 1208–1211.

23. C. D. Bayliss, T. van de Ven, and E. R. Moxon, "Mutations in PolI But Not mutSLH Destabilize *Haemophilus influenzae* Tetranucleotide Repeats," *The EMBO Journal,* 21(2002): 1465–1476.

24. H. Flores-Rozas and R. D. Kolodner, "The *Saccharomyces cerevisiae* MLH3 Gene Functions in MSH3-Dependent Suppression of Frameshift Mutations," *Proceedings of the National Academy of Sciences of the USA,* 95 (1998): 12404–12409.

25. T. Ogi, T. Kato, Jr., T. Kato, and H. Ohmori, "Mutation Enhancement by DINB1, a Mammalian Homologue of the *Escherichia coli* Mutagenesis Protein dinB," *Genes Cells,* 4(1999): 607–618.

26. Alex van Belkum, Stewart Scherer, Loek van Alphen, and Henri Verbrugh, "Short-Sequence DNA Repeats in Prokaryotic Genomes," *Microbiology and Molecular Biology Reviews,* 62 (1998): 275–293.

27. E. P. Rocha, I. Matic, and F. Taddei, "Over-representation of Repeats in Stress Response Genes: A Strategy to Increase Versatility under Stressful Conditions?" *Nucleic Acids Research,* 30 (2002): 1886–1894.

28. E. W. Brown, J. E. LeClerc, B. Li, et al., "Phylogenetic Evidence for Horizontal Transfer of mutS Alleles among Naturally Occurring *Escherichia coli* Strains," *Journal of Bacteriology,* 183 (2001): 1631–1644; E. Denamur, G. Lecointre, P. Darlu, et al., "Evolutionary Implications of the Frequent Horizontal Transfer of Mismatch Repair Genes," *Cell,* 103 (2000): 711–721.

29. The possibility that variations in the activity of mismatch repair proteins might result in "mutator tuning" rather than simply mutator inactivation and reactivation was raised in an (email) discussion, by E. Rocha. In preparing

these notes, I had the chance to reread, after a few years and in light of the thinking involved in writing the chapter, two articles that present a good conceptual framework to for discussion of these mutations: those focused on certain sequences in the genome and those that affect the genome more broadly (but which still, as discussed in this chapter, may increase mutations more at certain classes of sequences within the genome than at others): D. Field, M. O. Magnasco, E. R. Moxon, et al., "Contingency Loci, Mutator Alleles, and Their Interactions," in Lynn Helena. Caporale, ed., *Molecular Strategies in Biological Evolution, Annals of the New York Academy of Sciences,* 870(1999): 378–382; E. R.Moxon and D. S. Thaler, "The Tinkerer's Evolving Tool-Box," *Nature,* 387 (1997): 659–662. As Moxon and Thaler put it, "Contingency loci provide a molecular mechanism by which a hypermutable state is localized to a particular region of the genome." Further, they introduce the use of the word *feedback* in this context, pointing out that because the generation of variation is under genetic control, there can be an evolution of feedback from the effects on survival to the "mechanisms by which diversity is generated."

30. Rocha, Matic, and Taddei, "Over-representation of Repeats," loc. cit.
31. P. Foster and W. Rosche, "Mechanisms of Mutation in Nondividing Cells," in Caporale, ed., *Molecular Strategies,* op. cit., pp. 133–145.
32. D. G. Heath, F. Y. An, K. E. Weaver, and D. B Clewell, "Phase Variation of *Enterococcus faecalis* pAD1 Conjugation Functions Relates to Changes in Iteron Sequence Region," *Journal of Bacteriology,* 177 (1995): 5453–5439.
33. S. E. Finkel and R. Kolter, "DNA as a Nutrient: Novel Role for Bacterial Competence Gene Homologs," *Journal of Bacteriology,* 183 (2001): 6288–6293.
34. Werner Arber, "Involvement of Gene Products in Bacterial Evolution," in Caporale, ed., *Molecular Strategies,* op. cit., pp. 36–44.
35. X. De Bolle, C. D. Bayliss, D. Field, et al., "The Length of a Tetranucleotide Repeat Tract in *Haemophilus influenzae* Determines the Phase Variation Rate of a Gene with Homology to Type III DNA Methyltransferases," *Molecular Microbiology,* 35, no. 1 (2000): 211–222.
36. Email discussion with Christopher Bayliss.
37. Foster and Rosche, "Mechanisms of Mutation ,"loc. cit.
38. E. Evans and E. Alani, "Minireview: Roles for Mismatch Repair Factors in Regulating Genetic Recombination," *Molecular and Cellular Biology,* 20 (2001): 7839–7844.
39. E. Grzesiuk, A. Gozdek, and B. Tudek, "Contribution of *E. coli* AlkA, TagA Glycosylases and UvrABC-excinuclease in MMS Mutagenesis," *Mutation Research,* 480–481 (2001): 77–84; Gregory J. McKenzie, Reuben S. Harris, Peter L. Lee, and Susan M. Rosenberg, "The SOS Response Regulates Adaptive Mutation," *Proceedings of the National Academy of Sciences of the USA,* 97, no. 12 (2000): 6646–6651.
40. Malgorzata Bzymek and Susan T. Lovett, "Instability of Repetitive DNA Sequences: The Role of Replication in Multiple Mechanisms," *Proceedings of the National Academy of Sciences of the USA,* 98, no. 15 (2001): 8319–8325.
41. Y. Dubrova, M. Plumb, J. Brown, and A. Jeffreys, "Radiation Induced Germline Instability at Minisatellite Loci," *International Journal of Radiation Biology,* 74 (1998): 689–696.

Chapter 9   Journeys through Space and Time

1. James A. Shapiro, "Thinking of Bacterial Populations as Multicellular Organisms," *Annual Review of Microbiology*, 52 (1998): 81–104.
2. M. B. Miller and B. L. Bassler, "Quorum Sensing in Bacteria," *Annual Review of Microbiology*, 55 (2001): 165–199.
3. Randolph E. Schmid, "African Dust Brings Germs across Ocean," July 1, 2001, 12:35 P.M. EDT, Associated Press.
4. Dr. Vincent Fischetti quoted in *Rockefeller University News and Notes*, vol. 13, 10/19/01. See also http://www.ext.nodak.edu/extpubs/ansci/livestoc/a561w.html.
5. R. H Vreeland, W. D. Rosenzweig, and D.W. Powers, "Isolation of a 250 Million-Year-Old Halotolerant Bacterium from a Primary Salt Crystal," *Nature*, 407 (2000): 897–900.
6. See, for example, D. C. Nickle, G. H. Learn, M. W. Rain, et al., "Curiously Modern DNA for a '250 Million-Year-Old' Bacterium," *Journal of Molecular Evolution*, 54 (2002): 134–137; Robert M. Hazen and Edwin Roedder, "Biogeology: How Old Are Bacteria from the Permian Age?" *Nature*, 411(2001): 155; and R. H. Vreeland, and W. D. Rosenzweig, "The Question of Uniqueness of Ancient Bacteria," *Journal of Industrial Microbiology and Biotechnology*, 28 (2002): 32–41.
7. Owen White, J. A. Eisen, J. F. Heidelberg, et al., "Genome Sequence of the Radio-resistant Bacterium *Deinococcus radiodurans* R1," *Science*, 286 (1999): 1571.
8. S. Charlton, A. J. Moir, L. Baillie, and A. Moir, "Characterization of the Exosporium of *Bacillus cereus*," *Journal of Applied Microbiology*, 87 (1999): 241–245.
9. J. M. Aguilera and M. Karel, "Preservation of Biological Materials under Desiccation," *Critical Reviews in Food Science and Nutrition*, 37 (1997): 287–309.
10. Kathryn Brown, "Patience Yields Secrets of Seed Longevity," *Science*, 291 (2001): 1884–1885.

Chapter 10   Strategies as Targets, Round One: The Pathogens

1. Elizabeth Pennisi, "Closing in on a Deadly Parasite's Genome," *Science*, 290 (2000): 439.
2. http://www.defenders.org/case03.html.
3. Mariagrazia Pizza, V. Scarlato, V. Masignari, et al., "Identification of Vaccine Candidates against Serogroup B Meningococcus by Whole-Genome Sequencing," *Science*, 287 (2000): 1816–1820.
4. N. E. Kohl, E. A. Emini, W. A. Schleif, et al., "Active Human Immunodeficiency Virus Protease Is Required for Viral Infectivity," *Proceedings of the National Academy of Sciences of the USA*, 85 (1988): 4686–4690.
5. L. F. Rezende, W. C. Drosopoulos, and V. R. Prasad, "The Influence of 3TC Resistance Mutation M184I on the Fidelity and Error Specificity of Human Immunodeficiency Virus Type 1 Reverse Transcriptase," *Nucleic Acids Research*, 26 (1998): 3066–3072.
6. Laurie Garrett, *The Coming Plague* (New York: Farrar, Straus and Giroux, 1994).
7. Frank Ryan, *The Forgotten Plague: How the Battle against Tuberculosis Was Won-and Lost* (Boston: Little, Brown, 1992).

8. http://www.who.int/gtb/publications/globrep00/summary.html.
9. http://www.tigr.org/CMR2/BackGround/gmt.html.
10. S. T. Cole, R. Brosch, J. Parkhill, et al., "Deciphering the Biology of *Mycobacterium tuberculosis* from the Complete Genome Sequence," *Nature*, 393 (1998): 537–544.
11. D. W. Hood, M. E. Deadman, M. P. Jennings, et al., "DNA Repeats Identify Novel Virulence Genes in *Haemophilus influenzae*," *Proceedings of the National Academy of Sciences of the USA*, 93 (1996): 11121–11125.
12. Kirk Deitsch, M. Calderwood, and T. Wellems, "Cooperative Silencing Elements in *var* Genes," *Nature*, 412 (2001): 875–876.
13. Alan G. Barbour and Blanca I. Restrepo, "Antigenic Variation in Vector-Borne Pathogens," *Emerging Infectious Diseases*, 6 (2000): 449–457.
14. P. T. Kimmitt, C. R. Harwood, and M. R. Barer, "Toxin Gene Expression by Shiga Toxin-Producing *Escherichia coli*: The Role of Antibiotics and the Bacterial SOS Response," *Emerging Infectious Diseases*, 6 (2000): 458–465.
15. M. S. Swanson and B. K. Hammer, "*Legionella pneumophila* Pathogenesis: A Fateful Journey from Amoebae to Macrophages," *Annual Review of Microbiology*, 54 (2000): 567–613.
16. Joshua Lederberg (ed.), *Biological Weapons: Limiting the Threat* (Boston: MIT Press, 1999).

Chapter 11   Strategies as Targets, Round Two: Cancer

1. M. J. Mauro, M. E. O'Dwyer, and B.J. Druker, "ST1571, a Tyrosine Kinase Inhibitor for the Treatment of Chronic Myelogenous Leukemia: Validating the Promise of Molecularly Targeted Therapy," *Cancer Chemotherapy and Pharmacology*, 48, suppl. 1 (2001): S77–S78.
2. E. Mercedes, M. Mohammed Mansoor, Katharine Ellwood, et al.: "Clinical Resistance to STI-571 Cancer Therapy Caused by BCR-ABL Gene Mutation or Amplification," *Science*, 293 (2001): 876–880.
3. M. Yuasa, C. Masutani, T. Eki, and F. Hanaoka, "Genomic Structure, Chromosomal Localization and Identification of Mutations in the Xeroderma Pigmentosum Variant (XPV) Gene," *Oncogene*, 19, no. 41 (2000): 4721–4728
4. Ching-Tai Lin, Yi Lisa Lyu, Hai Xiao, et al., "Suppression of Gene Amplification and Chromosomal DNA Integration by the DNA Mismatch Repair System," *Nucleic Acids Research*, 29, no. 16 (2001): 3304–3310
5. R. M. Snapka, "Gene Amplification as a Target for Cancer Chemotherapy," *Oncology Research*, 4, nos. 4–5 (1992): 145–150.
6. Lin Zhang, Jian Yu, Ben Ho Park, et al., "Role of BAX in the Apoptotic Response to Anticancer Agents," *Science*, 290 (2000): 989–992.
7. Yurij Ionov, Hiroyuki Yamamoto, Stanislaw Krajewski, et al., "Mutational Inactivation of the Proapoptotic Gene BAX Confers Selective Advantage during Tumor Clonal Evolution," *Proceedings of the National Academy of Science of the USA*, 97 (2000): 10872–10877.
8. http://www.hhmi.org/research/investigators/modrich.html.
9. Bert Vogelstein, David Lane, and Arnold J. Levine, "Surfing the p53 Network," *Nature*, 408 (2000): 307–310.

10. S. W. Lowe, S. Bodis, A. McClatchey, et al., "p53 Status and the Efficacy of Cancer Therapy in Vivo," *Science*, 266 (1994): 807–810.

11. Muthusamy Thangaraju, Scott H. Kaufmann, and Fergus J. Couch, "BRCA1 Facilitates Stress-Induced Apoptosis in Breast and Ovarian Cancer Cell Lines," *Journal of Biological Chemistry*, 275 (2000): 33487–33496.

12. Lavanya Lall and Richard L. Davidson, "Sequence-Directed Base Mispairing in Human Oncogenes," *Molecular and Cellular Biology*, 18, no. 8 (1998): 4659–4669.

13. Simply driving cells to divide rapidly can change the ratio of G/C to A/T incorporated into genes, as was reported by Siquan Liu et al., "Genetic Instability Favoring Transversions Associated with ErbB2Induced Mammary Tumorigenesis," *Proceedings of the National Academy of Sciences of the USA*, 99 (2002): 3770–3775. Although these authors have not yet identified the mechanism responsible for their observation, I would suggest imbalances in the pool sizes as one likely explanation for this effect.

14. S. P. Linke, K. C. Clarkin, A. Di Leonardo, et al., "A Reversible, p53-Dependent G0/G1 Cell Cycle Arrest Induced by Ribonucleotide Depletion in the Absence of Detectable DNA Damage," *Genes and Development*, 10 (1996): 934–947.

15. N. C. Denko, A. J. Giaccia, J. R. Stringer, and P. J. Stambrook, "The Human Ha-ras Oncogene Induces Genomic Instability in Murine Fibroblasts within One Cell Cycle," *Proceedings of the National Academy of Sciences of the USA*, 91 (1994): 5124–5128.

16. Rossana Jorquera and Robert M. Tanguay, "Fumarylacetoacetate, the Metabolite Accumulating in Hereditary Tyrosinemia, Activates the ERK Pathway and Induces Mitotic Abnormalities and Genomic Instability," *Human Molecular Genetics*, 10 (2001): 1741–1752.

17. L. S. Michel, V. Liberal, A. Chatterjee, et al., "MAD2 Haplo-Insufficiency Causes Premature Anaphase and Chromosome Instability in Mammalian Cells," *Nature*, 409 (2001): 355–359.

18. M. Miele, S. Bonatti, P. Menichini, et al., "The Presence of Amplified Regions Affects the Stability of Chromosomes in Drug-Resistant Chinese Hamster Cells," *Mutation Research*, 219 (1989): 171–178.

19. Noriaki Shimizu, Nobuo Itoh, Hiroyasu Utiyama, and Geoffrey M. Wahl, "Selective Entrapment of Extrachromosomally Amplified DNA by Nuclear Budding and Micronucleation during S Phase," *Journal of Cell Biology*, 140 (1998): 1307–1320.

20. Hongyi Zhou, Jian Kuang, Ling Zhong, et al., "Tumour Amplified Kinase STK15/BTAK Induces Centrosome Amplification, Aneuploidy and Transformation," *Nature Genetics*, 20 (1998): 189–193.

21. G. Canute et al., "The Hydrogen-Induced Loss of Double-Minute Chromosomes," *Neurosurgery*, 42 (1998): 609–616.

22. L. A. Loeb, "A Mutator Phenotype in Cancer," *Cancer Research*, 61 (2001): 3230–3239.

Chapter 12 Theme and Variations

Any good biochemistry textbook will have an interesting diagram of how the amino acids in the active site of a serine protease work together to cut another protein. Similarly, if you would like a more detailed introduction to blood coagulation, a medical bio-chemistry textbook is a good place to begin.

1. Alan Khazei, cofounder of the national service organization City Year, quoted by Bill Shore in *The Cathedral Within* (New York: Random House, 1999).
2. S. Yokoyama, H. Zhang, F. B. Radlwimmer, and N. S. Blow, "Adaptive Evolution of Color Vision of the Comoran Coelacanth (*Latimeria chalumnae*)," *Proceedings of the National Academy of Sciences of the USA*, 96 (1999): 6279–6284.
3. Alex van Belkum, Stewart Scherer, Loek van Alphen, and Henri Verbrugh, "Short-Sequence DNA Repeats in Prokaryotic Genomes," *Microbiology and Molecular Biology Reviews*, 62 (1998): 275–293.
4. Nina Fedoroff, "Transposable Elements as a Molecular Evolutionary Force," in Lynn Helena Caporale, ed., *Molecular Strategies in Biological Evolution, Annals of the New York Academy of Sciences*, 870 (1999): 251–264.
5. In this book, I focus on generation of variation, the substrate on which natural selection acts, rather than on the origin of new species. However, an innovation that pops up and provides strong selective value may lead to the path to a new species when it opens access to an available niche or, for example, when the general population is under stress. This would enable rapid radiations and could provide a molecular basis for the observations of apparent jumps in the fossil record that led to the controversial theory of Stephen Jay Gould and Niles Eldredge, described in "Punctuated Equilibrium Comes of Age," *Nature*, 366 (1993): 251–264.

Chapter 13   Family Heirlooms: A Framework for Evolution

1. Dobzhansky's important contributions to evolutionary theory are put in context well by Nobel laureate Eric Kandel: http://www.columbia.edu/cu/alumni/Magazine/Legacies/Morgan/Century.html.
2. International Human Genome Sequencing Consortium, "Initial Sequencing and Analysis of the Human Genome," *Nature*, 409 (2001): 860–921.
3. Steven Henikoff, Elizabeth A. Greene, Shmuel Pietrokovski, et al., "Gene Families: The Taxonomy of Protein Paralogs and Chimeras," *Science*, 278 (1997): 609–614.
4. J. L. Riechmann, J. Heard, G. Martin, et al., "Arabidopsis Transcription Factors: Genome-Wide Comparative Analysis among Eukaryotes," *Science*, 290 (2000): 2105–2110.
5. International Human Genome Sequencing Consortium, "Initial Sequencing and Analysis of the Human Genome," loc. cit.
6. R. Desjarlais and J. M. Berg, "Toward Rules Relating Zinc Finger Protein Sequences and DNA Binding Site Preferences," *Proceedings of the National Academy of Sciences of the USA*, 89 (1992): 7345–7349.
7. It also is assumed that when an extra copy is made, both the original and the copy are free to mutate, since each will carry on the original function. However, it has not been ruled out that a copying process itself could tend to make mutations, thus generating, right at the start, variation in the new copy as a substrate for natural selection; this would maintain the original in its functioning regulatory context, which might prove useful.

8. Protein sequences organized by families can be found at http://pfam. wustl.edu/.

9. http://www.creaturelabs.com/.

10. Lynn Helena Caporale, "Mutation Is Modulated: Implications for Evolution," *Bioessays*, 22 (2000): 388–395.

11. W. J. Dickinson and J. Seger, "Cause and Effect in Evolution," *Nature*, 399 (1999): 30.

12. T. Ohta and C. J. Basten, "Gene Conversion Generates Hypervariability at the Variable Regions of Kallikreins and Their Inhibitors," *Molecular Phylogenetics and Evolution*, 1 (1992): 87–90.

Chapter 14   Interchangeable Parts

1. T. C. Sudhof, D. W. Russell, J. L. Goldstein, et al., "Cassette of Eight Exons Shared by Genes for LDL Receptor and EGF Precursor," *Science*, 228(1985): 893–895.

2. Examples can be seen on Dr. Go's laboratory's Web page, http://www.bio. nagoya-u.ac.jp:8001/~golab/researchE.html.

3. C. C. Blake, "Exons Encode Protein Functional Units," *Nature*, 277, no. 5698 (1979): 598.

4. Mitiko Go, "Correlation of DNA Exonic Regions with Protein Structural Units in Haemoglobin," *Nature*, 291, no. 5810 (1981): 90–92.

5. W. Gilbert, "Why Genes in Pieces?" *Nature*, 271, no. 5645 (1978): 501.

6. International Human Genome Sequencing Consortium, "Initial Sequencing and Analysis of the Human Genome," *Nature*, 409 (2001): 860–921.

7. Loc. cit.

8. See, for example, P. Nash, X. Tang, S. Orlicky, et al., "Multisite Phosphorylation of a CDK Inhibitor Sets a Threshold for the Onset of DNA Replication," *Nature*, 414 (2001): 514–521.

9. Hugh M. Robertson, "Two Large Families of Chemoreceptor Genes in the Nematodes *Caenorhabditis elegans* and *Caenorhabditis briggsae* Reveal Extensive Gene Duplication, Diversification, Movement and Intron Loss," *Genome Research*, 8 (1998): 449–463.

10. A discussion of our changing understanding of the word *gene*, from its conceptual origins as a term to describe something that is inherited, to our more precise molecular description of a colinear relationship between the letters in DNA and the amino acids in proteins, through the changed relationship between the linear structure and an inherited trait that is introduced into the definition by, for example, alternative combinations of introns, is presented in Evelyn Fox Keller's *The Century of the Gene* (Cambridge: Harvard University Press, 2000). As she puts it, success has taught us humility.

11. R. J. Britten, "Mobile Elements Inserted in the Distant Past Have Taken on Important Functions," *Gene*, 205 (1997): 177–182.

12. C. V. Kirchhamer, C. H. Yuh, and E. H. Davidson, "Modular cis-regulatory organization of developmentally expressed genes: Two genes transcribed terri-

torially in the sea urchin embryo, and additional examples," *Proceedings of the National Academy of Sciences of the USA*, 93 (1996): 9322–9328.

13. With a few exceptions, including our antibody-producing cells with their rearranged and mutated genes and our red blood cells.

14. This quote is from McClintock's address when she received the 1983 Nobel prize. She continued: "It is becoming increasingly apparent that we know little of the potentials of a genome." This talk is available from a variety of sources, including www.nobel.se. An exceptionally good place to read McClintock's publications is in Nina Fedoroff and David Botstein's *The Dynamic Genome* (Cold Spring Harbor, N.Y.: Cold Spring Harbor Laboratory Press, 1992).

15. F. H. Ruddle, C. T. Amemiya, J. L. Carr, et al., "Evolution of Chordate hox Gene Clusters," in Lynn Helena Caporale, ed., *Molecular Strategies in Biological Evolution, Annals of the New York Academy of Sciences*, 870 (1999): 238–248. Two excellent textbooks that discuss how genomic regulatory systems can lead to diverse living forms are Sean Carroll, Jennifer K. Grenier, and Scott D. Weatherbee, *From DNA to Diversity* (Oxford: Blackwell Science, 2001), and Eric H. Davidson, *Genomic Regulatory Systems* (San Diego: Academic Press, 2001).

16. John Doebley and Lewis Lukens, "Transcriptional Regulators and the Evolution of Plant Form," *The Plant Cell*, 10 (1998): 1075–1082.

17. D. Hareven, T. Gutfinger, Parnis, et al., "The Making of a Compound Leaf: Genetic Manipulation of Leaf Architecture in Tomato," *Cell*, 84:735–744.

18. A beautiful description of "how organisms make themselves" is found in Enrico Coen, *The Art of Genes* (Oxford: Oxford University Press, 2002). An important issue in evolution is the building up and interactions of modular components at higher and higher levels of organization. A comprehensive discussion of the interactions between modular systems in the body as they relate to development of body form in evolution can be found in Mary Jane West-Eberhard, *Developmental Plasticity and Evolution* (Oxford: Oxford University Press, 2002). An interesting example of adjustments in development, in nontechnical language, is provided by J. Travis, "Internal Fight Settles Size of Body Parts," *Science News*, 153 (1998): 231. Mark Kirschner and John Gerhart's article "Evolvability" [*Proceedings of the National Academy of Sciences of the USA*, 95 (1998): 8420–8427] addresses how the evolution of a variety of regulatory processes that control the timing and location of activation of "conserved core processes," and their responsiveness to what else is happening in and around the cell, can produce both robustness and flexibility in development. All the authors cited here discuss flexibility that can come from the range of responsiveness encoded in the genes an organism has. In this book, I have focused on variations in the genome itself, from generation to generation. (But slippery sequences also can slip at the protein factory, generating a group of slightly different proteins from one messenger RNA.) However, for example, the slippery DNA, in which the genome encodes some back and forth flexibility around its own sequence, is related to the concept that a specific genome can reach beyond explicitly encoding one thing to encode a range of possibilities.

19. Walter Gehring, *Master Control Genes in Development and Evolution: The Homeobox Story* (New Haven, Conn.: Yale University Press, 1998).

20. G. Theissen, J. T. Kim, and H. Saedler, "Classification and Phylogeny of the MADS-Box Multigene Family Suggest Defined Roles of MADS-Box Gene Subfamilies in the Morphological Evolution of Eukaryotes," *Journal of Molecular Evolution*, 43 (1996): 484–516.

21. Stacey L. Harmer, John B. Hogenesch, Marty Straume, et al., "Orchestrated Transcription of Key Pathways in Arabidopsis by the Circadian Clock," *Science*, 290 (2000): 2110–2113.

22. Satchidananda Panda, John B. Hogenesch , and Steve A. Kay, "Circadian Rhythms from Flies to Human," *Nature*, 417 (2002): 329–335. A mutation within the protein coding region of a gene that humans share with flies, which causes people to go to sleep very early relative to the sunrise, is described in Kong L. Toh, Christopher R. Jones, Yan He, et al., "An hPer2 Phosphorylation Site Mutation in Familial Advanced Sleep Phase Syndrome," *Science*, 291 (2001): 1040–1043. As other genetic variants have been associated with a tendency to stay up later, I can envision a clear survival advantage to diversity here as alert night owls and alert early risers rotate watch duty over ancient campfires.

Chapter 15   Jumping Genes

1. Primo Levi, *The Periodic Table*, trans. Raymond Rosenthal (New York: Schocken Books, 1984), p. 75.

2. http://www.nap.edu/readingroom/books/biomems/bmcclintock.html. See also Nina Fedoroff and David Botstein, eds.,*The Dynamic Genome* (Cold Spring Harbor, N.Y.: Cold Spring Harbor Laboratory Press, 1992).

3. J. A. Shapiro, "Barbara McClintock, 1902–1992," *Bioessays*, 14 (1922): 791.

4. R. Pohlman, N. Federoff, and J. Messing, "The Nucleotide Sequence of the Maize Controlling Element Activator," *Cell*, 37 (1984): 635–643.

5. In addition to these three textbook mechanisms, a bacterial mechanism recently found also to occur in plants and animals is described by Vladimir V. Kapitonov and Jerzy Jurka, "Rolling-CircleTransposons in Eukaryotes," *Proceedings of the National Academy of Sciences of the USA*, 98 (2001): 8714–8719.

6. Virginia Walbot, "UV-B Damage Amplified by Transposons in Maize," *Nature*, 397 (1999): 398–399.

7 Barbara McClintock in Nina Fedoroff and David Botstein, *The Dynamic Genome*, loc. cit. A jumping gene appears to help wild barley growing in a canyon to adapt to a moisture gradient, as discussed by Jonathan F. Wendeland and Susan R. Wessler, "Retrotransposon-Mediated Genome Evolution on a Local Ecological Scale," *Proceedings of the National Academy of Sciences of the USA*, 97 (2000): 6250–6252. Also see Susan Wessler's brief and clear historical review of conceptual breakthroughs in our knowledge of the dynamic genome: "Plant Transposable Elements. A Hard Act to Follow," *Plant Physiology*, 125 (2001): 149–151.

8. Jim Shapiro discusses this in "Genome System Architecture and Natural Genetic Engineering in Evolution," in Lynn Helena Caporale, ed., *Molecular Strategies in Biological Evolution, Annals of the New York Academy of Sciences*,

870 (1999): 23–35. This idea has found fertile ground in the creative imagination of the fiction writer Greg Bear; see *Darwin's Radio* (New York: Ballantine Books, 1999).

9. Invertebrates do have immune mechanisms, some of which we share [see e.g., R. Medzhitov, "Toll-Like Receptors and Innate Immunity," *Nature Reviews Immunology*, 1 (2001): 135–415], but the repeated severe infections suffered by many people who suffer from immunodeficiency diseases demonstrates the importance of the vertebrate immune system to our survival.

10. International Human Genome Sequencing Consortium (IHGSC), "Initial Sequencing and Analysis of the Human Genome," *Nature*, 409 (2001): 860–921. For a comprehensive discussion of the broad range of ways in which transposons have shaped genomes, from small local changes through major genome reorganizations and, likely, speciation events, see Margaret G. Kidwell and Damon R. Lisch, "Perspective: Transposable Elements, Parasitic DNA, and Genome Evolution," *Evolution: International Journal of Organic Evolution*, 55 (2001): 1–24; these authors comment that the distinction between host and parasite "becomes meaningless in many cases."

11. Nina Fedoroff, "Transposons and Genome Evolution in Plants," *Proceedings of the National Academy of Sciences of the USA*, 97 (2000): 7002–7007; C. Feschotte, N. Jiang, and S. R. Wessler, "Plant Transposable Elements: Where Genetics Meets Genomics," *Nature Reviews Genetics*, 3 (2002): 329–341; Nina Fedoroff, "Transposable Elements as a Molecular Evolutionary Force, " in Caporale, ed., *Molecular Strategies*, op. cit., pp. 251–264.

12. Jim Shapiro, "Genome System Architecture," loc. cit.

13. The discussion in this chapter focuses on how selection can decrease the damage done by mobile elements. This emphasis is in meant in part to balance widespread discussions that emphasized damage caused by mobile elements or simply considered these elements junk. A good balanced discussion of transposable elements can be found in Margaret G. Kidwell and Damon R. Lisch, "Transposable Elements and Host Genome Evolution," *Trends in Ecology and Evolution*, 15 (2000): 95–99, and, with more detail, in Kidwell and Lisch, "Perspective," loc. cit. Since we learned about DNA in terms of its stable transfer of linear information from generation to generation, when transposons jumped into our view of DNA sequences, our reaction was that they were disruptive; however, if we reflect on a very early time in the origins of life, before genetic information crystallized into what we see as distinct species, a vision of mobile blocks of information emerges.

14. IHGSC, "Initial Sequencing," loc. cit.

15. Fedoroff, "Transposable Elements," loc. cit.

16. Joana C. Silva and Margaret G. Kidwell, "Horizontal Transfer and Selection in the Evolution of P Elements," *Molecular Biology and Evolution*, 17 (2000): 1542–1557.

17. Guo-chun Liao, E. Jay Rehm, and Gerald M. Rubin, "Genetics Insertion Site Preferences of the P Transposable Element in *Drosophila melanogaster*," *Proceedings of the National Academy of Sciences of the USA*, 97, no. 7 (2000): 3347–3351.

18. Jim Shapiro , "Transposable Elements as the Key to a 21st Century View of Evolution," *Genetica*, 107 (1999): 171–179.

19 S. E. Holmes, B. A. Dombroski, C. M. Krebs, et al., "A New Retrotransposable Human L1 Element from the LRE2 Locus on Chromosome 1q Produces a Chimaeric Insertion," *Nature Genetics*, 7, no. 2 (1994): 143–148.

20. N. Puget, D. Torchard, O. M. Serova-Sinilnikova, et al., "A 1kb Alu-Mediated Germ-Line Deletion Removing BRCA1 Exon 17," *Cancer Research*, 57 (1997): 828.

21. K. Yoshida, A. Nakamura, M. Yazaki, et al., "Insertional Mutation by Transposable Element, L1, in the DMD Gene Results in X-linked Dilated Cardiomyopathy," *Human Molecular Genetics*, 7, no. 7 (1998): 1129–1132.

22. N. Narita, H. Nishio, Y. Kitoh, et al., "Insertion of a 5' Truncated L1 Element into the 3' End of Exon 44 of the Dystrophin Gene Resulted in Skipping of the Exon during Splicing in a Case of Duchenne Muscular Dystrophy, *Journal of Clinical Investigation*, 91(1993): 1862–1867.

23. H. H. Kazazian, C. Wong, H. Youssoufian, et al., "Haemophilia A Resulting from De Novo Insertion of L1 Sequences Represents a Novel Mechanism for Mutation in Man," *Nature*, 332 (1988): 164–166.

24. Y. Miki, I. Nishisho, A. Horii, et al., "Disruption of the APC Gene by a Retrotransposal Insertion of L1 Sequence in a Colon Cancer," *Cancer Research*, 52, no. 3 (1992): 643–645.

Chapter 16   Be Prepared for the Unexpected

1. http://www.nap.edu/html/biomems/htemin.html.

2. H. M. Temin and S. Mizutani, "RNA-Dependent DNA Polymerase in Virions of Rous Sarcoma Virus," *Nature*, 226 (1970): 1211–1213.

3. A very brief history can be found at http://www.nobel.se/chemistry/articles/altman/index.html.

4. A. S. Perelson, A. U. Neumann, M. Markowitz, et al., "HIV-1 Dynamics In Vivo: Virion Clearance Rate, Infected Cell Life-Span, and Viral Generation Time," *Science*, 271 (1996): 1582–1586. The "base camp" analogy that follows comes from an article that I read online. I apologize to the author for not being able to locate the original reference to list here.

5. H. H. Kazazian, Jr., "L1 Retrotransposons Shape the Mammalian Genome," *Science*, 289 (2000): 1152–1153.

6. J. V. Moran, R. J. DeBerardinis, and H. H. Kazazian, "Exon Shuffling by L1 Retrotransposition," *Science*, 283 (1999): 1530–1534. .

7. Abram Gabriel and Emilie Mules, "Fidelity of Retrotransposon Replication," in Lynn Helena Caporale, ed., *Molecular Strategies in Biological Evolution, Annals of the New York Academy of Sciences*, 870 (1999): 108–118.

8. Emma Whitelaw and David I. K. Martin, "Retrotransposons as Epigenetic Mediators of Phenotypic Variation in Mammals," *Nature Genetics*, 27 (2001): 361–365.

9. Alan Herbert and Alexander Rich, "RNA Processing in Evolution: The Logic of Soft-Wired Genomes," in Caporale, ed., *Molecular Strategies*, op. cit., pp. 119–132.

10. Liam P. Keegan, Angela Gallo, and Mary A. O'Connell (2000) "Survival Is Impossible without an Editor," *Science*, 290 (2000): 1707–1709.

11. Larry Simpson and Dmitri Maslov, "Evolution of the U-Insertion/Deletion RNA Editing in Mitochondria of Kinetoplastid Protozoa, in Caporale, ed., *Molecular Strategies*, op. cit., pp. 190–205.

12. In fact, the first step in cracking the genetic code was the discovery that UUU encodes F; when a synthetic messenger made of a string of Us was put into a protein-making mixture in the laboratory as a control, in place of a "real" messenger RNA, it turned out to direct the synthesis of a protein made of a string of Fs: as reported in Marshall W. Nirenberg and J. Heinrich Matthaei "The Dependence of Cell-Free Protein Synthesis in *E. coli* upon Naturally Occurring or Synthetic Polyribonucleotides," *Proceedings of the National Academy of Sciences of the USA*, 47 (1961): 1588–1602. The National Library of Medicine has made this article available on line at http://profiles.nlm.nih.gov/JJ/B/B/D/K/_/jjbbdk.pdf. This in turn was enabled by the demonstration that there *was* a messenger form of RNA: Sydney Brenner, François Jacob, and Matthew Meselson, "An Unstable Intermediate Carrying Information from Genes to Ribosomes for Protein Synthesis," *Nature*, 190 (1961): 576–581.

13. T. E. Jacks, "Ribosomal Frameshifting in Retroviral Gene Expression," *Dissertation Abstracts International*, 49 (1989): 3595.

14. International Human Genome Sequencing Consortium (IHGSC), "Initial Sequencing and Analysis of the Human Genome," *Nature*, 409 (2001): 860–921.

15. M. P. Ternsand R. M. Terns, "Small Nucleolar RNAs: Versatile trans-Acting Molecules of Ancient Evolutionary Origin," *Gene Expression*, 10 (2002):17–39.

16. Jerome Cavaille, Karin Buiting, Martin Kiefmann, et al., "Identification of Brain-Specific and Imprinted Small Nucleolar RNA Genes Exhibiting an Unusual Genomic Organization," *Proceedings of the National Academy of Sciences of the USA*, 97 (2000): 14311–14316.

17. M. A. Cleary, C. D. van Raamsdonk, J. Levorse, et al., "Disruption of an Imprinted Gene Cluster by a Targeted Chromosomal Translocation in Mice," *Nature Genetics*, 29 (2001): 78–82.

18. David Baulcombe, "RNA Silencing: Diced Defence," *Nature*, 409 (2001): 295–296; *Science* (vol. 296 [2002]: 1259–1273) has devoted a special section to articles on "RNA Silencing and Noncoding RNA," as has *Nature* (418 [2002]: 122–124, 213–258).

Chapter 17   Mixing Up Genes for the Children

1. Wendy P. Robinson, "Mechanisms Leading to Uniparental Disomy and Their Clinical Consequences," *Bioessays*, 22 (2000): 452–459.

2. G. Sluder and D. McCollum, "The Mad Ways of Meiosis," *Science*, 289 (2000): 254.

3. Mendel had observed that traits such as whether a pea plant was smooth or wrinkly or green or yellow assorted independently of each other, although he did not know that chromosomes underlay this observation (http://www.netspace.org/MendelWeb/Mendel.html). Traits encoded side by side on the same chromosome would be an exception to "independent assortment"; see A. H. Sturtevant, "The Linear Arrangement of Six Sex-Linked Factors in

Drosophila, as Shown by Their Mode of Association," *Journal of Experimental Zoology,* 14 (1913): 43–59, available on line at http://www.esp.org/foundations/genetics/classical/ahs-13.pdf.

4. http://www.discover.com/ask/main57.html.

5. Scott Keeney, "Mechanism and Control of Meiotic Recombination Initiation," *Current Topics in Developmental Biology,* 52 (2001): 1–53.

6. A. Schwacha and N. Kleckner, "Interhomolog Bias during Meiotic Recombination: Meiotic Functions Promotes a Highly Differentiated Interhomolog-Only Pathway," *Cell,* 90 (1997): 1123–1135; Dawn A. Thompson and Franklin W. Stahl, "Genetic Control of Recombination Partner Preference in Yeast Meiosis: Isolation and Characterization of Mutants Elevated for Meiotic Unequal Sister-Chromatid Recombination," *Genetics,* 153 (1999): 621–641.

7. B. Alberts, D. Bray, J. Lewis, et al., *Molecular Biology of the Cell* (New York: Garland Publishing, 1983).

8. Whether this is due to proteins that bind to the chromosomes or to direct interactions between the DNA sequences is still a matter of debate, according to Nancy Kleckner (personal communication), who concludes that the evidence points to direct interactions between the DNA sequences as discussed in Beth M. Weiner and Nancy Kleckner, "Chromosome Pairing via Multiple Interstitial Interactions before and during Meiosis in Yeast,"*Cell,* 77 (1994): 977–991.

9. Paramvir Dehal, Paul Predki, Anne S. Olsen, et al., "Human Chromosome 19 and Related Regions in Mouse: Conservative and Lineage-Specific Evolution," *Science,* 293 (2001): 104–111.

10. Annie Tremblay, Maria Jasin, and Pierre Chartrand, "A Double-Strand Break in a Chromosomal LINE Element Can Be Repaired by Gene Conversion with Various Endogenous LINE Elements in Mouse Cells," *Molecular and Cellular Biology,* 20 (2000): 54–60.

11. Florence Richard, Martine Lombard, and Bernard Dutrillaux, "Phylogenetic Origin of Human Chromosomes 7, 16, and 19 and Their Homologs in Placental Mammals," *Genome Research,* 10, no. 5 (2000): 644–651.

12. Z. Wong, N. J. Royle, and A. J. Jeffreys, "A Novel Human DNA Polymorphism Resulting from Transfer of DNA from Chromosome 6 to Chromosome 16," *Genomics,* 7 (1990): 222–234.

13. J. R. Murti, M. Bumbulis, and J. C. Schimenti, "Gene Conversion between Unlinked Sequences in the Germline of Mice," *Genetics,* 137 (1994): 837–843.

14. E. S. Davis, B. K. Shafer, and J. N. Strathern, "The *Saccharomyces cerevisiae* RDN1 Locus Is Sequestered from Interchromosomal Meiotic Ectopic Recombination in a SIR2-Dependent Manner," *Genetics,* 155 (2000): 1019–1032; Christine Richardson, Mary Ellen Moynahan , and Maria Jasin, "Double-Strand Break Repair by Interchromosomal Recombination: Suppression of Chromosomal Translocations," *Genes and Development,* 12, no. 24 (1998): 3831–3842.

15. Alastair S. H. Goldman and Michael Lichten, ""Restriction of Ectopic Recombination by Interhomolog Interactions during *Saccharomyces cerevisiae* Meiosis," *Proceedings of the National Academy of Sciences of the USA,* 97 (2000): 9537–9542.

16. Marina N. Nikiforova, James R. Stringer, Ruthann Blough, et al., "Proximity of Chromosomal Loci That Participate in Radiation-Induced Rearrangements in Human Cells," *Science*, 290 (2000): 138–141.

17. John R. K. Savage, "Proximity Matters," *Science*, 290 (2000): 62–63.

18. See Figure 1 of Angus I. Lamond and William C. Earnshaw, "Structure and Function in the Nucleus," *Science*, 280 (1998): 547–553.

19. David M. Prescott, "DNA Manipulations in Ciliates," in Wilfried Brauer, Hartmut Ehrig, Juhani Karhumäki, and Arto Salomaa, eds., *Formal and Natural Computing: Lecture Notes in Computer Science* (New York: Springer Verlag, 2002), vol. 2300, pp. 394–417.

20. John McPhee, *A Sense of Where You Are* (New York: Farrar Straus & Giroux, 1999).

21. Weiner and Kleckner, "Chromosome Pairing," loc. cit.

Chapter 18   Sculpting the Genome

1. Florence Nightingale, *Notes on Nursing* (1860; Dover, 1969). Available on line at http://www.deltaomega.org/nurse1.pdf .

2. P. Detloff, M. A. White, and T. D. Petes, "Analysis of a Gene Conversion Gradient at the HIS4 Locus in *Saccharomyces cerevisiae*," *Genetics*, 132 (1992): 113–123.

3. W. P. Wahls and G. R. Smith, "A Heteromeric Protein That Binds to a Meiotic Homologous Recombination Hot Spot: Correlation of Binding and Hot Spot Activity," *Genes and Development*, 8 (1994): 1693–1702.

4. M. Vedel and A. Nicolas, "CYS3, a Hotspot of Meiotic Recombination in *Saccharomyces cerevisiae*: Effects of Heterozygosity and Mismatch Repair Functions on Gene Conversion and Recombination Intermediates," *Genetics*, 151 (1999), 1245–1259.

5. Luther Davis and Gerald R. Smith, "Meiotic Recombination and Chromosome Segregation in *Schizosaccharomyces pombe*," *Proceedings of the National Academy of Sciences of the USA*, 98 (2001): 8395–8402.

6. K. L. Harteveld, M. Losekoot, R. Fodde, et al., "The Involvement of Alu Repeats in Recombination Events at the Alpha-globin Gene Cluster: Characterization of Two Alpha Aero-Thalassaemia Deletion Breakpoints," *Human Genetics*, 99, no. 4 (1997): 528–534.

7. N. S. Rudiger, N. Gregersen, and M. C. Kielland-Brandt, "One Short Well Conserved Region of Alu-Sequences Is Involved in Human Gene Re-arrangements and Has Homology with Prokaryotic Chi," *Nucleic Acids Research*, 23, no. 2 (1995): 256–260.

8. Margaret G. Kidwell and Damon R. Lisch, "Perspective: Transposable Elements, Parasitic DNA, and Genome Evolution," *Evolution: International Journal of Organic Evolution*, 55 (2001): 1–24; Haig H. Kazazian, Jr., "L1 Retro-transposons Shape the Mammalian Genome," *Science*, 289 (2000): 1152–1153.

9. Increased accessibility of a region of DNA would result from a combination of the particular kinds of molecules present in that cell, and sequences in or near that region of DNA. A. Blumental-Perry, D. Zenvirth, S. Klein, et al., "DNA Motif Associated with Meiotic Double-Strand Break Regions in *Saccharomyces cerevisiae*," *EMBO Journal*, 1 (2000): 232–238.

10. A. J. Jeffreys, "Spontaneous and Induced Minisatellite Instability in the Human Genome," *Clinical Science*, 93, no. 5 (1997): 383–390.
11. L. Edelmann, E. Spiteri, K. Koren, et al., "AT-Rich Palindromes Mediate the Constitutional t(11;22) Translocation," *American Journal of Human Genetics*, 68, no. 1 (2001): 1–13.
12. Craig Jankowski, Farooq Nasar, and Dilip K. Nag, "Meiotic Instability of CAG Repeat Tracts Occurs by Double-Strand Break Repair in Yeast," *Proceedings of the National Academy of Sciences of the USA*, 97 (2000): 2134–2139.
13. M. Duyao, C. Ambrose, R. Myers, et al., "Trinucleotide Repeat Length Instability and Age of Onset in Huntington's Disease," *Nature Genetics*, 4, no. 4 (1993): 387–392.
14. Tasuku Honjo, Kazuo Kinoshita, and Masamichi Muramatsu, "Molecular Mechanism of Class Switch Recombination: Linkage with Somatic Hypermutation," *Annual Review of Immunology*, 20 (2002): 165–196.
15. But that is not to say that the mechanism should be identical to the antibody class switch, in which the DNA in between the switch regions is cut out of the chromosome in a loop that is degraded.
16. G. P. Holmquist, Role of Replication Time in the Control of Tissue-Specific Gene Expression," *American Journal of Human Genetics*, 40 (1987): 151–173.
17. C. K. Mathews and J. Ji, "DNA Precursor Asymmetries, Replication Fidelity, and Variable Genome Evolution," *Bioessays*, 14 (1992): 295–301.
18. G. P. Holmquist, "Chromosome Bands, Their Chromatin Flavors, and Their Functional Features," *American Journal of Human Genetics*, 51 (1992): 17–37; G. D'Onofrio, K. Jabbari, H. Musto, et al. "Evolutionary Genomics of Vertebrates and Its Implications," *Annals of the NY Academy of Sciences*, 870:81–94.
19. Giorgio Barnardi, "Misunderstanding about Isochores; Part 1," *Gene*, 276 (2001): 3–13.
20. T. Ogi, T. Kato, Jr., T. Kato, and H. Ohmori, "Mutation Enhancement by DINB1, a Mammalian Homologue of the *Escherichia coli* Mutagenesis Protein dinB," *Genes to Cells*, 4, no. 11 (1999): 607–618.
21. M. Garcia-Diaz, O. Dominguez, L. A. Lopez-Fernandez, et al., "DNA Polymerase Lambda (Pol Lambda), a Novel Eukaryotic DNA Polymerase with a Potential Role in Meiosis," *Journal of Molecular Biology*, 301, no. 4 (2000): 851–867.
22. Margaret G. Kidwell and Damon Lisch,, "Transposable Elements as Sources of Variation in Animals and Plants," *Proceedings of the National Academy of Sciences of the USA*, 94 (1997): 7704–7711.
23. H. H. Kazazian, Jr., "An Estimated Frequency of Endogenous Insertional Mutations in Humans," *Nature Genetics*, 22 (1999): 130.
24. Thomas Rülicke, Michel Chapuisat, Felix Homberger, et al., "MHC-Genotype of Progeny Influenced by Parental Infection," *Proceedings of the Royal Society of London B Biological Sciences*, 265 (1998): 711–716. In addition to the exploratory molecular studies reported in this paper, references in its introduction put this in a broader context.
25. Kazazian, loc. cit.
26. See supplementary information for The International SNP Map Working Group, "A Map of Human Genome Sequence Variation Containing 1.42 Million Single Nucleotide Polymorphisms," *Nature*, 409 (2001): 928–933; also

available on line at http://www.nature.com/cgi-taf/DynaPage.taf?file=/nature/journal/v409/n6822/full/409928a0_fs.html.

27. Jennifer L. Gerton, Joseph DeRisi, Robert Shroff, et al., "Global Mapping of Meiotic Recombination Hotspots and Coldspots in the Yeast *Saccharomyces cerevisiae*," *Proceedings of the National Academy of Sciences of the USA*, 97, no. 21 (2000): 11383–11390. The authors discuss the possibility that proteins involved in turning genes on and off make certain regions of DNA accessible for cutting. Because different genes are turned on and off under different conditions, an important role for these proteins would point to an effect of the nutrients available to the yeast cell on where it undergoes recombination during meiosis. Indeed, there is some evidence for the effect of the metabolic state of the cell on the location and extent of recombination in meiosis, as described in: Mohamad F. F. Abdullah and Rhona H. Borts, "Meiotic Recombination Frequencies Are Affected by Nutritional States in *Saccharomyces cerevisiae*," *Proceedings of the National Academy of Sciences of the USA*, 98 (2001): 14524–14529.

28. While I use the word *slip* here, repeats can expand (and contract) by mismatch repair and recombination mechanisms. For example, some repeats in the human genome share a 10–15 letter core sequence that is similar to *E. coli*'s recombination hotspot chi [A. J. Jeffreys, V. Wilson, and S. L.Thein, "Hypervariable 'Minisatellite' Regions in Human DNA," *Nature*, 314 (1985): 67–73] and these sequences are in fact hotspots of recombination [A. J. Jeffreys, R. Barber, P. Bois, et al., "Human Minisatellites, Repeat DNA Instability and Meiotic Recombination," *Electrophoresis*, 20 (1999): 1665–1675]. An interesting observation is that certain repeat sequences in humans tend to expand if they are smaller than a certain length, and tend to contract if they are larger, thus providing variation within a range of lengths: J. Buard, C. Brenner, and A. J. Jeffreys, "Evolutionary Fate of an Unstable Human Minisatellite Deduced from Sperm-Mutation Spectra of Individual Alleles," *American Journal of Human Genetics*, 70 (2002): 1038–1043.

29. K. Walsh and H. Neurath, "Trypsinogen and Chymotrypsinogen as Homologous Proteins," *Proceedings of the National Academy of Sciences of the USA*, 52 (1964): 884–889.

30. See, for example, K. Ono-Koyanagi, H. Suga, K. Katoh, and T. Miyata, "Protein Tyrosine Phosphatases from Amphioxus, Hagfish, and Ray: Divergence of Tissue-Specific Isoform Genes in the Early Evolution of Vertebrates," *Journal of Molecular Evolution*, 50 (2000): 302–311.

31. Paramvir Dehal, Paul Predki, Anne S. Olsen, et al., "Human Chromosome 19 and Related Regions in Mouse: Conservative and Lineage-Specific Evolution," *Science*, 293 (2001): 104–111. These authors note many repetitive sequences in this very active region of the genome.

32. A detailed look at the structure of this hotspot of primate genome variation is reported in E. Eichler, S. Hoffman, A. Adamson, et al., "Complex β-Satellite Repeat Structures and the Expansion of the Zinc Finger Gene Cluster in 19p12," *Genome Research*, 8 (1998): 791–808. A broader overview of a two-step model in which duplicate domains are gathered by an active region of the genome and then duplicated in groups as a new combination of functions is given by R. V. Samonte and E. E. Eichler, "Segmental Duplications and the Evolution of the Primate Genome," *Nature Reviews Genetics*, 3 (2002): 65–72;

in this paper, there is a discussion of the morpheus gene family, in which the introns are more conserved than the exons among primates. (The observation that introns are more conserved than exons is considered an unexpected result as introns were thought to be mostly "spacers," and thus should be free to vary, whereas exons, with functional constraints, have been observed to change more slowly than introns.) The observation of a higher rate of change among the exons than the introns in the morpheus gene family is reminiscent of the relatively conserved introns in a family of rapidly varying venom proteins in vipers, as reported in Kin-Ichi Nakashima, Ikuo Nobuhisa, Masanobu Deshimaru, et al., "Accelerated Evolution in the Protein-Coding Regions Is Universal in *Crotalinae* Snake Venom Gland Phospholipase A2 Isozyme Genes," *Proceedings of the National Academy of Sciences of the USA*, 92 (1995): 5605–5609. While these results can be interpreted to indicate accelerated evolution of the exons compared to the introns because of positive selective pressure operating on the exons, a not mutually exclusive explanation is that there is pressure to conserve the introns in order to provide a framework that facilitates rapid variation among members of this gene family. A preliminary analysis in the viper paper did not find constraints on the intron sequences taken as a whole, but whether or not there are constrained sequences within the introns that might serve as a framework that facilitates exon variation merits further investigation.

When a higher rate of change was observed in the mouse histocompatibilty gene exons compared to the introns, the changes were noted to be in patches, so that small gene conversion events were proposed to explain them: E. Weiss, L. Golden, R. Zakut, et al., "The DNA Sequence of the H-2kb Gene: Evidence for Gene Conversion as a Mechanism for the Generation of Polymorphism in Histocompatibilty Antigens," *European Molecular Biology Organization Journal*, 2 (1983): 453–462.

33. Kari Hogstrand and Jan Bohme, "Gene Conversion of Major Histocompatibility Complex Genes Is Associated with CpG-Rich Regions," *Immunogenetics*, 49 (1999): 446–455. These authors also report that the gene conversion events appear to occur during the course of mitotic divisions in the germ line that take place prior to meiosis.

34. Alec J. Jeffreys, Liisa Kauppi, and Rita Neumann, "Intensely Punctate Meiotic Recombination in the Class II Region of the Major Histocompatibility Complex," *Nature Genetics*, 29 (2001): 217–222; Silvana Gaudieri, Roger L. Dawkins, Kaori Habara, et al., "SNP Profile within the Human Major Histocompatibility Complex Reveals an Extreme and Interrupted Level of Nucleotide Diversity," *Genome Research*, 10 (2000): 1579–1586.

Chapter 19   Decoding DNA

1. James Shapiro, "Part I. Summary," in Lynn Helena Caporale, ed., *Molecular Strategies in Biological Evolution, Annals of the New York Academy of Sciences*, 870 (1999): 97.
2. L. Rowen, B. F. Koop, and L. Hood, "The Complete 685-Kilobase DNA Sequence of the Human Beta T Cell Receptor Locus," *Science*, 272 (1996): 1755–1762.

3. Lynn Helena Caporale, "Is There a Higher Level Genetic Code That Directs Evolution?" *Molecular and Cellular Biochemistry*, 64 (1984): 5–13.

4. C. V. Kirchhamer, C. H. Yuh, and E. H. Davidson, "Modular *cis*-Regulatory Organization of Developmentally Expressed Genes: Two Genes Transcribed Territorially in the Sea Urchin Embryo, and Additional Examples," *Proceedings of the National Academy of Sciences of the USA*, 93 (1996): 9322–9328.

5. What Nobel laureate Werner Arber has called "evolutionary genes."

6. Fernando Alvarez-Valina, José Francisco Tortb, and Giorgio Bernardi, "Nonrandom Spatial Distribution of Synonymous Substitutions in the GP63 Gene from *Leishmania*," *Genetics*, 155 (2000): 1683–1692.

7. In addition to gene families, genes underlying variable traits, especially those known to lead to rapid radiations, are worth examining.

8. Paul Smith and Stephen Moss, "Structural Evolution of the Annexin Supergene Family," *Trends in Genetics*, 10 (1994): 241–246.

9. For an example of an early step in this direction, see Guo-chun Liao, E. Jay Rehm, and Gerald M. Rubin. "Insertion Site Preferences of the P Transposable Element in *Drosophila melanogaster*, *Proceedings of the National Academy of Sciences of the USA*, 97 (2000): 3347–3351.

10. At the conference that I organized in 1998 [Lynn Helena Caporale, ed., *Molecular Strategies in Biological Evolution*, *Annals of the New York Academy of Sciences*, 870 (1999)] one participant told me that it was great to be at a meeting where he did not feel like a naughty schoolboy who was being scolded and slapped on the hand with a ruler and told, you can't *say* that.

11. Several years before the conference in which I was asked whether I considered genomes "intelligent," the term *genetic intelligence* had been proposed and used by David Thaler; see David Thaler and Bradley Messmer, "Genetic Intelligence, Evolution of," in Robert A. Meyers, ed., *Encyclopedia of Molecular Biology and Molecular Medicine*, 2 (1996): 407–414.

12. Lewis Thomas, *The Lives of a Cell* (New York: Bantam Books, 1974).

13. More people would have died for several reasons. First, if CCR5 had been completely removed from the genome, no one could be protected by inheriting two, or even one [M. Marmor , H. W. Sheppard, D. Donnell, et al., "HIV Network for Prevention Trials Vaccine Preparedness Protocol Team: Homozygous and Heterozygous CCR5-Delta32 Genotypes Are Associated with Resistance to HIV Infection," *Journal of Acquired Immune Deficiency Syndromes*, 27 (2001): 472–481] copy of the broken receptor. Second, the absence of people in the community with broken receptors is likely to increase the risk that people with normal receptors would be exposed to the disease: Amy D. Sullivan, Janis Wigginton, and Denise Kirschner, "The Coreceptor Mutation CCR5Δ32 Influences the Dynamics of HIV Epidemics and Is Selected for by HIV," *Proceedings of the National Academy of Sciences of the USA*, 98 (2001): 10214–10219. Third, we would not have learned that blocking this receptor could block infection.

14. Laurie Garrett, *The Coming Plague* (New York: Farrar, Straus and Giroux, 1994).

Epilogue   What Became of the First Genome?

1. I recognize my debt to Primo Levi and to the friend who gave me a copy of Levi's *The Periodic Table*, trans. Raymond Rosenthal (New York: Schocken Books, 1984).

2. See http://mjhnyc.org/ringelbaum/main1.htm. The complete text can be found in Joseph Kermish, ed., *To Live and Die with Honor: Selected Documents from the Warsaw Ghetto Underground Archives "O.S."* (Jerusalem: Yad Vashem, 1986), 65–67.

3. Guo-Qiang Chen, Changhai Cui, Mark L. Mayer, and Eric Gouaux, "Functional Characterization of a Potassium-Selective Prokaryotic Glutamate Receptor," *Nature*, 402 (1999): 817–821.

4. The European Union Arabidopsis Genome Sequencing Consortium and The Cold Spring Harbor, Washington University in St. Louis, and PE Biosystems Arabidopsis Sequencing Consortium," Sequence and Analysis of Chromosome 4 of the Plant *Arabidopsis thaliana*: BRCA2 Is a Protein that We Need to Respond to DNA Damage," *Nature*, 402 (1999): 769–777.

5. International Human Genome Sequencing Consortium (IHGSC), "Initial Sequencing and Analysis of the Human Genome," *Nature*, 409 (2001): 860–921.

6. Two estimates based on very different methods, both giving numbers higher than 98 percent, are Asao Fujiyama, Hidemi Watanabe, Atsushi Toyoda, et al., "Construction and Analysis of a Human-Chimpanzee Comparative Clone Map," *Science*, 295 (2002): 131–134; and Mary-Claire King and Allan Wilson, "Evolution at Two Levels in Humans and Chimpanzees," *Science*, 188 (1975): 107–116.

7. Jack Cohen, "Knife-Edge of Design," *Nature*, 411(2001): 529. On the other hand, rapid expansion of a population can occur either when a new niche becomes available or when a genomic innovation overcomes challenges and/or captures new opportunities.

Index

Acknowledgments

I would like to recognize the importance of the support and encouragement I received from my family. In particular, I fondly remember my grandfather, Morris Babushkin, waiting at the Brooklyn College gate to bring me home each week the evening before an early morning freshman chemistry laboratory/section, and my grandmother, Rose Kistenberg Babushkin, preparing a special dinner, after which they both devotedly let me turn their apartment into a quiet study hall. Their granddaughter would become, as they later would say, "a Doctor of Science," although neither of them, hard-working immigrants who fled difficult circumstances, had had the opportunity to go to college.

Yet, there was a time when, simply put, I hated science, or what I thought was science: memorizing boring lists of things. While I "knew" that I hated science, an observant junior high school teacher found that I was a natural scientist. Indeed, all children are natural scientists—curious about the world and full of questions that scientific research can answer: Why is the sky blue, why is the grass green, why, why, why. Science often is presented as the work of calculating men in white coats who are members of an aloof priesthood. I was fortunate to have found, with the help of a few good teachers, that science, mostly, is not like that. Scientists explore, frame good questions, and imagine.

Because this is my first book for a broad readership, I would like to acknowledge specific individuals and institutions who contributed to my becoming a scientist many years ago. The people I thank here played an essential role in overcoming those people and assumptions (which I will not discuss here) that kept trying to push me, a young woman, out of science. I would like to thank my ninth-grade science teacher, whom I knew only as Miss Hemmer, for getting rid of my antipathy to science by encouraging me and a classmate, Joan Goldstein, to do a project, "The Harmful and Beneficial Effects of Molds," for a New York City science fair. This project involved gathering moldy fruit and bread from the back of the refrigerator and learning about penicillin.

I also would like to thank the teachers in the Summer Program in Biochemistry at the Loomis School, which I attended the first year it admitted "girls," and the National Science Foundation for funding this extraordinary program for young teenagers. I also am grateful to my eleventh- and twelfth-grade science teacher, Josef Rizik, who among many other things encouraged me to attend that summer program and assigned a term paper for physics class. (Coincidentally, I recalled as I wrote this book, I chose T dimers as the topic of that term paper, after reading an article in *Scientific American* in the school library. In writing the term paper, I drew on the extraordinary resources of the New York Public Library—although it involved putting my hair up in a bun so that I would look old enough to gain access to the stacks where the scientific literature was kept.) I am very grateful to New York City for the gift of a free college education, and I would like to thank two college chemistry professors: first, Leon Gortler, an extraordinary teacher, for inspiring a group of us to love organic chemistry and, much more recently, for giving very helpful feedback on a draft of this book; second, Herman Zieger, for encouraging me when I questioned what he said. I would like to give special thanks to Ralph Hirschmann, former senior vice president at Merck, for his support and encouragement through some challenging times in my career.

In spite of these good people, it is doubtful that I would have considered a career in scientific research if it had not been for the fact that when I was in high school I read John Gunther's book about his son, *Death Be Not Proud*. The excitement of science as seen through Johnny Gunther's eyes, and the helplessness of his doctors in the face of his brain tumor, led me to consider medical research as one option when I arrived at college, because of its potential to save lives.

For this book, I was fortunate to have had an excellent editor who believed in it: Amy Bianco, then at McGraw-Hill. Discussions with Amy helped a great deal in framing the flow of ideas. You too can thank her, for trimming redundancies and asking good questions to clarify the meaning of many paragraphs. This book would never have reached Amy if it had not been for my agent, Regula Noetzli. I am tremendously grateful to Regula for her early confidence in this book, and for her advice on how to present these ideas for a broad readership. I also would like to thank Ruth W. Mannino, Senior Editing Supervisor, for pulling the book together with the extraordinary ability to combine careful attention to detail with speed, Philip Ruppel, Vice President at McGraw-Hill, and the team that ushered the book through the publication process.

This book was made better by the input of those, some trained in science and some not, who gave their time to read a draft. I would like to thank Stephen Farrier for his tremendous enthusiasm, which definitely helped during the pressured days of finishing the book, for asking good questions, and for checking, and indeed contributing, calculations that help to put many large numbers in a context that is possible to grasp. I thank Margaret Price for her encouragement and comments, and thank John Franzén for wanting this book to succeed, devoting so much time to a careful reading, and making suggestions on every page.

Evelyn Witkin not only commented on the draft of several chapters, but also made an important, and treasured, contribution by putting together a brief history, with reprints and commentary, of her work and that of others. David Thaler read through the whole book, providing suggestions, and encouragement. Other scientists whose comments made significant contributions to specific chapters of the book were Larry Simpson, Margaret Kidwell, Richard Moxon, Chris Bayliss, Mary Jane West-Eberhard, Mel Green, Eduardo Rocha, Patricia Foster, Lynn Ripley, and Nancy Kleckner. David Prescott, Peter Grant, Roel Schaaper, Michael Neuberger, Nancy Maizels, Miro Radman, John Whysner, and Baldomero Olivera provided helpful input on specific sections and/or answered specific questions. In addition I want to thank the many other scientists who answered short questions and/or sent reprints of their work. I am grateful to John Roth for the time he spent in a valuable e-mail exchange relevant to the subject of this book. Scientists often disagree with one another on how to interpret the results of an experiment, and, indeed, some of the scientists listed here may disagree with one another and/or with me; thus I do not suggest that all the scientists on this distinguished list endorse every statement in this book; rather, I sincerely want to thank them because their comments helped to strengthen the book.

Finally, I want to thank my mother, Stella Babushkin Caporale, and Jill Caporale, who read parts of the book and made very helpful suggestions. Barbara and Judy Caporale read a few sections and provided encouragement. It was a particular treat for me that as my father, Ralph Caporale Jr., read the complete draft, he would call me with great enthusiasm to tell me how interesting he found a particular section. Needless to say, his encouragement and comments carried me across some difficult days of revisions and research. Beyond their contributions to the book, I would like to thank both of my parents for the devotion and encouragement that they have given to me all of my life.

About the Author

Lynn Caporale received her Ph.D. in Molecular Biology from the University of California at Berkeley. After teaching and doing research at New York University, Memorial/Sloan-Kettering Cancer Center, Rockefeller University, and Georgetown University Medical Center, she moved to Merck Research Laboratories, where she spent over a decade focused on the discovery of new medicines. Dr. Caporale has held research and senior executive positions with various biotechnology companies and in the pharmaceutical industry, and currently is an independent consultant in drug discovery and functional genomics. She lives in New York City.